THE LIVES OF GIRLS AND WOMEN FROM
THE ISLAMIC WORLD IN EARLY MODERN
BRITISH LITERATURE AND CULTURE

The Lives of Girls and Women from the Islamic World in Early Modern British Literature and Culture

BERNADETTE ANDREA

UNIVERSITY OF TORONTO PRESS
Toronto Buffalo London

ISBN 978-1-4875-0125-9 (cloth)

Library and Archives Canada Cataloguing in Publication

Andrea, Bernadette Diane, author
The lives of girls and women from the Islamic world
in early modern British literature and culture / Bernadette Andrea.

Includes bibliographical references and index.
ISBN 978-1-4875-0125-9 (cloth)

1. English literature – Early modern, 1500–1700 – History and criticism.
2. English literature – Women authors – History and criticism.   3. Women
and literature – Great Britain – History – 16th century.   4. Women and
literature – Great Britain – History – 17th century.   5. Islam and literature –
Great Britain – History – 16th century.   6. Islam and literature – Great Britain –
History – 17th century.   7. Women in literature.   8. Girls in literature.
9. Islamic civilization in literature.   10. Islam in literature.   I. Title.

PR428.W63A54 2017   820.9'3522   C2016-907813-2

This book has been published with the help of a grant from the Federation
for the Humanities and Social Sciences, through the Awards to Scholarly
Publications Program, using funds provided by the Social Sciences and
Humanities Research Council of Canada.

University of Toronto Press acknowledges the financial assistance to its
publishing program of the Canada Council for the Arts and the Ontario
Arts Council, an agency of the Government of Ontario.

To Ben, again.

Contents

Note on Sources

I retain original spelling and punctuation when citing early modern sources; however, I adjust the i/j and u/v letterforms to accord with modern conventions. The bibliography preserves the original spelling and typography. Protestant England followed the Julian calendar until 1752 with the year starting on March 25 (Old Style), after which the year was calculated from January 1 (New Style). For performances that fall between these dates, I indicate the year in N.S. and O.S. When citing publications, I list the date on the title page.

Acknowledgments

While it would not be possible to thank everyone who has shared their wit and wisdom as I completed this book, the following individuals have offered especially incisive input along with opportunities for presenting and publishing my preliminary efforts: Patricia Akhimie, Elizabeth Bearden, Charles Beem, Brian Catlos, Ruben Espinosa, Alison Findlay, Anke Gilleir, Julia Hairston, Jean Howard, Debra Johanyak, Ivo Kamps, Sharon Kinoshita, Carole Levin, Walter Lim, Ania Loomba, Kathleen Lynch, Bindu Malieckal, Giuseppe Marcocci, Linda McJannet, Alicia C. Montoya, Su Fang Ng, Nate Probasco, David Ruiter, Melissa Sanchez, Julia Schleck, Claire Sponsler, Mihoko Suzuki, Valerie Traub, Suzan van Dijk, Merry Wiesner-Hanks, and Owen Williams.

I especially thank Ben Olguín for generously reading and commenting on an earlier draft of the complete manuscript and Patricia Akhimie for offering a helpful reading of the introduction. It goes without saying that all the virtues belong to them and all the faults to me.

Since 2009, I have presented this material at the following conferences and symposia: Attending to Early Modern Women at the University of Wisconsin–Milwaukee; Christian-Islamic Interactions: Mobility, Connection, Transformation (1450–1800) at the Scuola Normale Superiore, Pisa (Italy); Dramatizing Penshurst: Site, Script, Sidneys at Penshurst Place (England); the Early Modern Rome conference at the University of California–Rome (Italy); Impact of Interaction: Exploring Cultural Convergence, the James A. Rawley Graduate Conference in the Humanities, at the University of Nebraska–Lincoln; the International Conference on New Directions in the Humanities at the Universidad de Granada (Spain); the Mediterranean Studies Congress at the Università degli Studi di Palermo (Italy); the Middle East Studies Association conferences; the Queen Elizabeth I Society at the South-Central Renaissance conference; the Renaissance Society of America conferences; the Seaborne Renaissance: Global Exchanges and Religion in Early Modernity, the Harrington Symposium, at the University of Texas–Austin; the Shakespeare Association of America conferences; and Shakespeare's Legacy: The Future of Shakespeare and Early Modern Studies at the University of Texas–El Paso.

My research during this period was funded by grants from the University of Texas at San Antonio (the Department of English, the College of Liberal and Fine Arts, and the Office of the Vice President for Research Support) and by two National Endowment for the Humanities (NEH) summer institute grants (2010 and 2015), for which I am grateful.

Mark Bayer has graciously fielded questions on Shakespeare and has been a supportive department chair. I also appreciate Daniel Gelo, Dean of the College of Liberal and Fine Arts, for supporting my research over the years. Most recently, I wish to thank him for appointing me as the Celia Jacobs Endowed Professor in British Literature, a position made possible by the generosity of Dr Milton Jacobs. Dr Jacobs is a true Renaissance man, who was inspired by his aunt's lifelong devotion to literature and learning.

Parts of several articles found their way into this book and are substantially revised. I specify in the notes how I include these prior investigations and how I have expanded them. None of the chapters in this book have been previously published in their entirety. That said, I wish to thank the following presses: Ashgate Publishing, Oxford University Press, and Palgrave Macmillan.

Last but not least, I thank Suzanne Rancourt, Executive Editor, University of Toronto Press, along with her superb staff including Luciano Nicassio, Barb Porter, and Miriam Skey, for ushering this book through the publication process in such a professional and pleasant manner, and Thérèse Lee Parent for her expert indexing.

THE LIVES OF GIRLS AND WOMEN FROM
THE ISLAMIC WORLD IN EARLY MODERN
BRITISH LITERATURE AND CULTURE

Can the Subaltern Signify? Tracing the Lives of Girls and Women from the Islamic World in British Literature and Culture, c. 1500–1630

Addressing an important but neglected topic in the burgeoning field of Global Renaissance Studies, this book presents a series of investigations that cohere around the problematic of the gendered subaltern's agency in what has been defined as England's "proto-imperialist" and "proto-orientalist" era.[1] It does so by recovering and resituating the lives of girls and women from *Dar al-Islam* (loosely translated as "the Islamic world") who travelled, with varying degrees of volition, as slaves, captives, or trailing wives to the British Isles throughout the sixteenth century and into the first decades of the seventeenth century.[2] These gendered subalterns include Elen More, a Black woman from Islamic West Africa, who participated in the Scottish King James IV's pageants at the turn of the sixteenth century; a Nogay Tatar girl, renamed "Ipolita the Tartarian," whom English merchants acquired in Islamic Central Asia and gifted to Queen Elizabeth I in the middle of the century; Lucy Negro, another Black woman whose genealogy stretches to Islamic West Africa and who resonates in Shakespeare's plays and poems at the close of the century; Teresa Sampsonia Sherley, a Circassian from the Safavid empire who travelled to England with her husband during the early seventeenth century; and Mariam Khanim, an Armenian from the Mughal Empire who came with her husband around the same time. Despite the apparent paucity of direct evidence, their material and semiotic strategies of "survivance," which Anishinaabe writer and scholar Gerald Vizenor defines as "the union of active survival and resistance to cultural dominance," impacted the documentary record and literature of Scotland and England during and after their lifetimes.[3] Assessing these strategies of survival and resistance demands a methodology that recognizes "traces and the trails they leave" in the extant records, which I advance through the resources of "micro" (Ginzburg), "connected" (Subrahmanyam), and "contrapuntal" (Said) historiographies.[4]

As I seek to show, the "fragments from the lives" of these gendered subalterns, to borrow a phrase from Clare Anderson's study of South Asian biographies during the height of the British imperial project from the late eighteenth century through the early twentieth century, inhered in the proto-imperial discourses of this earlier era, even if such displaced girls and women did not directly produce trade and diplomatic documents, maps and portraits, or literary works.[5] My analysis thus aligns with Margaret Ferguson's comparative study of literacy, gender, and empire during these centuries, in which she critiques the narrowly positivist dismissal of early modern women's agency in the absence of their direct authorship and addresses the alleged "problem of missing evidence."[6] Adducing the documented presence of girls and women from the Islamic world in the British Isles and their incorporation into the emerging anglocentric discourse of empire, I nevertheless complicate Ferguson's attention to English and other Western European women in relation to global expansionism by examining gendered subalterns from the Islamic world as integral to this project. "The empire writes back," I submit, starting in this era of incipient, if still only potential, expansionist efforts.[7]

Drawing on historical documents, literary works, and visual sources, I concomitantly argue that the lives of these subaltern girls and women are inextricably linked to elite Englishwomen such as Queen Elizabeth, who invested in the first English voyages to the New World and supported the first English diplomatic mission to the Ottoman Empire, and Lady Mary Wroth, who belonged to the aristocratic Sidney family implicated in these ventures from their inception. Tracing similar connections across a broad spectrum of British literary and cultural productions, I extend my analysis to important male writers of the period with a focus on William Shakespeare's plays for the public stage and Ben Jonson's performances for the English court. My book accordingly complements *A Companion to the Global Renaissance: English Literature and Culture in the Era of Expansion*, edited by early modern/postcolonial studies scholar Jyotsna Singh, which, in the words of reviewer Natasha Distiller, "reflects on early modern England's construction of the world and on England's actual interaction with that world." As Distiller summarizes, "History becomes interesting for what it reveals about the connections between textuality and materiality within a broad framework recognizing the connections between models of self and Other, nascent nationalism and nascent capitalism, and the exploitation of class and what would become race." Yet, as she concludes, "[g]ender, it seems, once again slips off the agenda."[8] This is the lacuna that my book seeks to fill.

As Singh and other scholars investigating the Global Renaissance have stressed, prior to becoming an imperial power beyond the British Isles in the eighteenth century, the English merchants and adventurers attempting to circumvent the Iberian monopoly on the lucrative trade routes to the East and West Indies (Asia and America broadly speaking) had to negotiate a polycentric world system within which England seemed backward compared not only to the Spanish but also to the Islamic empires of the era.[9] It is in this context, with England considered "marginal even within Europe," that I situate those girls and women from the Islamic world who rose – or were thrust – to historical visibility in sixteenth- and early seventeenth-century literary and cultural productions.[10] As Lesley Cormack explains in *Charting an Empire: Geography at the English Universities, 1580–1620*, "Until the sixteenth century, England had been marginal, both on the Ptolemaic map as an insignificant island on the edge of the known world and in the political and intellectual life of Europe."[11] As Linda Colley elaborates in *Captives: Britain, Empire, and the World, 1600–1850*, "Before the late sixteenth century, few of the English, and even fewer Scots, Irish and Welsh displayed much interest in the world beyond their own continent."[12] I add that the expansion of the world system characteristic of the "early modern/colonial period" resulted in the displacement of gendered and racialized subalterns to British shores even as Britons themselves remained extraneous and belated to the global imperial project initiated by the Iberians.[13] However, precisely because England, and even more so Scotland, was deemed marginal vis-à-vis the two dominant imperial dynasties of the "Greater Western World," the Habsburgs and the Ottomans, these girls and women could affiliate with and even assimilate into British culture, albeit at the cost of conversion and other types of deracination.[14]

Further building on the theoretical interventions of leading feminist scholars who approach early modern literature and culture from cross-cultural perspectives, with Natalie Zemon Davis and Merry Wiesner-Hanks in the forefront, I maintain that the girls and women from the Islamic world whom I engage in this study, and who have been dismissed in literary and historical studies of the period, *do* signify: both as significant, if neglected, constituents of the emerging anglocentric discourse of empire and as cultural agents in their own right.[15] As I establish, while they may not have literally inscribed their lives, the traces of their subaltern agency persist in documents from Richard Hakluyt's influential collection, *The Principal Navigations, Voyages, Traffiques and Discoveries of the English Nation*, and other primary sources, as well as in the groundbreaking printed works of Englishwomen writers from Queen Elizabeth to Mary Wroth and in the more canonical productions of Shakespeare and Jonson. I consequently evoke Gayatri Chakravorty Spivak's influential essay – "Can the Subaltern Speak?" – which addresses the paradox of "the supplement" (i.e., marginal *and* constitutive) from a postcolonial perspective.[16] As Stephen Morton elaborates, "Spivak subsequently clarifies this position, arguing that 'the subaltern cannot speak' … means that even when the subaltern makes an effort to the death to speak, she is not able to be heard, and speaking and hearing complete the speech act."[17] Turning to the early modern/ colonial period, I respond to this ethical and political call by recuperating the meaningful and multifaceted agency of girls and women from the Islamic world who travelled to early modern England and throughout the British Isles – whether involuntarily as de facto chattel or voluntarily, albeit with vulnerabilities, as trailing wives – through close contextualized readings of their often "refracted representations" in the historical documents and imaginative literature of this proto-imperialist and proto-orientalist era.[18]

Defining "Proto-Imperialist," "Paracolonial," and "Proto-Orientalist" England

The "presences of women" – to extend Anne Coldiron's astute discussion in "Women in Early English Print Culture" – is therefore the starting point for this book, which investigates the incorporation and subsequent erasure of the lives of girls and women from the Islamic world in early modern British literature and culture.[19] While the tendentiously edited letters from one of the Ottoman Empire's most powerful women, Safiye Sultan, were included in Hakluyt's *The Principal Navigations*,[20] neither she nor other female elite from this core region travelled to "the island encompassing England, Wales and Scotland."[21] However, a few girls and women from peripheral regions within Islamdom arrived during the sixteenth and early seventeenth centuries when "the English nation" – as Hakluyt emphasizes – was not (yet) a major player within the early modern/colonial world system.[22]

In the balance of this book, I examine how their lives intersect with each other and with significant British literary productions from this "proto-imperialist," "para-colonial," and "proto-orientalist" period. Here, I define some key terms in order to position these too often neglected lives within the emerging world system as a "subaltern instance" constituting and contesting the emerging anglocentric discourse of empire.[23]

When in 1533 Henry VIII, "King of England and of France [a residual claim based on the continental port of Calais], Prince of Wales and Lord of Ireland," proclaimed, "this realm of England is an empire,"[24] he was not instantiating the project of global domination upon which "the sun never set" that marked the height of the British Empire from the eighteenth to the twentieth century.[25] Rather, as G.R. Elton explains, he was "using the civilian concept of *imperium* existing in any polity whose ruler did not recognise a superior on earth" to reject the supra-national authority of the pope and to propel the English Reformation.[26] Anthony Pagden further details how "the Latin term 'empire,' *imperium*" originally "described the sphere of executive authority possessed by the Roman magistrates." It continued to signify "sovereignty" or "non-subordinate power" as captured by the principle "each ruler was also an 'Emperor in his own Kingdom' – *rex imperator in regno suo*": precisely the meaning Henry VIII invoked when he declared himself supreme head of the Church of England.[27] This assertion of "empire" had economic, legal, and political, as well as religious, ramifications, but it did not require – even if it did not preclude – an expansionist agenda beyond the British Isles.

"As a polysemic term with a rich history," Barbara Fuchs concludes, "*imperium* denotes both internal control of a polity and external expansion beyond that polity's original boundaries."[28] Indeed, Henry VIII rejected, or at least neglected, his advisors' urgings to engage in global trading ventures to match the efforts of the Spanish crown, which was consolidating its "discoveries" in the West and East Indies and establishing the basis for the modern colonial world system.[29] Instead, this prototypical "Renaissance prince" pursued the medieval course of war with France, which led to the depletion of his coffers and the eventual loss of Calais by his heirs.[30] As J.J. Scarisbrick assesses, "For much of his reign he so completely ignored the new worlds across the seas, preferring instead to pursue antique ambitions across the Channel, that for over a generation English maritime expansion languished."[31] Even into the early seventeenth century, as Nicholas Canny clarifies, when "King James [I of England/VI of Scotland] established 'Britain' as the

name of his multiple kingdom, phrases such as 'great Brittaines imperial crowne,' or 'the Empire of Great Britaine,' were but adaptations
of the prevailing concept of independent authority, and had no necessary expansionist associations."[32] In David Armitage's estimation, "the
nature of British maritime domination ... under the Stuarts [1603–1714,
with an interregnum from 1649 to 1660] had implied exclusive British
imperium solely over home waters; this was replaced by a conception of
mare liberum on the oceans which underpinned arguments for the free
circulation of trade around the Atlantic world" by the "second quarter
of the eighteenth century." Only then does "[t]he concept of the 'British
Empire'" take shape "as a political community encompassing England
and Wales, Scotland, Protestant Ireland, the British islands of the Caribbean and the mainland colonies of North America." The "second British Empire," extending to India, does not emerge until "the second half
of the eighteenth century."[33]

It bears repeating, then, that rather than asserting global imperial
power during the sixteenth century, England was literally and politically marginal to the two major empires that impinged on it: the Spanish
Habsburgs, who sought to incorporate and even to invade the British
Isles, and the Ottomans, who harried British merchants in the Mediterranean.[34] As Susan Brigden remarks, when "Henry Tudor [Henry VII,
1485–1509] came to the throne, the islands of Britain and Ireland were
isolated, on the edge of Europe, and little regarded by their greater
neighbours. So they were still as his granddaughter Elizabeth died
[in 1603]."[35] Kenneth Andrews concurs: "Queen Elizabeth was not an
imperialist," despite her interest in the early joint-stock companies that
challenged "the Iberian monopolies in West Africa, the Americas and
the East." She humoured, but did not support "the notions of overseas
empire or oceanic power floated by men like [John] Hawkins, [Walter]
Ralegh, [Richard] Hakluyt and [John] Dee." Her primary aims "were
defensive: to strengthen royal authority within the kingdom, to provide
for its defence against invasion and to frustrate the ambitions of foreign
powers in Ireland, Scotland and the Netherlands."[36] As William Sherman concludes, "[d]uring the reign of Queen Elizabeth the prospects
of a British Empire were – to put it mildly – pretty grim."[37] From the
reign of Henry VIII (1509–47), England nevertheless sought to function
as "a third party who would be prepared to upset that balance [of power
between France and 'the newly-formed Habsburg colossus'] and swing
it heavily against either of the other two great powers."[38] Lisa Jardine and
Jerry Brotton agree that this island nation remained a "comparatively

minor" player through the end of the sixteenth century.[39] At the same time, it was allying with the Ottomans and Moroccans against the Habsburgs, as France had done earlier in the century.[40]

Mapping an even broader field, Mary Fuller stresses that sixteenth-century projectors of a "British Empire" such as John Dee and Richard Hakluyt focused on "a legendary, archipelagic greater Britain, first subject to [King] Arthur" and stretching in one iteration "Westward to Greenland, East to Russia, and North to the Pole."[41] Dee extended this once and future empire as far as North America.[42] Practically speaking, the Iberian monopoly over the southern trade routes to the East and West Indies propelled the inaugural English voyages of "discovery" northeastward in the 1550s. The Muscovy Company – which originally sought to discover a new trade route to "Cathay," or northern China, and onwards to India – actually landed in the resurgent Russian Empire and proceeded overland across Central Asia as far as the Safavid Persian court.[43] These ventures spanned several Tudor sovereigns, with the first voyage launched under Edward VI (1547–53) returning to report to Mary I (1553–8). They continued under Elizabeth I (1558–1603), matched by the voyages northwestward in the 1570s under Martin Frobisher, whose accounts were informed by the earlier English encounter with Muslim Tatars in Central Asia. As Matthew Dimmock remarks, during this decade, "particularly after the Papal Bull *Regnans in Excelsis* had excommunicated Elizabeth I in 1570," the English crown actively sought trade, diplomatic, and even military alliances with the Safavids, the Ottomans, and Morocco. Focusing on the aftermath of this epochal event, English travellers from merchants to pilgrims recognized "the Ottoman-controlled lands to be a location of multiple transactions and possibilities, emphasizing the 'interested' way in which the Protestant English approached those lands free of Catholic hegemony."[44] Formal contact with the Mughals was initiated under King James I (1603–25), with the English ambassador Sir Thomas Roe required to adapt, if not quite abase, himself to the norms and demands of the emperor – or, more properly, "Padishah Ghazi" – Jahangir.[45] As Gerald MacLean and Nabil Matar assert, "the reports Roe did leave behind, in which he documents his frustrations at being welcomed by Jahangir but not taken seriously by his ministers, should remind us of how Britain remained relatively insignificant to the Mughals until much later in the [seventeenth] century."[46]

The concept of an expansionist "British Empire," broached by John Dee in the 1570s and elaborated by Richard Hakluyt in the 1580s and

1590s, accordingly emerged as a proposal rather than a description.[47] In Jane Burbank and Frederick Cooper's summation, "[t]he efforts of publicists like Hakluyt and [Samuel] Purchas to popularize trade and proselytizing did not resonate very far."[48] Queen Elizabeth, as Robert Baldwin meticulously documents, reigned over a "paper empire" of maps, tracts, and other plans for overseas expansion rather than a "real economy" based on colonialism beyond Britain.[49] In this sense, to expand on my prior discussion of these terms, England throughout the 1500s and into the 1600s must be designated as "proto-imperialist" and "proto-orientalist" – or as John Michael Archer proffers, "paracolonial." As he stresses, "[i]t is vital to avoid the notion of 'pre-colonial' studies ... for the sixteenth and seventeenth centuries did not contain the germs of the inevitable colonization of the rest of the Old World by Europe; Russia and the Ottomans were never colonized in the conventional sense at all."[50] It is in this context, with canonical English writers such as Edmund Spenser articulating "the imperial dream" well into the 1590s, that I explicate the lives of some subaltern girls and women from the Islamic world (and those early English voyagers took to be so) as registered in sixteenth- and early seventeenth-century British literary and cultural productions.[51] Thus challenging the dominant "locus of enunciation," I foreground subaltern agency by engaging an archive inscribed by Scottish and English men – and, importantly, English-women – from the perspective of these girls and women's significant, but understudied, lives.[52]

Gendered Subalterns from the Islamic World and the Anglocentric Discourse of Empire

Chapter 1, "The 'Presences of Women' from the Islamic World in Late Medieval Scotland and Early Modern England," is structured around case studies of several gendered subalterns who travelled, with varying degrees of volition, from West Africa, Central Asia, and Safavid Persia to Scotland and England during the proto-imperial period demarcated above. While a longitudinal analysis of these girls and women from the Islamic world residing in the British Isles prior to the early seventeenth century continues to be hampered by the paucity of "hard" evidence and biases in its interpretation, I adduce these case studies to assess how a salient few negotiated their lives in the British Isles and how their material and semiotic strategies of survival and resistance, or "survivance," continued to impact the imaginative literature, historical documents, and visual sources that constituted the emerging anglocentric discourse of global empire. They thereby become touchstones for the rest of the book, which endorses Frances Dolan's emphasis, in *True Relations: Reading, Literature, and Evidence in Seventeenth-Century England*, on "the literary as a method rather than a taxonomy."[53]

The first case study focuses on Elen (or Helen) More, featured as the "Black Queen of Beauty" in the early sixteenth-century Scottish pageants that presaged the masques Ben Jonson crafted almost a century later for King James VI of Scotland, crowned James I of England after Queen Elizabeth's death, and Anna of Denmark, his queen consort.[54] In addition to the documentary accounts of Elen More's performance in the "tournament of the wild [or 'black'] knight and the black lady" (1507/8), the sixteenth-century Scottish court poet William Dunbar memorialized her in his double-edged poem "Ane Blak Moir."[55] Originally from Islamic West Africa, where she may have been a Muslim or an animist or even a Christian, she was wrested by Scottish privateers from a Portuguese ship that had strayed into the North Sea. Clearly, the transatlantic slave trade motivated her forced movements. However, her status at the Scottish court seems to have been more akin to a lady-in-waiting than a chattel slave. In examining later sixteenth-century English performances, I connect her to Lucy Negro, also known as "Black Luce," who ran a notorious brothel at Clerkenwell in the heart of London and may have been the "Dark Lady" to whom Shakespeare addressed over two dozen sonnets.[56] It is probable that this subsequent "Black Queen" – "quean" or "a prostitute" was a common pun in Shakespeare's era (*OED*) – sat in the audience for one of his first plays, *The Comedy of Errors*. While documentation for Lucy Negro's life prior to her designation as "Abbess of Clerkenwell" is scarce – "abbess" was another euphemism for prostitute (*OED*) – collateral evidence for the scattered community of Black women in Scotland and England during the sixteenth century suggests a similar trajectory from West Africa, perhaps via the Iberian peninsula.[57] Records show that Elen More was baptized in Scotland; most likely, Lucy Negro was baptized in England, at birth or upon arrival. As I elaborate elsewhere, women from the Islamic world in England who retained their Islamic affiliation (some of them, as *dhimmis*, would have been Christians or Jews in any case) were virtually non-existent prior to the Victorian era.[58]

In this opening chapter, I also consider the Nogay "Tartar girl" who was acquired by Anthony Jenkinson, an agent of the Muscovy Company, in the war-torn Central Asian city of Astrakhan and transported to Queen Elizabeth's court towards the beginning of her reign.[59] Born a Muslim, she was baptized and renamed Ipolita once she reached England; however, she retained the ethnonym "Tartarian." Acquired in the context of English merchant voyages from Russia to Persia during the mid-1550s through the 1570s, she represents a more explicit exchange of a female chattel from the Islamic world than the chance arrival of Elen More on British shores half a century earlier. Although her fate was to become a human "pet," along with "a small Negro page boy [who] attended on the Queen in 1574" and a female dwarf identified as Thomasina, traces of her life persisted in the margins of the Muscovy Company records and in the inventories from Queen Elizabeth's wardrobe, among other sources.[60] As I argue in subsequent chapters, her historical agency also resonated in the literature of the era, such as Shakespeare's early plays (*The Comedy of Errors*, *Love's Labour's Lost*, and *A Midsummer Night's Dream*) and Mary Wroth's groundbreaking prose romance (*The Countesse of Mountgomeries Urania*), via ambiguously racialized representations that appropriate her origins in the Islamic world to English Protestant ends.

Shifting to the early seventeenth century, I conclude the opening chapter with a discussion of Teresa Sampsonia Sherley, a Circassian subject of the Safavid Shah 'Abbas, whose two "embassies" with her husband Robert from Isfahan through Western Europe and eventually to England during the early seventeenth century reverberated in a wide range of documentary accounts and literary works, including Wroth's *Urania*. After Robert's death in Safavid domains following their second return trip to report to the shah, Teresa Sampsonia travelled across Eurasia to reach Rome, where she resided until her own death decades later. She thus occupied multiple positions of subalternity as a Christian subject of the Persian shah and as the Persianate wife of a cosmopolitan Englishman. I assess her agency as evidenced by her negotiation of competing religious affiliations and shared patriarchal norms on her multiple trips from Isfahan through the leading cities of Europe, including Moscow, Cracow, Hamburg, Lisbon, Madrid, Rome, and London. Tracing her extensive itinerary over her long life necessarily shifts the focus away from her connection to her English husband, which is emphasized in most studies of the Sherley brothers. As I establish, she epitomizes what Roxanne Euben, in *Journeys to the Other Shore: Muslim and Western Travelers in Search of Knowledge*, calls the "'translated person' negotiating multiple worlds, languages, and practices" in a truly transhemispheric sense.[61]

Building on these cases studies, in chapter 2, "The Islamic World and the Construction of Early Modern Englishwomen's Authorship: Queen Elizabeth I, the Tartar Girl, and the Tartar-Indian Woman," I address the methodological problem of how to assess, as Margo Hendricks demands in her survey of "Feminist Historiography," "the immigrant [or migrant] woman's position in a world which symbolically exploits her 'otherness' as a literary and cultural foundation for the construction of a particular form of womanhood at the same time as it literally conceals her presence in Renaissance England?"[62] While Hendricks focuses on women of African descent in the context of Francis Drake's raids on Spanish American colonies during the 1570s and England's subsequent transatlantic slave trade, this chapter emphasizes the search for the northeast and the northwest passages to the riches of Asia, which propelled England's proto-imperial project starting in the mid-sixteenth century. As I contend, the "Tartar girl," who was transformed into Queen Elizabeth's "deare and welbeloved woman Ipolita the Tartarian," played a crucial, albeit neglected, role in enhancing the queen's proto-imperialist and proto-orientalist self-fashioning.[63] In line with Hendricks and other feminist scholars who attend to subaltern and/or non-European women's lives in the British Isles, I challenge the still common refrain that sources simply do not exist for a study of British women who travelled to the Islamic world prior to the eighteenth century or, even more so, for girls and women from the Islamic world who travelled to Britain around the same time. Fleshing out these connected histories, I assess how these gendered subalterns' strategies of "survivance" were appropriated by Queen Elizabeth and, as I expand in chapter 3, Lady Mary Wroth, to bolster their authorship and authority.[64]

Concomitant with this focus on English women writers and their multifaceted relations to women from the Islamic world, I investigate the subaltern agency of indigenous women – from Central Asia and what is now Canada – who were transported to England as a result of the elusive search for the northeast and northwest passages to "Cathay" from the mid-1550s through the 1570s. In addition to establishing the basis for England's proto-imperialist project, these ventures marked the beginning of a two-way, if not necessarily equal, flow of travellers, including from the Islamicate regions between Russia and Iran.[65] While men dominated these voyages and for the most part did not bring women with them, a small percentage of elite women are listed as investors, with Queen Elizabeth preeminent. Even less visible are the gendered subalterns forcibly acquired on these voyages: the afore-mentioned Nogay "Tartar" girl, whom Anthony Jenkinson brought (and probably bought) for the queen, and an Inuk woman whom Martin Frobisher abducted, along with her nursing child, as another royal prize. The latter, the first recorded Native American woman in the British Isles, is described along with her countrymen as "people of Cathay, Tartars, Tartar Indians, country people, strange people, and even Moors" in the records of the Frobisher voyages, which is not surprising given many of these Englishmen had travelled the northeast route across Central Asia, where the preponderance of natives they encountered were Crimean and Nogay Tatars.[66] The colonial catachresis "Tartar-Indian" woman thereby resonates with the forced movements of the "Tartar girl" within the expanding early modern "web of empire," which for the English, constrained by the Portuguese and Spanish monopoly over the southeastern and southwestern trade routes, initially extended northwards.[67]

Chapter 3, "The Islamic World and the Construction of Early Modern Englishwomen's Authorship: Lady Mary Wroth, the Tartar-Persian Princess, and the Tartar King," develops this argument by addressing how women who came to England from *Dar al-Islam* during the Elizabethan and Jacobean period informed Mary Wroth's alternately celebrated and excoriated negotiation of authorship. (In)famously, Wroth was the first Englishwoman to publish an original, as opposed to a translated, prose romance: *The Countesse of Mountgomeries Urania* (1621), to which she appended the sonnet sequence *Pamphilia to Amphilanthus*. She was forced to withdraw the first part of the *Urania* from circulation shortly after its initial publication due to pressure from powerful men for whom her depictions of the patriarchal abuse of wives, daughters, and servants struck too close to home. However, she continued with an equally substantial second part, which remained in manuscript until its publication towards the end of the twentieth century as a scholarly edition. She thus occupies the tenuous position of "author" for women during the Jacobean era. At the same time, she shows how early modern Englishwomen aligned themselves with their countrymen's imperial ambitions.

This chapter begins by situating Wroth within the Sidney family literary interest and literal investment in what Thomas James Dandelet, in *The Renaissance of Empire in Early Modern Europe*, calls the "dream of a Renaissance of empire." As Dandelet elaborates, "as an intellectual, cultural, and political project," this "was nothing less than the dominant master narrative that drove European political life for the entire early modern period."[68] As I propose, Wroth's familial connections to the northeast passage ventures during the sixteenth century, which traversed Russia, Central Asia, and Persia, and her connections to the Elizabethan (and later the Jacobean) court, meant she had direct knowledge of and perhaps even contact with individuals such as Ipolita the Tartarian and Teresa Sampsonia Sherley. On her own account, Wroth was an investor in the East India Company, which would have exposed her to further information about these voyages. Building on this historical foundation, I proceed with a close contextualized reading of the Tartar-Persian princess in the manuscript continuation of the *Urania* as a vehicle for Wroth's own negotiations of authorship and authority. This analysis necessarily extends to the Tartarian king, Rodomandro, who marries the character most frequently associated with Wroth in the romance: the Morean poet and princess, Pamphilia. As I argue, Rodomandro epitomizes the tangled racial and religious ascriptions of a romance that seeks to privilege (Christian) European women's agency as writers and rulers against the background of an effaced Ottoman Empire. Embodying foreignness as a Central Asian with a "sunn-burnt" face and familiarity as an Eastern Christian with "hands soe white," he manifests the contradictions of the proto-imperialist and proto-orientalist projection of a universalist, yet ultimately Eurocentric empire extending across Eurasia, which is achieved through the wish-fulfilment of romance.[69] His fraught assimilation into Wroth's "imaginative geography," to extend Edward Said's seminal concept, signals the more fully effaced, but still palpable, presence of women from the Islamic world in early modern England, which is reinforced through the amalgam of Tartar and Persian princesses in the romance.[70]

Chapter 4, "Signifying Gender and Islam in Early Shakespeare: *The Comedy of Errors* (1594) and the Gray's Inn Revels," the first of two chapters on Shakespeare, pursues a tropological consideration of the often contradictory connotations attached to the "Tartar" in Elizabethan drama in terms of the extended impact of Ipolita the Tartarian, who, to recall, was the queen's "deare and welbeloved woman" from the Islamic world.[71] Responding to the performative theory of subject formation elaborated by Judith Butler in *Gender Trouble: Feminism and the Subversion of Identity*, I parse how the classical and historical referents associated with Tartars – along with Turks – were mapped onto the trouble associated with gendered and racialized embodiment in the period. Conventionally, Shakespeare's theatre has been isolated as the locus for such "trouble" because boys and young men played the female roles. However, this assessment ignores the multiple sites for performance in the era, including the royal court and country houses where women appeared in aristocratic entertainments, often alongside professional male actors playing female speaking roles. This "mingle mangle of apparel," in the sixteenth-century anti-theatrical polemicist Philip Stubbes's words, dangerously confused ascriptions of status/ rank and sex/gender, to which we could add shifting ascriptions race, religion, and ethnicity.[72] The latter concatenation relates to the pioneering voyages of Englishmen to the Americas in the second half of the sixteenth century, where they sought to match the Iberian imperialists, and their concurrent voyages to the Safavid Persian and Ottoman Turkish empires, where they were received as supplicants. I submit that Protestant England's position as a proto-imperial realm vis-à-vis these more powerful empires induced a concomitant "racial trouble" in its designations of Self and Other with specific reference to a whitened beauty standard that excluded blackness from the primary definition of "fair" as beautiful, a history I expound in chapter 5.

The account of the Christmas revels at Gray's Inn in 1594/5, which ran from late December to early March, exemplifies this combination of gender trouble and racial trouble through an interlinked series of cultural performances. These include the semi-parodic allegory of the Prince of Purpoole and "an Ambassador from the mighty Emperor of *Russia* and *Moscovy*," enacted by the young gentlemen of the Inns of Court; the madcap premiere of Shakespeare's *The Comedy of Errors*, one of his first ventures into this genre; and *The Masque of Proteus*, involving professional and court performers, with Queen Elizabeth in the audience.[73] While literary critics and historians have mined the *Gesta Grayorum*, the published eyewitness account of the 1594/5 revels, when glossing Shakespeare's early comedies, few have explicated this series of performances as a whole, which is how they were received if not conceived. As I maintain, by reading the published account holistically and historically, the otherwise marginalized figures of Turks and Tartars come to represent what Louis Montrose, in "The Work of Gender in the Discourse of Discovery," calls a "radical and hostile Otherness."[74] In this case, it is to "all *Christendom*," in the words of the revelers.[75] As such, Western and Eastern Christians – namely, the Protestant English and the Orthodox Russians – ally as "proximate figures of Otherness" despite their religious, political, and cultural differences.[76] Complicating the revel's patriarchal homosociality, established across and against ethnic and racial differences, this web of relationships "between men," to evoke Eve Kosofsky Sedgwick's influential paradigm, intersects explicitly with the documented presence of African-descent women in Shakespeare's London such as Lucy Negro, who shared historical links to Islamic West Africa with Elen More.[77] Moreover, this web is prefigured – tropologically and topographically – by the classical Amazons, who persisted within the English male elite's dream and drama of empire. This connected history complicates approaches to gender and the "discourse of discovery" by foregrounding the fraught historical embodiment of subaltern women from the Islamic world (along with the projection of the Amazons into this space) and their neglected, albeit constitutive, role in early modern English literature, including Shakespeare's plays.

Chapter 5, "Signifying Gender and Islam in Late Shakespeare: *Henry VIII* or *All is True* (1613) and British 'Masques of Blackness'," examines the volatile gender politics of the Henrician era in one of Shakespeare's last plays, which abridges a century of "masques of blackness" for a Jacobean court weighing its investments in trans-Atlantic expansionism. Reflecting the uncertainties of the era, the English oscillated between anxieties about their status as "sluggish" imperialists, which term Hakluyt coined at the end of the sixteenth century, and as supplicants to the more powerful polities of the Islamic world, including the Ottoman Empire.[78] This tension imbues the play from its opening scene, which focuses on the Field of Cloth of Gold (*Le Camp du Drap d'Or*): a political spectacle staged in 1520 at the English pale in Calais to celebrate the détente between Henry VIII and the French king, Francis I. The latter would go on to forge an alliance with the Ottomans in the mid-1530s; Henry's daughter, Elizabeth, would follow suit fifty years later. As I propose, the French imperial display in Shakespeare's *Henry VIII*, having "made Britain India" (1.1.21), casts the English as a potential colonizing power and a potential colonial "other."[79] Reinforcing this overdetermined spectacle, the play continues with a masque showcasing "a noble troop of strangers" (1.4.54), coded as Turks and Moors by analogy with similar entertainments in which the historical Henry VIII appeared.

Linked to these competing discourses of empire, the spectacles in Shakespeare's *Henry VIII* are charged with multivalent and troubling representations of three queens – Katherine of Aragon (former), Anne Boleyn (current), and Elizabeth (future) – all of whom are represented as blackened by their fall from patriarchal dynastic imperatives. As indices of England's emerging and uncertain global imperial project, their metaphorical denigration points towards, even as it effaces, the material conditions of those girls and women from the Islamic world that I limn in this study. To recover what Christopher Miller in *Blank Darkness: Africanist Discourse in French* calls "[t]he notion of a nullity," a heuristic I extend to the proto-imperialist and proto-orientalist discourses that are my focus, I proceed to trace more than a century of performances in the Scottish and English courts that incorporate Black women and men, whether literally or figuratively, into "residual" British models of exoticism and "emergent" anglocentric discourses of empire.[80] These include the aforementioned Elen More's performance as the "Black Queen of Beauty" at the Scottish court of James IV; Henry VIII's masquerade "after Turkey fashion" with two ladies of the court dressed as "nigrost or blacke Mores"; and Queen Anna's *Masque of Blackness* (1604/5) with Ben Jonson.[81] As I conclude, adding Shakespeare's play to this genealogy recalls the provenance of women from the Islamic world whose agency has been ignored in studies of the early modern/colonial period, which too often fail to address what Ferguson, in *Dido's Daughters*, identifies as "ideologies of gender." This lacuna results precisely because such studies privilege "the empirical [and, I would add, imperial] archive" at the expense of less tangible evidence.[82]

The final chapter, "The Intersecting Paths of Two Women from the Islamic World: Teresa Sampsonia, Mariam Khanim, and the East India Company," returns to women from the Islamic world who travelled to England from the empires of the Safavids and Mughals during the early seventeenth century with attention, to their connections and intersections. Within the context of England's early commercial engagements on the sub-continent, I consider Mariam Khanim, an Armenian from the Mughal emperor's court, who departed for England with her first husband, the East India Company operative William Hawkins, around the same time Teresa Sampsonia left England for the Safavid court with her "ambassador" husband, Robert Sherley.[83] As I establish, Mariam Khanim and Teresa Sampsonia crossed paths, and may have met, at the Cape of Good Hope in 1613, when their East India Company ships carried them in opposite directions. Sixty years later, Mariam had been incorporated into the poet laureate John Dryden's "mercantile morality play," *Amboyna*, as the deracinated heroine Ysabinda.[84] As I assert, the bilateral movement of women across Eurasia during the early seventeenth century exemplified by this encounter offers a more complicated model of cultural exchange than the unilateral movement of British women captives into the "Barbary States" that has been emphasized in studies of early modern England and the Ottoman-dominated Mediterranean.[85] This shift in geopolitical perspective, moreover, acknowledges the British and Persian female servants who travelled with these relatively privileged women. Although less visible in the extant records than Teresa Sampsonia and Mariam Khanim, the traces of these serving women's lives emerge between the lines of the early East India Company archives, the Carmelite chronicles, and other sources. Together, as I demonstrate throughout this book, the imprints of a diverse range of gendered subalterns in the documentary record and their resonance in the literature of the era speak to the inter-imperial impact of the women who travelled as servants on East India Company ships; the gendered negotiations of "foreign wives" such as Teresa Sampsonia and Mariam Khanim; and the "survivance" of de facto chattel such as Elen More, the "Tartar girl"/Ipolita the Tartarian, Ignorth the Tartar-Indian woman, and Lucy Negro ... if we but listen!

Chapter One

The "Presences of Women" from the Islamic World in Late Medieval Scotland and Early Modern England

Long considered to be the first book issued from the printing press of William Caxton, *The Dictes and Sayings of the Philosophers* (c. 1477) establishes the Arabic treatise *Mukhtar al-hikam wa mahasin al-kalim* ["The Choicest Maxims and Best Sayings"], via successive Spanish, Latin, and French translations, at the foundation of English print culture.[1] As Franz Rosenthal asserts in his detailed bibliographical study of *Mukhtar al-hikam*, these translations from the thirteenth century onwards of this eleventh-century "book of popular philosophy," written by "the Syro-Egyptian historian, philosopher, and bibliophile, Abû l-Wafâ' al-Mubashshir b. Fâtik" four hundred years after the Hijrah, "were landmarks in the literary and intellectual history of the Western European nations."[2] The book had a similar impact on medieval Muslim literature and thought, where its classical Greek proof texts were supplemented by "some sayings of Muslim sages and mystics not belonging to al-Mubashshir's work."[3] As Leila Ahmed elaborates in *Women and Gender in Islam*, this shared legacy, based on "Aristotle's theories," inculcated misogynist dictums into "both Arab and European civilizations."[4]

In *The Dictes and Sayings*, Socrates, along with Aristotle, authorizes this misogyny when he introduces women as a "grete empeshement" or impediment to men. Predictably, a list of the "evils of women" follows, exemplified by "a long [tedious] mayde that lerned to write."[5] In her astute study of women in early English print culture, Anne Coldiron explains how "Caxton restores some misogynist passages that his translator-patron, Anthony Woodville, had suppressed," thereby enhancing the marketability of this landmark text. As she concludes, "[t]he handling of the problematic missing misogyny in the *Dictes* is a telling early signal of the rapidly broadening, sometimes paradoxical, and usually controversial *presences of women* in early English print culture" (emphasis added).[6] For a point of comparison, al-Mubashshir's daughter, as Rosenthal records, "outlived him by many years and transmitted Prophetical traditions in Alexandria."[7] As one of the many female scholars who shaped the early Islamic tradition, she constitutes another absent presence in her father's influential transmission of classical Greek misogyny.[8]

The "presences of women" in this foundational multicultural tome (to recall Coldiron's terminology) constitutes the starting point for this chapter and more broadly for this book, which investigates the incorporation and subsequent erasure of the lives of women from *Dar al-Islam* in early modern Scottish and English literature and culture.[9] I begin with one of "the More lassis" [Moor lasses or girls] – listed as "Helenor in the Count Accounts, possibly Ellen [Elen or Helen] More" – who was featured in the early sixteenth-century Scottish pageants that presaged the masques Ben Jonson crafted almost a century later for King James VI of Scotland, crowned James I of England upon Elizabeth I's death, and his queen consort, Anna of Denmark.[10] Her legacy extends to Lucy Negro, a woman of African descent who worked as a brothel-keeper in late sixteenth-century London and who influenced William Shakespeare's early plays and poems. (I discuss Lucy Negro at greater length in chapter 4.) In this opening chapter, I also consider the "Tartar girl" whose acquisition for Queen Elizabeth I during the mid-sixteenth century was imprinted in the margins of the Muscovy Company records and rehearsed in Shakespeare's plays decades later.[11] Shifting to the early seventeenth century, I focus on a woman of relatively higher status who came from one of the ascendant Islamic empires of the era: Lady Teresa Sampsonia Sherley,[12] a Circassian subject of the Safavid shah who married Robert Sherley, whom seventeenth-century playwright and pamphleteer Thomas Middleton dubbed "this famous English *Persian*."[13] She crossed paths during her travels on an East India Company ship with Mariam Khanim, an Armenian subject of the Mughal emperor, who arrived in England with her second husband, Captain Gabriel Towerson; her first husband was the "East India Company operative, William Hawkins," whom she buried in Ireland.[14] (I discuss Mariam Khanim at greater length in chapter 6.) As I stress in the introduction to this book, while a longitudinal analysis of all the women from the Islamic world who travelled to the British Isles prior to the eighteenth century is hampered by the paucity of "hard" evidence and biases in its interpretation, an approach through these salient case studies from the beginning of the sixteenth century, the middle of the century, and the beginning of the seventeenth century offers valuable insights about how some of these displaced women and girls expressed their agency through various material and semiotic strategies of "survivance," in Gerald Vizenor's formulation, and how their "active survival and resistance to cultural dominance" impacted British literary and cultural productions during their lifetimes and afterwards.[15] These case studies covering the proto-imperial period delineated in the introduction thereby set the stage for the close contextualized readings in subsequent chapters of their "refracted representations," to recall Bindu Malieckal's apt phrase, in the primary documents and literary works of this transitional era.[16]

The "Moor Lass" and the "Tournament of the Wild Knight and the Black Lady"

As indicated above, the "Moor lass" – provisionally designated Elen or Helen More – surfaces in the historical record as the "Black Queen of Beauty" who presided over the Scottish court's entertainments in June 1507 and May 1508 during the reign of King James IV. Louise Olga Fradenburg, in her influential analysis of "The Black Lady" in *City, Marriage, Tournament: Arts of Rule in Late Medieval Scotland*, adjudicates the debate over the identity of the woman who appeared in this tournament, offering that she may have been one of a small but significant group of displaced Africans at court or she may have been a European woman who signified her "blackness" through "black sleeves and gloves," possibly "Queen Margaret herself." The scholarly consensus, as Fradenburg summarizes, nevertheless favours the first ascription, for which she adduces the sixteenth-century Scottish court poet William Dunbar's "Ane Black Moir" as evidence:

> Since we have a poem by Dunbar on the subject of a black woman and a tournament and since we have a tournament of a wild knight and a black lady, it may seem simplest to argue that the black lady of the tournament was a black woman. The black people at James's court were often involved in entertainments, and this may lend some support to the view that Dunbar's poem was written about the tournament of 1507 or 1508.[17]

Although she does not mention the likely Islamic provenance of this "black woman," Fradenburg documents the tradition of representing explicitly Muslim Moors and Turks in medieval and early modern court entertainments across Christian Europe and connects James IV's "tournament of the wild knight and the black lady" to his crusading aspirations.[18] As I propose, while clearly an important example of "The Early Black Presence in the British Isles" (to reference Paul Edwards's groundbreaking article) Elen More also functions as a crucial index of how the lives of girls and women from the Islamic world in early modern Scotland and England resonated in the literature of the period.[19]

Elsewhere I have examined how Elen More's ambivalent agency as an African-descent woman extends through a genealogy that culminates in one of the earliest "queen's masques" for the court of King James I of England, who (to recall) was also James VI of Scotland. As I concluded, her "explicit historical presence as the 'Black Queen of Beauty' in Scottish court entertainments of the sixteenth century suggests her implicit counter-presence in Queen Anna's subsequent *Masque of Blackness* [1604/5]."[20] Clare McManus, in *Women on the Renaissance Stage: Anna of Denmark and Female Masquing in the Stuart Court (1590–1619)*, makes a similar argument, tracing this genealogy to the Danish court of Anna's youth.[21] More recently, Imtiaz Habib in his magisterial study *Black Lives in the English Archives, 1500–1677* situates Elen More with respect to the significant, albeit fleeting, presence of "Blacks" in England from the reign of Henry VIII through the Restoration of Charles II. He shows how she, along with a few other African men and women, became "Portuguese human booty brought back by Scottish privateers to Edinburgh" around the turn of the sixteenth century.[22] Fifty years earlier, the Portuguese had received papal approval "to conquer and reduce to perpetual slavery all 'Saracens and pagans ... and other infidels and enemies of Christ' in West Africa."[23] During this period, "Islam became the royal cult" throughout the region, "but the people continued to practise their old religions" as syncretic or even nominal Muslims.[24]

Nonetheless, scholars who have focused on "Blacks" in early modern Britain – including myself in the earlier article I mentioned – have ignored Elen More's links to the Islamic world, which this nexus implies.[25] One of the reasons for this emphasis on "blackness" over, or to the exclusion of, the Islamicate roots of these historical individuals and the characters based on their lives may be the fraught representations of Shakespeare's Othello on the English stage and in literary criticism, which for centuries effaced his Black African identity by privileging his "Moorish" or Muslim background. As Virginia Mason Vaughan explains in *Performing Blackness on English Stages, 1500–1800*, "It was politically correct in the nineteenth and early twentieth centuries to lighten Othello's skin tone and make him a 'tawny Moor.'"[26] Historically, this oversight accrues from Elen More's conversion to Christianity, along with other Africans in Scotland at this time. For instance, Habib indicates that "Petir Morien or Petir the More" only "appears in the records [1500/1] evidently after he has been christened"; the christenings of Elen More and her companion, Margaret More, occurred three years later. Petir the More "was clearly a favorite companion of the monarch, and well accepted in the early sixteenth-century court of this culturally sophisticated Scottish king."[27] As I submit, Elen More, also a favourite at court, was received more ambivalently. Yet it is her life that continued to resonate in the inaugural entertainments for the Jacobean court, rendered canonical through the imprimatur of Ben Jonson.

During her captivity, Elen More worked as a maidservant for Queen Margaret Tudor, James IV of Scotland's wife and James I of England's maternal great-grandmother, though it is not certain she was her slave.[28] As Habib stresses, she was "visibly pampered," with the records documenting extensive clothing purchases. Habib additionally considers Elen More a "celebrity" for her role as the "Black Queen of Beauty," a performance reprised as a racial masquerade in *The Masque of Blackness* almost a century later.[29] In the earlier Scottish tournament, Elen More was cast as the chivalric prize for James IV who, according to the sixteenth-century chronicler Robert Lindesay of Pitscottie, "jousted himself disguised unknown and he was called the Black Knight who gave battle to all of them that would fight for their lady's sake and especially of the knights and gentlemen of France, England and Denmark."[30] Her objectification as a prize was within the norms of medieval chivalry, as we can see from her representation as beautiful. Her blackness added an exotic edge, which led to more ambivalent representations. *The Accounts of the Lord High Treasurer of Scotland* specify that she was lavishly attired in "a gown of damask flowered with gold, trimmed with green and yellow taffety; she had sleeves and gloves of black 'semys' [seamed] leather, and the sleeves were themselves covered with 'plesaunce' [fine cloth], of which material she also had a kerchief about her arm." In addition, "[s]he rode in state in a 'chair triumphal' covered with Flemish taffety, one hundred and sixty ells of this stuff – white, yellow, purple, green, and gray – having been purchased in Flanders at a cost of £88," a princely sum in the era.[31] Two elegantly attired women accompanied her – the records do not specify their ethnicity or race – as well as two squires of the court. The finale of the tournament, with its focus on her sexuality, was more earthy: the winner, in the courtly manner, received a kiss and an embrace; the loser, following the comically sexualized fabliau tradition, had to "cum behind and kis hir hippis," as depicted in Dunbar's oft-cited poem on "Ane Black Moir."[32] In this double-edged paean, Dunbar likens her to "an aep" [ape], "gangarell" [possibly a toad], and a "catt" while emphasizing her "mekle lippis" [thick lips] and her blackness.[33] Although informed by the "flyting" tradition of medieval Scotland,[34] Dunbar's poem anticipates the racism of subsequent discourses of empire.[35]

What remains less clear is how Elen More's "forced relocation" informs this performance, which does not include any overt Islamicate references.[36] Only her last name suggests her origins in the Islamic world, with "Moor" in the early modern period meaning "a Muslim" and/or "black person" (*OED*).[37] Given that King James IV promoted a "crusading diplomacy" against the Turks throughout his reign, I broach a preliminary genealogy by way of analogy with the entertainments in the court of King Henry VIII around this time, which featured highly orientalized images of Turks and Moors.[38] Specifically, as Tudor chronicler Edward Hall conveys, in 1510 Henry VIII and the Earl of Essex appeared dressed "after Turkey fashion," with "greate rolles of Gold" and brandishing scimitars. The faces of their male attendants were blackened "lyke Moreskoes" and the court ladies had "their heades rouled in pleasauntes and typpers like the Egipcians, enbroudered with gold. Their faces, neckes, armes and handes, covered with fyne plesaunce blacke ... so that the same ladies semed to be nigrost or blacke Mores."[39] This disguising arguably constitutes the prototypical "masque of blackness" for the English court, with similar entertainments staged in Scotland during the same period. The Henrician entertainment, which features an array of orientalist signifiers with its fetishized "Turkish" accessories, "Egyptian" headgear, and blackface, thus brings to the fore the implicit orientalism of the earlier Scottish tournament. (In chapter 5, I return to these early sixteenth-century entertainments as they relate to one of Shakespeare's last plays, *Henry VIII*.)

The Masque of Blackness, Queen Anna's inaugural court entertainment with Ben Jonson, also introduces Islamicate signifiers through the copious sources Jonson added to his published script for this performance. Elsewhere I have examined Jonson's marginal gloss to the authoritative *Description of Africa* by the "converted Moor," Johannes Leo Africanus – born al-Hasan ibn Muhammad al-Wezzan al-Fasi – as "supplementary in the Derridean sense of being simultaneously marginal *and* constitutive."[40]

Here, I argue that Elen More's likely provenance in the Islamic world functions the same way: even as it is rendered marginal through her conversion to the dominant religion and manners of the sixteenth-century Scottish court, as encoded through the term "Moor" it becomes constitutive of the early modern "ideologies of racial difference" that subtended the anglocentric discourse of empire.[41] As subsequent chapters detail, the imprint of her agency and abjection as "The Black Queen of Beauty" in the early sixteenth-century Scottish records continued to inform this oscillation between religious and racial registers in the proto-imperialist and proto-orientalist entertainments of the Tudor and Jacobean courts.

The "Tartar Girl"/Ipolita the Tartarian: Queen Elizabeth's "Deare and Welbeloved Woman"

The "Tartar girl," whose itinerary in the mid-sixteenth century took her from the Central Asian region between the Black and the Caspian Seas to Elizabethan England, constitutes a more explicit exchange of a female chattel from the Islamic world than that suggested by Elen More's obscured origins.[42] As a subaltern subject on multiple levels, she receives a fleeting reference in "A letter of *Master Anthonie Jenkinson* upon his returne from *Boghar* [Bukhara] to the worshipful *Master Henry Lane*, agent for the *Moscovie* Companie, resident in Vologda, written in the *Mosco* [Moscow] the 18. of September 1559," and published in Richard Hakluyt's *The Principal Navigations, Voyages, Traffiques and Discoveries of the English Nation* forty years later. This letter conveys the results, mostly disappointing, of Jenkinson's first attempt to "voyage toward the lande of *Cathay*" via Central Asia, where "incessant and continuall warres" made him turn back once he reached what is now Uzbekistan and was then a contested region between the Russian, Safavid, and Ottoman empires. After this brief report, Jenkinson signs off, "[t]hus giving you most heartie thanks for my wench Aura Soltana, I commend you to the tuition of God, who send you health with hearts desire," a classic example of the exchange of women between men. Nonetheless, Hakluyt's marginal note – "This was a young Tartar girle which he gave to the Queene afterwarde" – complicates the patriarchal circuit of this exchange by incorporating women privileged by class.[43] This is the only direct evidence we have in the English sources of this gendered subaltern from the Islamic world. However, by reading these traces contextually and linking them to other traces that have been similarly passed over as enigmas, I have determined that this "Tartar girl" is "Ipolita the Tartarian," whom Queen Elizabeth called her "deare and welbe-loved woman."[44] Beyond the scanty documentary record, she resonates in a variety of literary works from the period, including Shakespeare's *A Midsummer Night's Dream* (first performed sometime between 1594 and 1596) and Mary Wroth's *The Countesse of Mountgomeries Urania* (the first part published in 1621; the second part continued in manuscript through the 1630s).

Like Elen More and other displaced Africans in the sixteenth-century Scottish and English courts who hailed from the Islamic world, the "Tartar girl" fulfilled an ornamental role once she reached England. Importantly, even though this role may not have resulted in extreme privation, it did not foreclose her de facto chattel status.[45] This status, moreover, is one she carried from the Safavid and Ottoman empires, where Central Asians, especially girls, were frequently sold into slavery.[46] As such, the name Jenkinson gives in his letter, "Aura Sol-tana," alludes to the multi-ethnic, multi-confessional elite harems of the Islamic empires of the era, particularly the Ottomans. Here, females of non-Muslim provenance, invariably slave girls throughout the six-teenth and seventeenth centuries, could rise to the exalted position of "sultana" if they produced a son for the sultan or, more decisively, if that son became the ruler.[47] Clearly, in the English system this was not an option, but its reference would lend prestige to the Elizabethan court, if only by association. It also evokes the practice of replacing the names of enslaved Africans with those from the classical empires that inspired early modern English efforts, as with Elen More, whose name alludes to Helen of Troy.[48] Likewise, in medieval Italy, "female Tartar slaves imported from the Black Sea" lost their names at christening to "a boring set of narrow choices, with Caterina, Lucia, and Margherita leading the way."[49] Queen Elizabeth may have attended the baptism ceremony of her "Tartar girl," where she was renamed Ipolita (Ippol-yta, Hippolyta), which suggests the Amazonian queen conquered by the Athenian king and adventurer Theseus. (Shakespeare features this queen, who hailed from the same region as the "Tartar girl," in *A Mid-summer Night's Dream*.) In any case, as the accolade "oure deare and welbeloved woman" implies, Ipolita the Tartarian was a cherished member of Queen Elizabeth's retinue, which does not discount her subordination and even dehumanization.[50]

Concomitantly, Ann Rosalind Jones and Peter Stallybrass, in *Renais-sance Clothing and the Materials of Memory*, calculate that "the livery of Ippolyta the Tartarian must have cost significantly more than the wages of Lady Cobham for a year's work."[51] As the lavishness of this livery suggests, the erstwhile "Tartar girl" enjoyed a life of material comfort, sharing a similar status with a "small Negro page boy [who] attended on the Queen in 1574" and a female dwarf identified as Thomasina, who received equally rich garments and accessories.[52] Similarly, Janet Arnold, in *Queen Elizabeth's Wardrobe Unlock'd*, records that "Ippolyta was still in the Queen's service in 1569" as attested by the additional garments she received.[53] Nevertheless, as "exotic ornaments and pets," their life of comfort came at cost of their full humanity, even though none of them were slaves in the strict sense. This girl's position in the English court is therefore analogous to Elen More's in the Scottish court. As humanistic geographer Yi-Fu Tuan affirms, "affection is not the opposite of dominance; rather it is dominance's anodyne."[54]

Yet, as a "Tartar" this girl signified even more complexly than a "Moor," both in racialized and religious terms. As I have argued elsewhere, the figure of the Tartar in English cultural productions of the sixteenth and seventeenth centuries was generally positive, based as it was on a deracinated representation of Timur/Tamerlane as an antidote to Ottoman expansionism in the period.[55] Tamerlane in English pamphlets – if not necessarily in Christopher Marlowe's play *Tamburlaine the Great* (1587/8) – presented a *tabula rasa* in terms of religion, with marked sympathies for Christians suffering under Ottoman hegemony, whereas the historical Timur (Temür) was a Sunni Muslim with Sufi leanings.[56] The terms of racialized abuse in Shakespeare's *A Midsummer Night's Dream* – "Away, you Ethiope!" and "Out, tawny Tartar, out" (3.2.258, 264) – are therefore outliers when compared with the bulk of representations of Tartars in English literature of the era, including the Tartar-Persian princess in Mary Wroth's *Urania*. In Wroth's prose romance, this princess and her brother, the Tartar king, Rodomandro, are Eastern Christians enlisted to save the beleaguered West, a conjunction I explore in chapter 3. Racially, Tartars, like Persians, were figured as white, albeit not quite, rather than black. They were frequently conflated with those Native Americans – Inuits or Algonquian from the region around Labrador – forcibly transported to England from the turn of the sixteenth century onwards, who once acculturated to English norms allegedly did not appear "other" to contemporary observers, as I detail in chapter 2. Ironically, while Tartars and Persians, when converted, could assimilate as "white" into English culture, this assimilation resulted in an even more complete erasure than the increasingly denigrated figure of the female "blackamoor."[57] As subsequent chapters show, the "Tartar girl" – Ipolita the Tartarian – repeatedly surfaces in the documentary record and resonates in the literature of the era through ambiguously racialized representations that ultimately appropriate her origins in the Islamic world to English Protestant ends.

"Theresia Sampsonia Amazonites Samphuffi Circassiae Principis Filia": Teresa Sampsonia Sherley, Amazon and Circassian

Compared with Elen More and Ipolita the Tartarian's forced transport, Lady Teresa Sampsonia Sherley's multiple journeys to Western Europe and across Eurasia involved a degree of agency not available to these captives. Instead, like Lady Mary Wortley Montagu, the wife of the British ambassador to the Ottoman Empire from 1716 to 1718, Teresa Sampsonia travelled with her husband, the aforementioned "English *Persian*" Robert Sherley, with her journey from the Islamic world to England the obverse of Montagu's.[58] After Robert's death at Qazvin, she trekked across Eurasia to reach Rome, where she lived until her own death four decades later. She accordingly occupied multiple positions of subalternity as a Christian subject of the Persian shah and as the Persianate wife of a cosmopolitan Englishman.[59] While details of her life have been submerged in the biographies of her husband and his brothers, I seek to assess Teresa's agency as she negotiated competing religious affiliations and shared patriarchal norms during her travels and travails from Isfahan through the leading cities of Europe, including Moscow, Cracow, Hamburg, Lisbon, Madrid, Rome, and London. As I explained in the introduction, tracing her extensive itinerary over her long life necessarily shifts the focus away from her connection to her English husband, which is privileged in studies of the Sherley brothers.[60] She consequently emerges as a prime example of what Roxanne Euben in *Journeys to the Other Shore: Muslim and Western Travelers in Search of Knowledge* calls the "'translated person' negotiating multiple worlds, languages, and practices."[61]

Although often reduced to the nameless wife of Robert Sherley, Teresa Sampsonia was represented through a conflicting array of English-language pamphlets, travelogues, chronicles, and literary works, which Muhammad Nezam-Mafi productively labels "Sherlian discourse."[62] Augmenting this discourse are eyewitness accounts by English travellers in Safavid and Mughal domains, such as Thomas Herbert and Thomas Coryat, who reported their several encounters with Robert and Teresa.[63] An additional textual source, which offers perspectives on Teresa's life not included in the English accounts, is *A Chronicle of the Carmelites in Persia*, the compiled records of the Catholic religious order that established a mission in Isfahan with the permission of Shah 'Abbas. (The first Discalced Carmelite mission left Rome in 1604 and arrived in 1607; an Augustinian mission, which was sent from Goa in 1602, preceded it.)[64] The only known document Teresa wrote in English is a petition addressed to King James I, defending her husband against the accusations of imposture from a competing Persian envoy, Naqd 'Ali Beg.[65] Visual evidence includes a series of portraits painted by Anthony van Dyck while Teresa and Robert were in Rome, along with anonymous portraits made in England.[66] Letters and other official papers signed by Shah 'Abbas focus on her husband, and so give only a peripheral understanding of Teresa's life while in Iran.[67] This array of sources raises a host of methodological questions about the effacement of subalterns (gendered, racialized, religious, and otherwise) in the historical record, the range of information required to access their historical agency, and the pitfalls of restoring them to history by creating composite narratives.

Drawing on the above sources with due caution, we can piece together the following lineaments of Teresa Sampsonia's life: born around 1589, "Sampsonia" (her ancestral name) was the "daughter of a Circassian chieftain named Sampsuff Iscaon" or "Isma'il Khan."[68] Herbert, a gentleman traveller who conversed with Teresa while in Safavid domains and drew his information directly from her, specifies in his travelogue from 1677 that "[t]he Countrey she first drew breath in was *Cyrcashia* [Circassia], that which *Pomponius Mela* calls *Sargacia*, near *Palus Mæotis*, adjoyning *Georgia*, and 'twixt the Northerly parts of the Black and *Caspian* Seas."[69] In the 1634 edition, he is more expansive:

> Though, it may seeme impertinent, I cannot passe by in silence, without injury to her memory, whom I so much honoured, the thrice worthy and undaunted Lady *Terezia*, his faithfull Wife, to this sad time, constant to our company, her Faith was ever Christian, her parents so, and noble, her Countrey *Circashia*, which joynes to *Georgia*, and to *Zuiria*, neere the *Euxine* [Black] and *Caspian* Seas.[70]

Kadir Natho, in his synoptic history, specifies that "Circassians, who call themselves *Adyghe*, are the aborigines of the Northwestern Caucasus," which extends "from the great Caspian Sea to the Black Sea."[71]

As Seteney Shami clarifies in her entry on "Circassians" for the *Encyclopedia of the Modern Middle East and North Africa*,

> The term encompasses several groups linked by language and culture who refer to themselves in their own languages by different ethnonyms; primary among them are the Adyge, Abaza, and Ubykh. The terms *Circassian* (English), *Çerkes* (Turkish), *Cherkess* (Russian), and *Sharkass* (Arabic) are used by outsiders loosely to include various north Caucasian peoples.[72]

Amjad Jaimoukha, in *The Circassians: A Handbook*, adds that "[t]he first mention of the name Circassia was made by John de Plano Carpini, Pope Innocent IV's envoy to the Great Khan of the Mongols, who made his journey in 1245 AD."[73] The narratives of Carpini and other medieval missionaries to Central Asia were republished in Hakluyt's *The Principal Navigations, Voyages, Traffiques and Discoveries of the English Nation*, which anachronistically sutured them into the emerging anglocentric discourse of empire.[74] Hence, an interest in Circassians, a designation introduced into the Western lexicon during the medieval era, newly resonated for an early modern English audience interested in global travel, trade, and colonialism.

As Jaimoukha underscores, Circassians have long been associated with "beauty, heroism and gallantry." Moreover, "[d]espite the relative dominance of the male sex, women in Circassian society in general enjoyed a relatively good position, perhaps unparalleled by any other 'Eastern people.'"[75] They were not secluded, they could choose their marriage partners, and polygamy was not tolerated. However, they were also considered ideal concubines for Muslim "harems," and often bore this stigma whether they were slaves or not. Representations of Teresa Sampsonia as a Circassian thus evoke the positive qualities of beauty and bravery, even though the latter challenged patriarchal dictates (Eastern and Western) forbidding women to travel and bear arms. At the same time, she laboured under the assumption that as a Circassian she was Robert's concubine rather than his wife. For instance, a report circulated among the Carmelites that Robert "purchased a slave from Circassia, a province situated between Muscovy and Persia, who belonged to the *Muhammadan* faith, kept her as his wife, and because it was made a point of religious scruple and duty he had her baptized ... and married her."[76] Other Carmelite sources contest this description of Teresa as "a bought slave."[77] Indeed, it may be that Teresa is more accurately denoted "a 'slave' of the king" in the sense Robert was, as mentioned in this same report, which meant he owed his absolute loyalty to the shah, as in the Ottoman *kul* system.[78]

Connected to her Circassian background, Teresa's natal religion is not entirely clear, with sources such as Herbert asserting "[s]he was of *Christian* Parentage, and honourable descent," but with the records of the Carmelites suggesting she may have been born a Muslim, which is plausible.[79] Circassians began to convert to Islam on a significant scale in the sixteenth century; however, given the Russian influence at the same time, Teresa may have been from an Eastern Orthodox background. As Jaimoukha remarks, "During this period, it was common to find both Muslim, Christian and even pagan members in the same family."[80] Whatever the case, she was certainly baptized as a Roman Catholic by the Carmelites in 1608, after which she married Robert and left for their first European embassy. Her "Christian" name, Teresa, derives from the founder of the Discalced Carmelites, Teresa of Ávila, and she "wore on her breast a small relic of the flesh of S[t]. Teresa, given her in Madrid by the Carmelite Mother Beatrice, niece of the saint."[81] Ironically, for some this baptism raised doubts about whether Teresa was an Orthodox Christian, rather than a Muslim, prior to converting to Catholicism. In other words, she would not have needed to be baptized if she was already a Christian. However, doctrinal differences may have led her to do so.[82]

Furthermore, English pamphlets, such as Anthony Nixon's *The Three English Brothers* (1607), wrongly describe Teresa Sampsonia as niece of "the Emperour of *Persia*." Later in this narrative, Nixon calls her "the Kings [shah's] cousin Germaine" (or first cousin), which is even more fanciful.[83] More likely, she was related to one of the women in the shah's household, who could have been "a favorite wife" or a concubine.[84] Rudi Matthee, focusing on Christians in Savavid Iran, discusses how "the harems of rulers and court officials became filled with women from the Caucasus" during the sixteenth and seventeenth centuries.[85] Many of these women, some of whom became mothers of Safavid rulers, were from Christian backgrounds. John Anthony Butler, in his critical edition of Herbert's 1677 travelogue, proposes that this aunt could be "Tzarievna Marta, a Circassian herself."[86] With the imperial harem of the shah, like the female quarters of the Ottoman sultan's household, functioning as a complex "training institution" for "the servants of the royal family," Teresa's kinswoman could also have been one of the numerous women who served as administrators, educators, and other functionaries in such gender-segregated environments.[87] As with the contemporaneous case of Mariam Khanim, which I discuss along-side Teresa Sampsonia's travels and travails in chapter 6, it is likely that the shah arranged her marriage with the Englishman in reward for his services.

Accompanying her husband on his first journey as Shah 'Abbas's envoy to the sovereigns of Christian Europe – including the Holy Roman Emperor, the pope, the king of Spain, and the English king – Teresa Sampsonia travelled through Moscow to Poland, where Robert left her for two years as he continued to Prague, Florence, Rome, Milan, Genoa, Barcelona, and Madrid. She rejoined him in Lisbon via Hamburg and they travelled from thence to Madrid and Valladolid; they left for England from Bayonne, arriving around the beginning of August 1611, where they remained until January 1613; after an interlude in Safavid domains and a further residence in Spain, they returned once more to England in 1623, staying until 1627. In early November 1611, Teresa gave birth to their child, Henry, with Queen Anna and Prince Henry (the eldest son of King James I) standing as his godparents. Little else is known about possibly the first Anglo-Persian born in England; however, the evidence that Mariam Khanim visited him is tantalizing, which I adjudicate in chapter 6.[88] Robert and Teresa's return trips on East India Company ships took them from Madagascar, around the Arabian peninsula, through the Mughal Empire, including cities such as Agra, Lahore, and Goa. Teresa saved her husband's life at least twice: once as they set off on their first journey when his Persian enemies sought to kill him, for which the Carmelites praise her as "a true Amazon," and again when the couple encountered hostile Portuguese traders on their way to Goa.[89] Fittingly, in her portraits she holds a pistol in her right hand, which art historian Sheila Canby identifies as a symbol of her "dauntless courage" based on these episodes.[90] More broadly, it alludes to the Circassians' fame as warriors, both women and men, with their roots stretching into pre-historic matriarchies.[91]

Upon arriving in Qazvin after their second extended trip through Europe, the Sherley couple experienced constant harassment. A Carmelite narrative states that Persian rivals "contrived to get them into discredit with the Shah by saying that Donna Teresa, before she became a Christian, had professed the Muhammadan religion." This was an extremely serious charge that could have resulted in Teresa's execution as an apostate. The narrative continues: "although the story was false and a calumny, still for all that it was published abroad in the Court that the king intended to have her burnt." The possibility apparently upset Robert so much that he contracted "a very serious illness from which he died at the end of 15 days [in 1628], while the Countess [Teresa Sampsonia] remained always courageous in spirit and resisting the many blows which were aimed at her from all sides."[92] More realistically, Robert died from dysentery, which also claimed the life of the English ambassador, Sir Dodmore Cotton. Thomas Herbert, who witnessed Robert's death and its aftermath, corroborates the ensuing persecution of Teresa, which involved the expropriation of her property and threats to her life. As he records, a group led by *"Mamet-Ally-beg* [Mehmet Ali Bey]," Robert's inveterate enemy, "(without any Apology for their rudeness, or pity to her distress) broke-ope her Chests, and plundered her of what was valuable ... not caring if the Lady starved." Herbert praises her as the "thrice worthy and heroick Lady, *Teresia*" for her ingenuity and courage in this dire situation.[93] She later coped with her tenuous position by dissimulating her whereabouts, hiding in an Armenian convent rather than seeking shelter with the Carmelites.[94]

Several years later, she was able to leave Safavid domains, despite the ban on women's travel; she resided for three years in Istanbul before leaving for Rome in 1634, where she lived for over three decades. In 1658, she arranged for Robert's remains to be transported to their final resting place in the Carmelite Church of Santa Maria della Scala across the Tiber in Trastevere.[95] His epitaph, in which she may have had a hand, celebrates him as "Legato ad Scia Abbam Regem Persarum [Ambassador of Shah Abbas, King of Persia]," among other accolades. Upon her death in 1668, she was interred alongside him, with her epitaph commemorating her as "Teresia Sampsonia Amazonites" [i.e., "a native of the region of the Amazons"].[96] This final tribute recalls her Circassian roots, with the Amazons traditionally linked to the Black Sea region.[97] It thereby underscores her indomitable spirit and acknowledges her subversion of patriarchal gender norms common to the Muslim and Christian cultures she encountered.

In this relatively longer case study, made so by the greater quantity of available evidence, I have sought to understand Teresa Sampsonia's subaltern positioning across multiple registers along with her relative privilege as a diplomat's wife. My primary aim was to explicate the references in Western European sources to her Circassian background, where it carried a range of positive, albeit ambivalent, connotations. However, many more questions remain about Teresa's journeys, including the two years she spent at a convent in Cracow while her husband proceeded to Madrid on his mission for Shah 'Abbas; the three years she spent in Istanbul after leaving Iran for the last time; and the final three decades she spent in the vicinity of Santa Maria della Scala.[98] We might also ask what appeal Carmelite spirituality had for Teresa, who took her Christian name from the mystical founder of the order? How did it resonate with the Sufi-infused spirituality of the Safavids and the shamanistic heritage of the Circassians? While Teresa Sampsonia crossed multiple religious boundaries, we may find a link in the mysticism that infuses all three traditions. In short, she should be included among the "women on the margins" whose lives Natalie Zemon Davis has reconstructed, and when necessary imagined, in terms of "a borderland between cultural deposits that allowed new growth and surprising hybrids," as should the equally resonant examples of Elen More and Ipolita the Tartarian.[99]

Three "Extreme Cases": Recovering Gendered Subalterns from the Islamic World

Dwelling on the most celebrated instance of an involuntary traveller from the Muslim world to Western Europe during the sixteenth century, Davis in her critical biography of al-Hasan ibn Muhammad al-Wazzan al-Fasi – known as "'Iean [Jean] Leon, African ...' in French (1556); 'Iohannes [Johannes] Leo Africanus' in Latin (1556); and 'Iohn [John] Leo, a More' in English (1600)" – offers an additional term we can apply to those girls and women from the Islamic world who travelled to the British Isles during the sixteenth and early seventeenth centuries.[100] Despite the more extensive documentation, he represents "an *extreme case* – most North African Muslims were not captured by Christian pirates or, if they were, were not handed over to the pope – but an extreme case can often reveal patterns available for more everyday experience and writing" (emphasis added).[101] The patterns revealed by the lives of the individuals I have covered – all even more extreme cases due to the restrictions on women's travel in traditional Christian and Muslim societies – reveal these exceptional women's negotiations of exceptionally difficult circumstances. All converted from their natal religion, whether various Islams or Eastern Christianities, to Catholicism or Protestantism, both Western European sects. In contrast to al-Hasan al-Wazzan, the possibility of such women retaining their religion, particularly if they were Muslims, was nil prior to the eighteenth century and perhaps prior to the nineteenth century.[102] Given the isolation they experienced, whether as captives or wives without any significant contact with their ethnic group, it would be surprising if they retained or returned to their natal religion, even in its cultural aspects. Yet, what is significant, particularly for this proto-imperialist era, is the degree of agency they exercised as displaced girls and women.

As we have seen, critics continue to debate whether Elen More, as the "Black Queen of Beauty," was lavishly praised or cruelly mocked; however, both sides tend to efface her ability to negotiate her displacement, despite her story's resemblance to that of al-Hasan al-Wazzan, who was also captured by pirates and gifted to a Western European potentate. Admittedly, he had access to literacy in multiple languages and proximity to his home in the Maghreb, while Elen More was reduced to a spectacle and stranded on the northern edge of Europe. However, insights into his strategies of assimilation and dissimulation might illuminate the more sparsely documented lives of women from the Islamic world like Elen More.[103] Attempting "[t]o recover the lost black women of the English Renaissance," Imtiaz Habib offers a "radical" approach for assessing this gendered subaltern's agency as inscribed in Dunbar's poem even though he does not attend to the Islamicate aspects of her background:

> ... in her interaction with the textuality of her inscriber's discourse, the poem's subject, Elen More, may be resisting and subverting the conventions of the poem's very inscription, she may be resisting the writing of herself. In that resistance is her ghostly voicing, her echoing auditory existence. She speaks from inside the moment of her historical soiling.[104]

I posit that she similarly negotiated the conditions of her initial performance in the "tournament of the wild [or 'black'] knight and the black lady,"[105] which persisted as a model of resistance for Queen Anna and her ladies in *The Masque of Blackness* (see chapter 5), albeit one layered with white women's proto-imperialist and proto-orientalist desires. Ipolita the Tartarian, who has received negligible attention from critics, displays a similar negotiation of her place in Queen Elizabeth I's court, where she became the queen's "deare and welbeloved woman" after having been valued by the Muscovy Company agent Anthony Jenkinson, along with "many goodly Tartars children" devastated by the conquest of Astrakhan, at the price of "a loafe of bread worth six pence in England."[106] We should not be too quick to dismiss her as one of the exotic "freaks" – in the sixteenth-century sense of *lusus naturae* or "sport of Nature" (*OED*) – collected by Renaissance sovereigns.[107] Instead, we should grant that Ipolita effectively negotiated her way into the queen's affections and therefore into a life of some stability and comfort. Nor should we be too quick to ascribe the racialized epithets in Shakespeare's *A Midsummer Night's Dream* to her, as other references to Tartars in English-language texts of the period are relatively positive, even as they are premised on their assimilation as white and Christian, albeit Eastern.

Teresa Sampsonia Sherley was not an involuntary traveller, as were Elen and Ipolita, both of whom landed on British shores as slaves though we cannot be sure they remained such. Yet, as a dependent wife in the Islamic empire from which she hailed and the English culture in which she lived for extended periods, Teresa cannot be set in the same category as the "voluntarie travellers" from those exclusively male professions listed in Thomas Palmer's *An Essay of the Meanes how to make our Travailes, into forraine Countries, the more profitable and honourable*.[108] While wives were generally obliged to follow their husbands, she may have desired to go with hers, just as Desdemona does in Shakespeare's *The Tragedy of Othello, the Moor of Venice* (1603/4). Teresa Sampsonia's life with Robert certainly presented as many dangers as Desdemona's once she left her father's home, even if it did not end in tragedy; having survived her husband by decades, the full extent of her life actually begins to seem more like Othello's with "most disastrous chances," "moving accidents by flood and field," and "hair-breadth [e]scapes" (1.3.133–5). To review a few episodes: she extricated her husband from his difficulties in England when a rival ambassador appeared on the scene during their second visit, she protected him when the Portuguese attacked him on their voyages through Mughal domains, and she persisted during the persecution that ensued after he died on their return trip to Persia. Although it took several years of intense hardship, she finally settled beside the Carmelite Church of Santa Maria della Scala in Rome, thus confirming her ties to this missionary order. Most critics have read her life through that of her husband – the "famous English *Persian*," Robert Sherley – but she equally belongs in a feminocentric genealogy signalled by the amulet she wore as a source of protection and connection to Teresa of Ávila, which was gifted to her by the saint's niece. As such, her itinerary underscores how the lives of women from the Islamic world in the British Isles during the sixteenth- and seventeenth-centuries impacted English culture and went beyond it.

Chapter Two

The Islamic World and the Construction of Early Modern Englishwomen's Authorship: Queen Elizabeth I, the Tartar Girl, and the Tartar-Indian Woman

This chapter, along with the next, argues that girls and women brought to England from the Islamic world during the late sixteenth century through the early seventeenth century informed the negotiation of authorship and authority by two of the era's most important women writers: Queen Elizabeth I, who "produced a substantial corpus of poems, speeches, letters, prayers, and translations" over her forty-five reign as "'king' or 'prince'" and "virgin queen," and Lady Mary Wroth, who was the first Englishwoman to publish an original, rather than a translated, secular prose romance and sonnet sequence.[1] As detailed in chapter 1, these girls and women range from de facto slaves to servants of various ranks to merchants' and ambassadors' wives, all of whom were "trafficked" in the dual sense Jonathon Burton deploys in *Traffic and Turning: Islam and English Drama, 1579–1624*: "the transportation of merchandise for the purposes of trade between distant or distinct communities" and "any form of intercourse, communication, or business involving an exchange, sometimes with illicit connotations like those that attached themselves to travel and trade."[2] If privileged Englishwomen are at one end of this global nexus, the "Tartar girl" Anthony Jenkinson acquired, ostensibly as a gift for Queen Elizabeth, is at the other end. As I have shown, her subaltern agency and impact can be traced in the documentary record through isolated marginalia, brief mentions in inventories, and later allusions in literary works. She can be seen, thereby, as a constitutive and resistant component of the emerging anglocentric discourse of empire. In this chapter, I extend my argument by specifying how this multiply marginalized subject, renamed "Ipolita the Tartarian" upon her arrival in England, was used to enhance the queen's imperialist self-fashioning. As I argue here, she also served as a template for the tendentious descriptions of Native American (and, specifically, Inuit) women incorporated into the anglocentric discourse of global trade, colonization, and empire that accrued from the northeast and northwest passage ventures initiated during the mid-sixteenth century.[3]

In examining these connected histories with an emphasis on gendered subalterns and their neglected lives, I accordingly revisit Margo Hendricks's productive interrogation of feminist historiography in *A Companion to Early Modern Women's Writing* through the optic of girls and women brought from the Islamic world to early modern England. As Hendricks demands,

> how do feminist scholars of early modern English culture understand the immigrant [or migrant] woman's position in a world which symbolically exploits her "otherness" as a literary and cultural foundation for the construction of a particular form of womanhood at the same time as it literally conceals her presence in Renaissance England?[4]

While Hendricks focuses on women of African descent in the context of Francis Drake's raids of Spanish American colonies during the 1570s and England's subsequent transatlantic slave trade, this chapter emphasizes the search for the northeast and the northwest passages to the riches of Asia, which propelled the anglocentric imperial project starting in the mid-sixteenth century. It also marked the beginning of a two-way – albeit not equal – flow of travellers, including girls and women from West Africa, Central Asia, West Asia (including the Safavid Empire), and South Asia (including the Mughal Empire). In line with Hendricks and other feminist scholars who attend to gendered subalterns in the early modern/colonial period, I consequently challenge the still common refrain that sources simply do not exist for a study of British women who travelled to the Islamic world prior to the eighteenth century or, even more so, women from the Islamic world who travelled to Britain around the same time.[5] Ultimately, my analysis of Queen Elizabeth's and Lady Mary Wroth's self-fashioning goes even further in reconceptualizing English-women's authorship during an era of "firsts" by acknowledging these gendered subalterns as one of its facilitating conditions.[6]

The Queen's Letters, Anthony Jenkinson, and the Shah

The first two volumes of the second edition of Richard Hakluyt's *The Principal Navigations, Voyages, Traffiques and Discoveries of the English*

Nation (1599), often overshadowed by the final volume on colonialism in the Americas (1600), feature "the worthy Discoveries, &c. of the *English* toward the North and Northeast by Sea" extending into Russian, Persian, and Ottoman domains.[7] These volumes include Queen Elizabeth's correspondence with a range of Muslim rulers and signal her increasing awareness of the politics of positioning during an era when England was, as Lisa Jardine and Jerry Brotton assert in *Global Interests: Renaissance Art between East and West*, a "comparatively minor" player in the macropolitics of the region.[8] Because the balance of power favoured Islamic empires such as the Ottomans and their rivals, the Safavids, Elizabeth did not – and, indeed, could not – take an orientalist stance in her correspondence. Instead, she had to finesse the perception that she was a supplicant and her kingdom a potential tributary. Later in the century, this eastern trade became more propitious for several reasons, including England's post-Reformation isolation from Catholic Europe, which led the queen to make strategic alliances with Muslim rulers as like-minded iconoclasts and monotheists. Still, in negotiating this double-edged role, she sought to conceal her efforts from domestic audiences by distancing the crown from negotiations with non-Protestant Christians and non-Christians more generally. Instead, joint-stock companies such as the Russia (or Muscovy) and the Levant (or Turkey) companies took the lead.[9]

Prior to Elizabeth's unlikely accession to the throne in 1558, English merchants quietly sought a foothold in the expansionist Russian Empire ruled by Ivan IV (b. 1530), who was named Grand Prince upon the death of his father in 1533 and ultimately crowned tsar in 1547.[10] He died in 1584. The first voyage, led by Hugh Willoughby and Richard Chancellor, left English shores in 1553 "for the search and discoverie of the Northerne part of the worlde, to open a way and passage to our men for travaile to newe and unknown kingdomes," meaning "Cathay" or China and, by extension, India.[11] Unexpectedly, they veered across the White Sea, with Chancellor learning "from some natives that the country he had reached was called Russia, or Muscovy, and that Ivan Vassilivitch was their king."[12] Despite this apparent success, the results of the voyage were mixed. As T.S. Willan, in *The Early History of the Russia Company*, clarifies: "Chancellor's 'discovery' of the northern route to Russia may not have been a genuine discovery, for the route was known before even if it had not been used commercially in the past, but it opened up the possibility of direct trade with a Russia which had at that time no 'window' on the Baltic."[13] Willoughby froze to death with his crew for lack of knowledge about how to survive extreme northern winters.

Chancellor, charged with conveying "Osepp Gregoriwich Napea," the first Russian ambassador to England, drowned when their ship wrecked off the coast of Scotland. Fortunately for future Anglo-Russian relations, the ambassador washed ashore relatively unharmed.[14] After haggling with the Scots over his lost goods, Napea rode to the English capital, where he was received by the reigning sovereigns, Mary and Philip, and feted by the Russia Company. During his stay in London, Mary died and Elizabeth was raised to the throne, "providentially" in the view of the Protestant party, which favoured the Russian trade.[15]

It was during this transition to Queen Elizabeth's reign that Anthony Jenkinson, after an apprenticeship in the Mediterranean wherein he gained a "safe conduct or priviledge, given by Sultan Solyman the Great Turke ... at Aleppo, in Syria, in the yeere 1553," shifted his attention northeastward.[16] Having been appointed "Captaine generall" of a fleet of four merchant ships bound for "S[t]. Nicolas in Russia," Jenkinson, in addition to his instructions from the "companie of the Marchants adventurers," bore two royal charges: the aforementioned Osep Napea, whom he was to return safely to the Russian court, and a bundle of gifts and letters for the Russian tsar from the new English queen.[17] He discharged both duties successfully, with Napea assisting him in later trade negotiations and Ivan preferring him as the queen's representative. Among the highlights of his northern career, Jenkinson was

> the first to describe from personal observation eastern parts of Russia, at that time only recently annexed by Ivan; the first to descend the Volga since it had become a Russian river, a great highway between east and west; the first Englishman to navigate the inland waters of the Caspian; to recognise that it really was a landlocked sea and had no communication with Northern or Indian Ocean, removing prevalent errors, by assigning it truer proportions than hitherto; the first to describe with some approach to accuracy the various countries bordering on its coasts, and to enumerate some of the rivers falling into it.[18]

He was also the first Englishman to be received at the court of a Safavid shah – Tahmasp, son of the founder of the dynasty, Ismail I – with the Sherley brothers in the early seventeenth century serving Tahmasp's grandson, Shah 'Abbas I, after a break of two decades in formal Anglo-Persian relations.[19] In total, Jenkinson made four expeditions through Russian territories and beyond, retiring in 1572 with the hope, in his words, of taking "my rest in mine owne house, chiefly comforting my selfe in that my service hath bene honourably accepted and rewarded of her Majesty and the rest by whom I have been emploied."[20]

In the preface to the 1589 edition of *The Principall Navigations*, Hakluyt praises Jenkinson, along with William Burrough, as "gentlemen of great experience, and observations in the north Regions"; in the preface to the 1599 edition, he lauds him as "that valiant, wise, and personable gentleman."[21] Hakluyt thus places Jenkinson at the forefront of what was later dubbed the "great prose epic" of the English nation.[22] Around the same time, another "nationalist epic," William Warner's *Albion's England* (1602), elaborated Jenkinson's contributions to England's "Commerce and Fame" in over two hundred lines of laboured verse.[23] Illuminating by contrast how early modern Englishwomen's engagement with the Islamic world shaped their construction as authors and authority figures, Warner frames his description of "our Queene *Elizabeth* her letters" with hyperbolic representations of a "Pluralitie of wives" among Persianate Muslim rulers far in excess of the bare ethnographic details of Jenkinson's company reports.[24] He likewise embellishes the number of concubines: "sixe score" in one instance; "fifteene score" in another.[25] He thereby follows Hakluyt's lead, whose influential collection disseminated "A compendious and briefe declaration of the journey of M. Anthonie Jenkinson, from the famous citie of London into the lande of Persia, passing in this same journey through Russia, Moscovia, and Mare Caspium."[26] Where Jenkinson reports that "the king ["Obdolowcan" or Abdullah Khan]" spent the evening "banketting [banqueting] with his women, being a hundred and fortie in number," Hakluyt adds the misleading marginal note: "Multitude of concubines."[27] As Leslie Peirce documents in *The Imperial Harem: Women and Sovereignty in the Ottoman Empire*, a high-ranking Muslim man's "women" (or "harem") was not limited to his wives and/or concubines, but included female relatives such as his mother, unmarried sisters, aunts, daughters, and nieces.[28] Similar conditions prevailed in the Safavid Empire: as Maria Szuppe emphasizes in her study, "Status, Knowledge, and Politics: Women in Sixteenth-Century Safavid Iran," "[a]lthough women lived in their own quarter, its walls were less tightly closed in the sixteenth century than in the following one. Women were seen going in and out of the harem with escorts composed sometimes only of their maids."[29] Clearly, not only the Englishmen's reporting of numbers, but their understanding of the harem institution was faulty.

Reinforcing the displacement of Queen Elizabeth's authorship and authority within "an imagined plurality that has no limit," which Alain

Grosrichard in *The Sultan's Court: European Fantasies of the East* identifies as a core feature of Western male conceptions of the harem "as a phantasmic place,"[30] Warner depicts Jenkinson's reception "before King *Obdolowcans* Throne" by means of an analogy replete with patriarchal and imperial connotations: "Scarce *Cleopatras Anthony* was feasted with more cheere/Of varied Meates and spice Conceits than *Jenkinson* was heere."[31] Warner's evocation of this (in)famous queen, cast in Shakespeare's *The Tragedy of Antony and Cleopatra* (1606/7) as an "Eastern femme fatale," reinforces his prior orientalist scenario of female sexual excess to undermine his opening gesture towards "our Queen *Elizabeth* her letters."[32] Elizabeth may have been touted as the "virgin queen," but she was also slandered as a loose woman precisely to contain her authority. As Ilona Bell explains in *Elizabeth I: The Voice of a Monarch*, "Because Elizabeth was not only a monarch but also a queen, the ambassadors [and other men] judged her words and actions according to the assumptions about women that dominated their world. Misogyny pervades early modern discourse; indeed it was the default setting, as Shakespeare's comedies repeatedly illustrate."[33] Hence, even though Warner concludes his encomium to Jenkinson by imagining Elizabeth as "The Maiden Empresse, and her Knights their Enterprises rare,/Which now have pearst [pierced] through everie Pole, of all admired are," his attitude to female authorship and authority is ultimately dismissive and even degrading.[34] This is a tension that continues throughout the queen's correspondence with the Russian and Persian emperors, as they are called in the salutations of her letters from the 1560s and 1570s.

Although often overlooked in studies of England and Islam in the early modern period, "The Queenes Majesties letters to the Great Sophie of Persia, sent by Master Anthony Jenkinson," dated 1561, is Elizabeth's first missive to a Muslim sovereign, preceding her correspondence with the Ottoman sultan and *valide sultan*, or queen mother, by two decades, for which it functions as a touchstone.[35] As with her prior letter to the Russian tsar, Elizabeth begins by denoting herself "Queene of England, &c." and her interlocutor as "the right mightie, and right victorious Prince, the great *Sophie*, Emperour of the *Persians*, *Medes*, *Parthians*, *Hyrcanes*, *Carmanarians*, *Margians*, of the people on this side, and beyond the River of *Tygris*, and of all men, and nations, betweene the *Caspian* Sea, and the gulph of *Persia*, greeting and most happie increase in all prosperitie."[36] Relying on classical references, the lens through which Persia was frequently viewed during the Renaissance, she amplifies the extent of the Safavid Empire, which under Tahmasp was constantly beleaguered by the Uzbeks on their northeastern and the Ottomans on their western flank.[37] Moreover, as in her initial letter to the Russian emperor, she undercuts her claims to sovereignty by presenting herself as mere "queen" of a realm completely unknown to the shah, despite her signature from "our famous Citie of London."[38] This defensive posture parallels the response Englishmen experienced during their forays in the Levant at the beginning of the seventeenth century, then under Ottoman rule, where they were reduced to the generic ranks of the *"Frankes* of *Christendome,"* as William Lithgow records in *A Most Delectable and True Discourse, of an admired and painefull peregrination from Scotland, to the most famous Kingdomes in Europe, Asia and Affricke* (1614).[39] Not only were the English marginal to the Islamic empires of this period, as these commentators stress, they often did not register on their geo-political maps.

As with the Anglo-Ottoman correspondence over a decade later, Queen Elizabeth's letter to "the Great Sophie" or Persian shah repeatedly evokes "the Almightie God" as a point of commonality, avoiding the Trinitarian references that characterized her letters to the Russian tsar.[40] Bearing this letter, Jenkinson followed his sovereign's lead by attempting to finesse religious distinctions between various expressions of Christianity and Islam. For instance, during his audience with the shah he strategically identified himself as "neither unbeleever nor Mahometan, but a Christian." However, when the shah learned from one of his Christian subjects ("the king of Georgians sonne") that "a Christian was he that beleeveth in *Jesus Christus,* affirming him to bee the sonne of God, and the greatest prophet," an answer combining traditional Christian and Muslim understandings, Jenkinson was thrown out of the shah's court as an "unbeleever, and uncleane."[41] He eventually discerned the realpolitik underlying this spectacle when he learned that the recent rapprochement between the shah and "the great Turke his brother," Süleiman the Magnificent, had blocked his attempt to establish English trade in Persian domains.[42] In this case, Ottoman Sunni and Safavid Shi'a bonding trumped Protestant English efforts, even though religious ideologies did not prevent either the Ottomans or Safavids from forging trade agreements with these Christian upstarts only a few decades later.[43]

After this initial foray, English trade in Persian domains stagnated for over a decade, with attention turning to the Ottomans via the Mediterranean due to increasing instability in Central Asia. Composed in the wake of this first, albeit foreclosed, early modern Anglo-Islamic exchange, in her initial letter to the Ottoman Sultan Murad III in 1579 Queen Elizabeth positions herself prior to him in her salutation, having learned from her earlier correspondence with the shah the deleterious effects of the reverse order.[44] She underscores her position as "the most invincible and most mighty defender of the [reformed] Christian faith against all kinde of idolatries," which would resonate with a Muslim readership. Situating herself as a strict monotheist, she further evokes "the most mightie God, and onely Creatour of heaven and earth" – unlike, it is implied, the idolatrous Catholics with their saints and perhaps even the Orthodox with their icons.[45] The queen also issued a series of letters to Murad's successor, Sultan Mehmed III, along with other highly ranked members of the dynasty. The most significant for a gendered analysis is her correspondence with the Ottoman *valide sultan*, Safiye, which was accompanied by gifts of clothing, perfume, and portraits. As I have argued elsewhere, these letters informed not only the commencement of Englishmen's trade in the region, but also early modern Englishwomen's engagement with the Islamic world.[46]

Dwelling on Queen Elizabeth as an exceptional woman authority and author of diplomatic letters to Muslim sovereigns, including powerful women such as the *valide sultan*, nevertheless effaces the significance of gendered subalterns for these exchanges. As I have stressed, attention to the traces of girls and women from the Islamic world brought to England and of lower-status Englishwomen transported to the Islamic world prior to the mid-seventeenth century, when Quaker missions to the Mediterranean began, reveals a cumulative portrait that foregrounds their agency in the absence of first-person narratives. Focusing on one such life, I examine how the "Tartar girl"/Ipolita the Tartarian's presence in Queen Elizabeth's court was refracted in the first original prose romance by an Englishwoman to appear in print, Mary Wroth's *The Countesse of Mountgomeries Urania* (chapter 3), and earlier dramatic productions, including Shakespeare's (chapter 4). As a foundation for this literary investigation, I proceed to articulate how this gendered subaltern from the Islamic world – along with the prime commodity sought by the increasingly cosmopolitan English merchants, silk from Safavid domains – functioned as a literal accessory for Queen Elizabeth's proto-imperialist self-fashioning.[47]

Queen Elizabeth, the Tartar Girl, and the Persian Lady

Daryl Palmer, in *Writing Russia in the Age of Shakespeare*, aptly concludes that Anthony Jenkinson, as Queen Elizabeth's envoy to the Russian tsar and the Safavid shah, exemplified "a kind of intercultural self-fashioning that continues, in our own day, to define the sophistication of multi-national existence."[48] My discussion here and elsewhere of the "Tartar girl" Jenkinson acquired in Central Asia uncovers the other side of this multi- or trans-national existence: one characterized by human trafficking, which was integral to the network of commodity exchange that emerged in the early modern period and that persists as the "darker side" of postmodern (and even postcolonial) celebrations of cosmopolitanism.[49] Although this girl left only scattered traces in the historical record, as a subaltern subject she speaks to all the levels of exchange – commodity, cultural, diplomatic, political, and religious – that contemporary critics have engaged in their study of early modern English relations with the Islamic world. The issue I have already raised, and continue to explore here, is not whether this subaltern literally transcribed her life, which can be accessed in the margins of written documents and beyond them through material signifiers, but whether we can develop the theoretical apparatus to recognize her impact and agency.

In what Palmer calls "a truly imaginative tramp through the life and times of Jenkinson" and one of the few studies prior to my own investigations to take the "Tartar girl" seriously, Margaret Morton links the acquisition of this girl to Ivan the Terrible's conquest of "[t]he Nagayan Tartars, 'of the law of Mahomet,'" in Jenkinson's words.[50] Thousands were enslaved as a result, with Jenkinson in his extended narrative calculating that "the price of a Nagayan Tartar slave was 'a loafe of bread woorth six pence in England.'"[51] Morton interprets Jenkinson's acquisition of this girl as a compassionate act and she imagines he was "[d]eeply moved" by the suffering he witnessed. Yet, his use of the term "wench," which carried denigrating class and sexual connotations, suggests less gracious designs on his part.[52] As Palmer observes, on the whole "Jenkinson, [Jerome] Horsey, and Giles Fletcher (along with their colleagues in the Russia Company) tend to elide the existence of women in their world."[53] Ironically, it may be that Jenkinson's designation of the "Tartar girl" he acquired as a gift for Queen Elizabeth raised this subaltern to the historical record, if only on the margins.

Since she was a subaltern on multiple levels, most critics have either doubted or ignored this girl's history after Jenkinson acquired her. Morton, for her part, questions whether she actually reached England, but does not provide any evidence otherwise.[54] Certainly, the journey was treacherous, as the near loss of the first Russian ambassador to

England in the North Sea attests. However, as I specify in chapter 1, contextual evidence places the "Tartar girl" in Queen Elizabeth's court as one of several pampered human "pets." David Loades, in stressing that "Elizabeth did not share John Dee's vision of a British empire, but she was impressed by it," concludes the queen "did not, apparently, indulge in the common contemporary practice of keeping 'innocents', or freaks" such as mutes, dwarves, so-called fools, and racialized "others" as did the imperial courts of the Ottoman sultan and the Holy Roman emperor.[55] As Jardine and Brotton emphasize, established and aspirant imperial courts accumulated inventories of "living, breathing luxury items" to broadcast and even to create the illusion of their power.[56] Despite his claim that Elizabeth did not follow this trend, Loades concedes,

> two mysterious young women feature in the records who may have been something of the kind. The first was known as Ippolyta [Ipolita] the Tartarian, described in 1564 as "oure deare and wellbeloved woman," and the second was Tomasina de Paris. Both were made clothing allowances over a number of years, and Tomasina appears to have been a dwarf; but the nature of the service they provided is nowhere described. They are unlikely to have been jesters in the ordinary sense, and whether they were supposed to be a source of humour is not known.[57]

Hence, while Elizabeth did not pursue "a global ambition" to the same degree as the Ottoman sultan and the Holy Roman Emperor, she did use the signifiers of empire to assert her sovereignty, just as her father did, and therefore to project her power.[58]

As indicated above, the accolade "oure deare and welbeloved woman" in the "warrant dormant for her livery in June 1564" implies that Ipolita the Tartarian was treated with affection, which accords with the position of a human "pet."[59] Here, I move beyond this ambivalent subject position to focus on the material culture of the Elizabethan court and how Ipolita was deployed to enhance the queen's imperialist self-fashioning. As the list of items in her livery, including "fyne hollande," "granado silke," and "venice golde & silver" confirm, she was well-dressed as befits the queen's "welbeloved woman."[60] Yet, these items also connect the "Tartar girl"/Ipolita the Tartarian to the global exchange of foreign luxury goods, where she functioned as a commodity *and* a consumer. Concomitantly, this global exchange involved the queen through her accumulation of people and apparel to enhance her proto-imperialist profile. Her adoption of Ipolita's fashion in shoes is a case in point:

> All the Queen's shoes in the early years of her reign were made of velvet but after Ippolyta [Ipolita] had had two pairs of Spanish leather shoes in 1562 and half a dozen pairs in 1563 Elizabeth ventured to try a pair in 1564. She ordered another three pairs in 1565 and two more pairs in 1569, still with up to forty pairs of velvet shoes each year.[61]

As I maintain, the connections between the "Tartar girl," her exotic accessories, and the English queen illuminate the recurring debate over the subject of the portrait Roy Strong dubbed "the Persian Lady" and who was long thought to represent Elizabeth.[62] While Strong and other critics have questioned this attribution,[63] the nexus from the "Tartar girl" to the queen's wardrobe recalls the overriding purpose of Jenkinson's several northern missions: the potentially lucrative trade in Russian furs and Persian silk.[64]

In particular, even though Jenkinson and other agents of the Muscovy Company were tasked with delivering the queen's letters to various eastern sovereigns, including her first letter to a Muslim ruler, the real focus was the less glamorous trade of cloth through the Russian Empire into Central Asia and, without lasting success, the Safavid court.[65] In Jenkinson's narrative, and in the more prosaic account of Sir Thomas Randolph who replaced him as Queen Elizabeth's ambassador to Russia and Persia, textiles are the main character, with English woolens travelling eastward and Russian furs and Persian silk travelling westward. Whether the subject of this portrait is Elizabeth may be, at least for our purposes, a moot point. But that she wore Persian silk is confirmed by the inventories Arnold analyses, with "the 'Armada' portrait ribbons" a salient example.[66] Given the circuit of global traffic I have traced thus far and the interpellation of the "Tartar girl" therein, it would not be entirely facetious to dub this iconic image of imperialist self-fashioning another "Persian Lady." Still, in adjudicating how this Tartar girl-cum-woman impacted the emerging anglocentric discourse of empire, we need to register the argument Karen Hearn makes in *Dynasties: Painting in Tudor and Jacobean England, 1530–1630* about the Armada portrait, with which Jyotsna Singh opens *A Companion to the Global Renaissance*: "Her right hand rests on a globe, her fingers 'covering the Americas, indicating England's dominion of the seas and plans for imperialist expansion of the New World'" and beyond.[67] Given the indubitably subordinate position of the English realm vis-à-vis "the three great Muslim land empires (Ottoman, Safavi, and Mogul)" throughout the Elizabethan era, along with the persistent fear of English incorporation into the Spanish Empire even after 1588, it may be better to qualify this portrait as an example of the "diplomatic wishful thinking regarding ... imperial power" that Jardine and Brotton specify for the less powerful French (and English) facing the Iberian monopoly on global imperialism.[68] After all, the English followed the French strategy of countering their relative weakness in the imperial contests of the "Greater Western World" by forging strategic alliances with the Islamic empire of the Ottomans, with the French signing their capitulations (*ahdname* or official trade agreement) in 1536 and the English in 1580.[69]

The trajectory from Jenkinson's "Tartar girl" to the queen's "deare and welbeloved woman Ipolita the Tartarian" accordingly reveals the gendered subaltern in transit through the circuits of the early modern/colonial world system. Moreover, the presence in Queen Elizabeth's household of this gendered subaltern from Islamic Central Asia, which was a liminal zone between the competing Russia, Ottoman, and Safavid empires, points towards the queen's investments in the inaugural English ventures in global trade, which would lead to plans for imperial expansion. Yet, the "Tartar girl," and other gendered subalterns in early modern England, also exercised agency through their "active survival and resistance to cultural dominance" or "survivance," to recall Gerald Vizenor's neologism.[70] The next section addresses these material and semiotic practices as encoded in the documents surrounding the northeast ventures involving Jenkinson and continuing two decades later with the northwest ventures led by Martin Frobisher. The resonance of the "Tartar girl" in English literature and culture, as I detail below, bridges both of these attempts to establish global trade and, eventually, a colonial empire.

Queen Elizabeth, the Frobisher Voyages, and the Tartar-Indian Woman

Following on the northeast passage ventures that yielded a Nogay "Tartar" girl as a gift for Queen Elizabeth, another indigenous woman's movements in the circuits of the early modern/colonial world system were influentially inscribed in the historical record of the first official English overseas venture westwards for the purpose of trade, colonization, and empire: Martin Frobisher's voyages from 1576 to 1578 ostensibly in search of a northwest passage to the riches of Asia.[71] Like Christopher Columbus almost a century prior, Frobisher stalled in the Americas, lured by the promise of gold, which in Frobisher's case turned out to be false.[72] Nonetheless, his ventures were cast as the foundation for a British seaborne empire as articulated by the advisor to the short-lived Cathay Company, John Dee, who also advised the Muscovy Company, which had launched a series of voyages in search of a northeast route to the riches of Asia in the 1550s and 1560s.[73] As previously mentioned, this project stalled in Persia and ceased by the 1580s due to internecine wars in Central Asia; however, the thwarted northeast ventures remained intertwined with Frobisher's northwest scheme.[74]

While men dominated these voyages and for the most part did not bring women with them, a small percentage of elite women are listed as investors, with Queen Elizabeth preeminent.[75] Even less visible are the gendered subalterns who were transported to England as a result of these voyages: the aforementioned "Tartar girl" whom Jenkinson acquired as a gift for Elizabeth and an Inuk woman from Baffin Island whom Frobisher abducted, along with her "baby-in-arms," as a prize for the queen.[76] The latter, the first recorded "New World native" woman in the British Isles, is described along with her countrymen and women as a "Tartar" in the records of the Frobisher voyages.[77] This ascription is not surprising given many of these Englishmen had travelled the northeast route across Central Asia, where the preponderance of natives they encountered were Muslim Tatars. It also relates to the tendentious view, from Columbus onwards, that the American continent was an outcrop of Asia.[78] As William Sturtevant and David Quinn summarize, the English when attempting to categorize the natives they encountered on their sixteenth-century northwest voyages "vacillated between people of Cathay, Tartars, Tartar Indians, country people, strange people, and even Moors, but not of course Eskimos [Inuit]."[79] The colonial catachresis "Tartar-Indian" woman accordingly connects arbitrarily but meaningfully with the "Tartar girl" to chart the expanding early modern web of empire, which for the English, constrained by the Portuguese and Spanish monopoly over the southeastern and southwestern trade routes, initially extended northwards.[80]

Symptomatically, neither elite nor subaltern women are included among the "travelling bodyes" the "poet-of-all-trades and miscellaneous soldier" Thomas Churchyard celebrates in his "Epistle Dedicatorie" to his widely read composite volume from 1578.[81] This volume includes a synopsis of one of Queen Elizabeth's many progresses through her realm ("The entertaynemente of the Queenes Majestie into Suffolke, and Norffolke"); a poem in praise of Sir Humphrey Gilbert, a widely travelled soldier and explorer who two years earlier lobbied for the northeast route ("A matter touching the Journey of Sir *Humfrey Gilbarte Knight*"); and an account of Martin Frobisher's several ventures in search of the northwest passage ("A Prayse, and Reporte of Maister Martyne Forboishers Voyage to Meta Incognita").[82] As Churchyard specifies, the category "travelling bodyes" applies exclusively to those men who participated in the overseas voyages that characterized England's proto-imperialist era: "Sir Humfrey Gilbert, Maister Henry Knolles, and others, right worthy Gentleman."[83] In the balance of this chapter, I expand Churchyard's parameters to include women relegated to the margins of the early modern/colonial world system, such as the "Tartar girl" and the "Tartar-Indian" woman, along with elite Englishwomen like Queen Elizabeth who invested in these voyages.

Nonetheless, the question of these gendered subalterns' agency remains fraught, as both were captives, with the former likely traded to Jenkinson and the latter forcibly kidnapped by Frobisher's men. As we have seen, the "Tartar girl" seems to have found a place at Queen Elizabeth's court as her "welbeloved woman Ipolita the Tartarian."[84] By contrast, the "Tartar-Indian" woman, whom the English labelled "Ignorth," the generic Inuktitut word for "woman," succumbed to a fatal disease approximately six weeks after her arrival on British shores.[85] Attending to the traces of their lives in English and other European documents alongside oral histories from the northern native tradition, I highlight their negotiations of their enforced conditions of travel to track how they emerged as historical agents within and beyond the English narrative.[86] Such methodological questions have been neglected in studies of the early English voyages of "discovery," especially those focusing on English and other European sources, even as scholars are beginning to theorize British women's "domestic travel" through an expanded archive.

To situate this argument, in the next section I engage the critical debate over what constitutes "travel" as a necessary preliminary to tracing the agency of gendered subalterns such as the "Tartar girl" and the "Tartar-Indian" woman, whose coerced journeys brought them to proto-imperial England. As Andrew McRae in his influential study, *Literature and Domestic Travel in Early Modern England*, relates, "in the early modern period to 'travel' typically meant to leave the nation's shores."[87] Problematically, this definition elides the movements of those gendered subalterns who arrived via the early modern/colonial circuits of global exchange, as well as those who travelled "domestically" after their arrival. Instead, by explicating the conditions and consequences of their journeys to and within the British Isles, I emphasize how these girls and women impacted the emerging anglocentric discourse of empire and its concomitant "ideologies of racial difference," for which the narratives of the Frobisher voyages were foundational.[88]

Objects that Speak in the Early Anglocentric Discourse of Empire

Jaś Elsner and Joan-Pau Rubiés, in their synoptic introduction to the collection *Voyages and Visions: Towards a Cultural History of Travel*, define their key term "*travel* as a culturally significant event rather than as mere physical movement" (emphasis added).[89] The *Odyssey* is the bedrock of this cultural history, with its eponymous hero "the model of the wanderer who finally returns home through numerous adventures (military, sexual and magical)." From the medieval through the early modern era, he also stood as "the ideal model of a traveller whose journey brought inner as well as outer fulfillment."[90] Frobisher himself was frequently compared "with Ulysses [Odysseus] and also with other heroes of Greek legend, especially Hercules and Jason."[91] Hence, even though Elsner and Rubiés acknowledge the occasional female traveller – such as medieval pilgrim Egeria (fl. 381–4 C.E.) – they embed an implicit gender binary in their primary definition: men travel abroad (Odysseus), chaste women remain behind (Penelope), and women encountered abroad are promiscuous witches (Circe).[92] This gendered differential subtends the opposition between the designation of "travel as a culturally significant event" (associated with the ideal *male* traveller) and "mere physical movement" (relegated to subalterns such as women "following" their husbands, lower-class women and men seeking employment, and slaves transported as commodities).[93] Ironically, the physician, Edward Dodding, who performed the autopsy on the Inuk man transported to England with the "Tartar-Indian" woman, deploys this very binary in his epitaph: "Had hardy Ulysses escaped his plight,/How great his Lady's joy: her fame how slight!"[94] Dr Dodding thus celebrates male travel, even when such travel was coerced, and contrasts it to the ideal of the chaste and, he presumes, homebound woman. Ignorth's physical movement – doubly erased due to her status as a woman and a native from the lands the English sought to exploit – fails to register in this masculinist and imperialist paradigm as a significant event. It therefore does not count as travel.

The "Tartar-Indian" woman, hailing from an isolated community in the "New World," did not carry the necessary immunities against

Eurasian diseases; within six weeks of her arrival in England, she "was troubled ... with boils," to cite "Doctor Doddyngs Report," "which broke out very densely on her skin" and from which she died shortly thereafter.[95] However, she clearly was meant as a display, and perhaps another gift for Elizabeth, as indicated by the attending doctor's response to her male companion's death: "I was bitterly grieved and saddened, not so much by the death of the man himself as because the great hope of seeing him which our most gracious Queen had entertained had now slipped through her fingers, as it were, for a second time."[96] Her baby, the last survivor, was rushed towards the queen's palace during his final illness and died en route.[97] Despite these displacements and traumas, as I have been arguing, the "Tartar-Indian" woman emerges as a historical agent, and not just an object of investigation, in the records of the Frobisher voyages and their aftermath. As with the English encounters with the Algonquians in the 1580s, the encounters with the Inuit a decade earlier were "embedded" in the English texts produced at this time and articulated in the oral histories of the northern indigenous people, which began to be transcribed in the nineteenth century.[98] Hence, a wide array of sources must be read "*contrapuntally*" to access the abducted Inuk woman's and her male companion's strategies of survival and resistance.[99]

To begin with an analogous instance, Thomas Harriot's *A briefe and true report of the new found land of Virginia: of the commodities there found and to be raysed, as well as merchantable, as others for vituall, building and other necessarie uses for those that are and shalbe the planters there; and of the nature and manners of the naturall inhabitants* (1588) features John White's drawings of women from both Native American (Algonquian) and British (Picts) communities with facial tattoos.[100] This famous example from White, who had earlier depicted the Inuit abducted on Frobisher's voyages, underscores the "difference within sameness" characterizing what Walter Mignolo conceptualizes in *Local Histories/Global Designs: Coloniality, Subaltern Knowledges, and Border Thinking* as "Occidentalism" from "the (Latin) American perspective."[101] As he specifies, "Occidentalism" from this locus of enunciation, rather than simply the obverse of Orientalism, "is basically the master metaphor of colonial discourse since the sixteenth century and specifically in relation to the inclusion of the Americas as part and margin of the West."[102] The operative mode in the anglocentric discourse of global empire in its initial stages is therefore "the denial of coevalness" – in Mignolo's formulation, "the end result of relocating people in a chronological hierarchy rather than in geographical places" – rather than a strict opposition between "us" and "them."[103] This early modern categorization of difference, while still supremacist, nevertheless leaves room for assimilation into the imperial norm. It consequently explains how the "iii [3] men takyn In the Newe ffound Ille land [Newfoundland and environs]" in the context of the Cabots' voyages at the turn of the sixteenth century seemed indistinguishable from English males from an anglocentric perspective once divested of their native clothing.[104] The Inuit men captured seventy-five years later on Frobisher's voyages also wore English clothes. The Inuk woman, with her distinctive facial tattoos, likely assimilated less easily and is not known to have donned Englishwomen's attire.[105]

The Frobisher voyages, because they resulted in a fiasco over the false gold that became their focus, were narrated in several versions, which are supplemented by copious state records.[106] Two of these, based on direct evidence, provide detailed accounts of the English encounters with the natives of the northern regions Queen Elizabeth dubbed "*Meta Incognita* – the unknown limits."[107] The earliest published, *A true reporte of the laste voyage into the West and Northwest regions ... worthily atchieued by Capteine Frobisher of the sayde voyage the first finder and Generall. With a description of the people there inhabiting, and other circumstances notable. Written by Dionyse Settle, one of the companie in the sayde voyage* (1577), was "the first piece of English travel-literature to be translated into the main European languages," including French, German, Italian, and Latin.[108] Settle accordingly offers the first, and most famous, printed account of the Inuk woman's capture:

> Two women, not being so apt to escape as the men were, the one for her age, and the other being incombred with a yong childe, we tooke. The olde wretch, whome divers of our Saylers supposed to be eyther a Divell, or a Witche, plucked off her buskins [boots], to see, if she were cloven footed, and for her oughly [ugly] hewe and deformite, we let her goe: the young woman and the childe, we brought away.[109]

As in the gendered definition of travel Elsner and Rubiés proffer, the old woman is cast as a debased Circe, the witch who leads travelling men astray; the young woman, though, is retained for the sailors' presumed pleasure.[110] While subsequent narratives emphasize the woman's chastity in refraining from sexual contact with the captive male, the possibility of her abuse by the Englishmen (intended or realized) cannot be discounted.[111] Perhaps Frobisher's plan to deliver her as a gift to the queen, as Jenkinson did with the "Tartar girl," afforded her some measure of protection. As Settle elaborates, further contact with the natives involved negotiations for a possible "hostage" exchange, with Frobisher intent on recovering five of his crew members who went missing on a prior voyage. The English and the Inuit accounts of their fate varies: Frobisher concluded the men had been murdered by the Inuit; however, Inuit oral history conveys that the men survived the winter with the help of the native people, only to perish in the icy seas as they tried to return to England on an improvised boat. Settle also records attempts by the Inuit to rescue their compatriots on the English ship, none of which were successful.[112]

The second published narrative detailing the capture of the Inuk woman – George Best's *A True Discourse of the late voyages of discoverie, for the finding of a passage to Cathaya, by the Northweast, under the conduct of Martin Frobisher Generall* (1578) – is "the only contemporary account of all three of Frobisher's voyages by one who participated in them." As Vilhjalmur Stefansson, an early twentieth-century Arctic explorer and editor of *The Three Voyages of Martin Frobisher*, continues: "Best went on the second expedition as Frobisher's Lieutenant aboard the *Aid*, and on the third as Captain of the *Anne Frances*."[113] During this second voyage, in which colonization of North America was added to the initial goal of finding a northwest passage to Cathay, Frobisher and his crew intensified their efforts to capture some Inuit, whom they characterize as "this newe pray [prey]."[114] As Settle's account earlier conveyed, in addition to the Inuk man, who was captured in a prior ambush, an Inuk woman was abducted at what the English memorialized as "the Bloudie point."[115] Rehearsing Settle's binary opposition between the old woman and the young one, Best adds that an English arrow had

> pierced through the childs arme, whereupon she [the child's mother] cried out, and was take[n], & our Surgeo[n], meaning to heale hir childs arme, applyed salves therunto. But, she not acquainted with such kinde of surgerie, plucked those salves away, & by co[n]tinuall licking with hir owne tongue, not muche unlike our dogges, healed uppe the childes arme.[116]

Here and elsewhere in this narrative, Best likens the Inuit to animals; yet, his description also inadvertently gives voice, and perhaps a resistant form of agency, to the woman as she heals her child through traditional – and effective – means. As Inuit oral history documents, "[s]ome people were born with the gift of healing," which meant (among other things) "[t]hey could cure cuts and other wounds by licking the affected area."[117] Notably, when her male companion was on his deathbed in England, he also refused English medical practices – in his case, bloodletting – inscribing another act of resistance in an otherwise lethal narrative of captivity.

Best finally posits a motive, if only post hoc, for the abduction of the woman: "Having now got a woman captive for the comforte of our man, we broughte them both togither, and every man with silence desired to beholde the manner of their méeting and entertaynement, the whiche was more worth the beholding, than can be well expressed by writing." The Englishmen's voyeuristic motive for bringing the man and woman together, who did not seem to have any previous acquaintance, is foreclosed through the woman's resistance, who "at the first verie suddaynely, as though she disdeyned or regarded not the man, turned away, and beganne to sing, as though she minded another matter."[118] From the perspective of the Inuit, as recorded in their oral histories, "[s]ongs are thoughts, sung out with the breath when people are moved by great forces and ordinary speech no longer suffices."[119] What the woman sang, therefore, the English could not know on several levels. However, after communicating directly with each other, the two adult captives joined efforts in trying to escape and ultimately to survive their transport to England:

> the man brake up the silence first, and with sterne and stayed [staid] countenance, beganne to tell a long solemne tale to the woman, whereunto she gave good hearing, and interrupted him nothing, till he had finished, & afterwards, being growen into more familiar acquayntance by spéech, were turned togither, so that (I think) the one would hardly have lived, without the comfort of the other.

As Best concludes, "yet did they never use as man and wife, though the woman spared not to do all necessarie things that apperteyned to a good huswife indifferently ["impartially" (*OED*)] for them both, as in making cleane their Cabin, and every other thing that apperteyned to his ease."[120] Best, along with other commentators, underscores the Inuits' "shamefasteness and chastitie," even though he diminishes his praise by labelling them "those savage Captives."[121]

In his closing ethnography, "A generall and briefe Description of the Countrey, and condition of the people, which are found in *Meta Incognita*," Best judges the native people he encountered on his northwest voyages "to be a kinde of Tartar" like those the Englishmen met on their northeast voyages, an assessment he shared with other commentators.[122] Hence, unlike the "Ethiopian as black as a cole" he adduces earlier in the narrative – which Cassander Smith posits as the limit case for an emerging ideology of bodily, rather than climactically, determined racial categories – the northern natives the English initially encountered may have seemed "infidels" and "savages" from an anglocentric vantage point, but they could be converted and civilized by adopting English religious and cultural habits, as with the aforementioned "American natives" brought to England at the turn of the sixteenth century.[123] As such, Best reiterates that the captive Inuit were "verye chaste in yᵉ [the] maner of their living," adding that while in England "[t]hey beganne to grow more civill, familiar, pleasaunt, and docible ["teachable, docile; submissive to teaching or training, tractable" (*OED*)] among us in a verye shorte time."[124] This narrative of assimilation is nevertheless complicated by native recalcitrance, which is a frequently misunderstood aspect of "survivance."[125] For instance, while the Inuk man had learned some English phrases, reportedly dying on the words "God be with you," the Inuk woman registered her final act of resistance through her gestures when she refused to see her companion buried, even though the attending physician prevailed: "at my persuasion she was led with me, albeit unwillingly, to the burial." Dr Dodding explains that he forced her to come with him to prove the English did not practise human sacrifice or anthropophagism, as he assumes the Inuit did.[126]

As Europeans killing and consuming humans was not unheard of during the first stage of their colonization of the Americas, with incidents persisting in the Arctic region as late as the nineteenth century, this report suggests an underlying anxiety that Europeans would not merely succumb to "cannibals," but become "man-eaters" themselves.[127] Certainly, the doctor's insistence bespeaks a further colonial projection onto this desolate woman. She died, "presumably from measles," shortly thereafter.[128] However, her visual and discursive image persisted as part of the emerging English discourses of global expansionism, which promoted exploration, trade, and colonization. As I have sought to show, so did her agency through multiple acts of survival and resistance. Her forced movement into proto-imperial England, along with the "Tartar girl" – who was better equipped, if only immunologically, to survive and perhaps even to thrive in Queen Elizabeth's court – must therefore be recognized as a significant cultural event within the larger schema of early modern travel, both local and global. As the next chapter details, such gendered subalterns continued to be enlisted as the necessary supplement – simultaneously marginal and constitutive – for early modern English women's negotiations of authorship and authority into the seventeenth century, starting with Lady Mary Wroth's groundbreaking publications.

The Islamic World and the Construction of Early Modern Englishwomen's Authorship: Lady Mary Wroth, the Tartar-Persian Princess, and the Tartar King

Continuing the investigation of early modern women's negotiation of authorship and authority begun in chapter 2, this chapter elaborates how gendered subalterns who travelled to England from the Islamic world during the Elizabethan and Jacobean period informed Lady Mary Sidney Wroth's alternately celebrated and excoriated role as a groundbreaking female writer.[1] As noted in the introduction, Wroth was the first Englishwoman to publish an original prose romance – *The Countesse of Mountgomeries Urania* in 1621 – to which was appended the sonnet sequence *Pamphilia to Amphilanthus*. After a hostile response to the published first part of the *Urania*, she continued with a substantial second part, which remained in manuscript until 1999.[2] (She also wrote a pastoral tragicomedy, *Love's Victory*, which likewise remained in manuscript until the late twentieth century.)[3] Throughout the two-part romance, its "principal character" Pamphilia is lauded as an exemplary woman writer, particularly of lyric poetry.[4] She thereby functions as an idealized self-portrait for Wroth, whose sonnets Ben Jonson praised for making him "[a] better lover, and much better poet."[5] While Wroth did not travel beyond her father's post in Flushing (Vlissingen, in the Netherlands), she maps the transnational movements of female characters from Tartaria and Persia onto "the incomparable Pamphilia" (*U1* 166), who hails from the Peloponnese peninsula in southern Greece, denoted Morea in the medieval and early modern periods.[6] In the first part, Pamphilia is crowned queen of her eponymous kingdom in Asia Minor (now part of Turkey); by the second part, she marries a Central Asian monarch, Rodomandro "the great King of Tartaria" (*U2* 42), who is racialized as black and white.[7] She herself travels frequently between Europe and Asia over the course of the two-part romance. Pamphilia – and, by extension,

Wroth – thus aligns with elite women from what Wroth's contemporaries would identify as the Islamic world, even if it is "under erasure" for most of the *Urania*.[8] Yet, as with Queen Elizabeth I's proto-imperialist self-fashioning, which I examine in chapter 2, this form of identification by Western women negotiating their authorship and authority ultimately results in the appropriation of the "other" woman's voice and the effacement of her historical agency.

To assess how Wroth instantiates this otherness as a facilitating factor for early modern Englishwomen's authorship in prestige genres such as Renaissance prose romance and Petrarchan sonnets,[9] I begin by situating her within the Sidney family literary interest and literal investment in what Thomas James Dandelet calls the "dream of a Renaissance of empire."[10] To recall, Wroth (her married name) was born a Sidney and was a niece of the celebrated sixteenth-century writers Sir Philip Sidney and Mary Sidney (Herbert), the Countess of Pembroke. The subsequent discussion focuses on Wroth's representation of the Tartar-Persian princess as a vehicle for her own negotiations of authorship and authority in relation to England's belated imperial project. The concluding sections address the Tartar king, Rodomandro, who marries the character most closely linked to Wroth: the Morean princess and poet, Pamphilia.[11] This king, who straddles East and West, also serves as an important vehicle for the incorporation of the romance's female characters – including those from Tartaria and Persia – into the "universal Christian empire" towards which the convoluted plot tends.[12] As such, he belongs with the "refracted representations" of girls and women from the Islamic world in early modern Englishwomen's imaginative writing that is the focus of this chapter.[13]

The Renaissance of Empire, the Sidney Family, and Mary Wroth's *Urania*

To reiterate, Mary Wroth, following the lead of the illustrious "Sidney circle" of literary writers and patrons, especially her uncle Philip Sidney and her aunt Mary Sidney Herbert, incorporates and questions the "Imperial Renaissance" in her prose romance and sonnet sequence.[14] Like Philip Sidney, she references the Holy Roman Empire in both parts of the *Urania*, which in her case was a fantasy projection encompassing Eurasia and effacing actual Ottoman predominance in the region.[15] Like Mary Sidney, she thematizes blackness in relation to gender, extending her aunt's rendition of the foundational narrative for Western European imperialism: the fall of the Roman Antony due to his desire for the Egyptian Cleopatra and the consequent rise of Augustus Caesar.[16] In Wroth's case, she introduces an updated episode of a European woman's competition with an African woman over a European man when Urania's maid projects her jealousy onto "a Black-moore" (*U1* 49). In related similes, she uses "Egyptian" and "Indian" as vehicles for female dissimulation and desire.[17] She thereby foregrounds gendered discourses of race and empire as integral to Englishwomen's negotiations of authorship and authority, which extends to women writers in the romance such as Pamphilia.

In this section, I address Wroth's extension of the Sidney family interest in empire into the eastern regions of "Persia" and "Tartaria" to highlight these gendered and racialized negotiations of authorship. While the romance's trajectory towards Constantinople (under the Ottoman Empire from 1453) is a staple of the revived "Greco-Roman erotic romance," her turn to the northeast reflects the Sidney family connection to the first official English trade and diplomatic missions to Central Asia and Safavid Persia, which grew out of Muscovy Company ventures in the mid-sixteenth century.[18] Henry Sidney (father of Philip and Mary Sidney and grandfather to Mary Wroth) was associated with these ventures from their inception, with his inaugural address included in the report, "The newe Navigation and discoverie of the kingdome of *Moscovia, by the Northeast, in the yeere 1553*," published in the first edition of Richard Hakluyt's *The Principall Navigations, Voyages, and Discoveries of the English Nation* (1589).[19] His contemporary, William, first earl of Pembroke, was also involved in the merchant companies that financed the early voyages to Russia, Central Asia, and Persia.[20] Mary Wroth's aunt and mentor, Mary Sidney, became Countess of Pembroke upon marrying his son, Henry Herbert.[21] Wroth, then, had multiple avenues through her family to contemporary reports about "Persia" and "Tartaria." As an investor in the East India Company on her own account, she also had access to updated information about voyages to the Mughal and Safavid empires, which followed the route around the Cape of Good Hope.[22]

Drawing on this extended history, I argue that Wroth's representation of empire, particularly in the second part of the *Urania*, responds to these contemporary trends by "shadowing" – in Josephine Roberts's resonant phrase – the lives of women from the Islamic world who arrived in England as a result of these and subsequent ventures.[23] As specified in previous chapters, such women range from a de facto slave, to servants of various ranks, to a diplomat's wife. In the case of the "Tartar girl" whom Anthony Jenkinson, the first Englishman to travel through Central Asia to the Safavid court, acquired with the intent of presenting to Queen Elizabeth, the evidence for her life in England consists primarily of isolated marginalia and brief mentions in inventories, which I assess in chapter 1. As an accoutrement for Elizabeth's court, this gendered subaltern was meant to enhance the queen's imperialist self-fashioning, as I detail in chapter 2. In the case of Lady Teresa Sampsonia Sherley – who travelled on East India Company ships with her husband, the "famous English *Persian*" Robert Sherley – an ample, if often tendentious, discourse developed around her.[24] East India Company records show that other Persian women of lesser rank accompanied Lady Sherley to England; at least one of them married an Englishman.[25] I submit that Wroth's representation of the Tartar and Persian princesses in the second part of the *Urania*, along with a Tartar king, bears the imprint of these women from the Islamic world who resided in England shortly before and during her lifetime. While the northeast ventures through Central Asia and into Persia did not yield sustained economic dividends for English traders or political alliances for the English crown, Wroth's representations of Tartars and Persians in the *Urania* signals her own investment in the multi-generational Sidney family effort to promote the dream of a Protestant English empire on a global scale.

The Tartar-Persian Princess, Proto-Imperialism, and the Prototypical Woman Writer

Wroth, then, epitomizes the tenuous negotiation of authorship for even the most elite women during the Jacobean era. At the same time, she shows how early modern Englishwomen aligned themselves with their countrymen's imperial ambitions. This dual positioning intensifies in the manuscript continuation of the *Urania*, which shifts from the classical emphasis of the published version to an increasingly belligerent assertion of Christian hegemony. It is therefore significant that the first mention of Persians in the *Urania* is coupled immediately with Tartaria when a forlorn lady identifies herself as "daughter to the King of Tartaria; my mother was a Persian" (*U2* 9). It is also significant that this lady is introduced through the "black but beautiful" formula used to describe non-European women in general: "her hair browne, butt her face, neck, and hands of the rarest and cleerest complexion.

Her eyes black, butt comaunding his [the widowed king of Epirus, Selarinus's] hart to say his soule wowld Joye if hee might bee blessed with their kinde lookes" (*U2* 7).[26] Yet, this opening scenario of cultural and racial difference is immediately dismissed as "a dreame" and "a fiction" (*U2* 10). Further discredited, the so-called "lady" is unmasked as a malevolent spirit who has sexually ensnared one of the narrative's chivalric heroes (*U2* 10, 303–5, 397). I have shown elsewhere how the ambivalent cultural and racial markers Wroth ascribes to this princess correspond to contemporary descriptions of Teresa Sampsonia Sherley as having "more of *Ebony*, then *Ivory*, in her Complexion, yet amiable enough, and very valiant, a quality considerable in that Sex, in those Countries."[27] Given the resonance of Jenkinson's "Tartar girl" in English literature from the late Elizabethan era onwards, this character further encodes the anxieties over assimilation and difference associated, in Shakespeare's oft-quoted epithet from *A Midsummer Night's Dream*, with the "tawny Tartar" (3.2.264).[28] Hence, she is best described as a "Tartar-Persian" princess who plays a pivotal role later in the romance, despite her dismissal here.

As historian Alison Games, among others, has emphasized, the early anglocentric discourse of empire cannot be confined to the transatlantic context, which did not dominate English efforts until the later seventeenth century; rather, it needs to be situated within "the web of empire" from earlier in the century, when England lagged behind leading empires such as the Habsburgs and Ottomans, as well as the Safavids and Mughals.[29] Cognizant of these competing empires, Wroth returns to the Tartar-Persian princess – who is revealed as "the true Sophia of Percia," Lindafillia – and pits her against her uncle, the "usurping Sophye of Percia" (*U2* 54). This dichotomy transforms the European misnomer for the Safavid shah (Sophy, from the Sufi tradition upon which the Safavids based their claims) into a Christian term (Sophia, from the Byzantine tradition, which resonates with the 1453 Ottoman conquest of Constantinople and the conversion of the Byzantine imperial church, Hagia Sophia, into a mosque).[30] Moreover, this episode comes nearest to naming Islam as the enemy, when "a Giant, and the fiercest and cruellest esteemed of any in all thos[e] parts, Called Limorando," upon capturing the ship carrying Lindafillia, "thought itt against his owne religion to holde faithe with infidells, as hee termed Christians" and "resolved to satisfy him self in his bacer [baser] desir[e]s" (*U2* 54). The profusion of orientalist and other exotic stereotypes characterizing this episode – Italian pirates (*U2* 54), Turkish swords

(*U2* 55–6), and Persian giants (*U2* 57) – marks a noticeable shift from the first part of the romance.[31]

Similar references to Christianity multiply as indices of this clash of competing imperialisms, which comes to a head when "the King of Natolia" (*U2* 72) attempts to enlist the "brave Tartarians" against the Greek Moreans (*U2* 73). The king describes the Tartarians as "his neerest nieghbours [*sic*]" and the Moreans as their common and "ancient ennimies" (*U2* 73). Natolia, or Anatolia, was under Ottoman rule in Wroth's era, with this historical referent "under erasure" in the first part. Nevertheless, the Tartarians ally with the distant Moreans, "having understood of their Kings safety and the glorious entertainment hee had receaved in the Morean Court soe lately" (*U2* 73), an episode to which we shall return. More pragmatically, the Tartarians base their decision on "the hope of the alliance with the Moreans by the mar[r]iage beetweene Pamphilia and the Kinge" (*U2* 73), which we shall examine more closely in the next section. As such, he must be incorporated into this prospective empire's ruling dynasty, despite his seemingly ineluctable marks of difference.

Even though West and East, and by implication white and black, unite in the marriage of Pamphilia and Rodomandro, the episode immediately following, which features "the King of Tartarias sister" (*U2* 76) and Licandro, the "duke and prince of Athens" (*U2* 78), suggests these "interracial"/"intercultural" couplings are less stable than they seem.[32] Escorted to her country by the Athenian prince, introduced earlier in the romance as "the Cur[t]ious Licandro" (*U2* 62; square brackets in original), this Tartar-Persian princess abruptly refuses his proposal when "hee kissed her hand, butt soe fervently as if his lips wowld have dwelt ther[e]" (*U2* 77). As the narrator reports, "She, never Used to such moist salutes, tooke her hand away, some what more neere snatching then courtious taking itt, and with a fro[w]ne, able (from such a heavenlike beauty) to kill then please, turned away, which made a bashfull blush rise in the prince" (*U2* 78; square brackets in original). While the narrator implies that the princess lacks courtesy as defined by Western norms, her questioning of Licandro's worthiness due to his ignorance of Eastern practices confirms that cultural exchanges between Asians and Europeans do not necessarily favour the latter. The episode ends with Licandro learning through a friend's dream that "[t]his Lady is nott for you" (*U2* 80), after which the princess proceeds "towards Tartaria" to seek her brother, Rodomandro (*U2* 81); concurrently, he escorts Pamphilia to her kingdom in Asia Minor (*U2* 84). The romance thus broaches and retreats from cross-cultural couplings – especially potentially racialized ones – as part of its proto-imperial strategy.

When the king of Tartaria next appears in the romance, it is to pledge the support of "this Christned world" – which could read "Christian" or "christened" – "to succor the delicate, distressed princess, rightfull Sophie of Persia" (*U2* 115–16), who it is implied is his sister. As he adds, "for I heere [hear] certainly all the west hath resolved to succour her. Then wee of the East joining, what shall hinder us to obtaine a whole and hap[p]y victorie?" (*U2* 116). Concomitantly, the "usurping Sophy" of Persia seeks to marry his niece, which enables another attack on his character: "This beast wee last spake of ... who lately hath an intent to marry her, beeing his naturall neece, which is as hatefull to her to think on as his lyfe is to all true and harty Christians" (*U2* 156). At this point, the "true Sophia," or the Tartar-Persian princess, is doubled with Pamphilia, who also experienced the threat of marriage from the "usurping Sophy" (*U2* 108). As this episode underscores, the boundaries between Asia and Europe become increasingly permeable, and yet remain under (European) Christian control, as the romance extends its dream of empire globally.

Accordingly, as "the Innocently wronged Sophie of Percia" surfaces from her imprisonment, the plot accelerates towards the incorporation of Central Asia into this ultimately Eurocentric project (*U2* 165). In an encounter anticipating a Christianized Persian court, for which Western Europeans vainly hoped from the medieval era through the early modern period, Pamphilia's brother, Rosindy, while traipsing through Asia, succours this princess, whom he describes as "such a peece of perfect perfections as could nott bee equaled on Earthe, much les[s] to bee thought on of beeing surpassed" (*U2* 168). She is associated with "the purest pearle the Orient cowld afforde" and wears "apparell of the Asian fashion" (*U2* 168); to balance these orientalist signifiers, her skin is praised as whiter than "[t]he milky way" and "[t]he snowe on the Mountaine topes" (*U2* 168). She thus figures the positive pole in the bifurcated view of Persia in early modern Europe, with Rosindy's description of her person also suggesting emerging racialized discourses of empire.[33] After her appeal to Rosindy to deliver her from her uncle's attempts to seize her person and realm, the Tartar-Persian princess retreats from an active role in the romance and cedes her kingdom to European control, with none other than Rosindy serving as "governour of Percia" (*U2* 354). Her brother, Rodomandro, nevertheless lingers as the guarantor of Christian hegemony in Asia, which Pamphilia identifies as "my husbands country and mine" (*U2* 378). Despite his status as a Christian, his marks of whiteness, and his marriage to a Greek princess, the Tartar king remains a destabilizing "subaltern instance" in the ongoing construction of Pamphilia's authorship and authority and, by extension, Wroth's.[34]

To summarize thus far, I have situated Wroth's negotiations of authorship within both the "the web of empire" that rendered English travellers subordinates, not colonial masters, in Safavid and Ottoman domains and within the anglocentic imperial aspirations and dreams articulated by the "Sidney circle" and their clients. In so doing, I have begun to trace her extension of her famous uncle's and aunt's representations of the "Imperial Renaissance," traditionally based on ancient Roman and medieval Holy Roman foundations, into Central Asia and Persia as a result of contemporary English ventures. Led by the Muscovy and the East India Companies, these ventures were initially motivated by commercial concerns. However, the unsuccessful efforts of the former to secure a northeast passage to the riches of Asia transmuted into the search for the northwest passage, which was explicitly motivated by trade, colonization, and empire, as described in chapter 2. The early East India Company ventures, as we know in hindsight, became the bedrock for the British Empire "upon which the sun never set" from the late eighteenth century through the mid-twentieth. However, because Wroth was writing in a proto-imperialist era, she cast her Tartar and Persian characters as princesses and kings, not subalterns. These representations hinge, I submit, on the presence of women from the Islamic world at the English court, including the "Tartar girl" from Central Asia and Teresa Sampsonia Sherley from Safavid Persia. Wroth as a member of the Sidney family, who invested in these ventures from their inception, would be familiar with their stories and perhaps those of other less well-documented subalterns in England during the same period. These girls and women thereby function as one of the facilitating conditions for Wroth's literary innovations. The next section traces these innovations in the character of Rodomandro, king of Tartaria, whose ambivalent racialized and religious attributes do not disqualify him from becoming husband of "the incomparable Pamphilia" (*U1* 166).[35] However, neither do they remove him from the margins of the romance, whether its geography or its narrative. In the end, while crucial for securing Western Christian hegemony over Asia through marriage and conquest, he effectively disappears from the romance once it fulfils its imperialist dreams.

Imaginative Geographies, Proto-Orientalism, and the King of Tartaria

Edward Said in "Imaginative Geography and Its Representations," a section he subtitles *"Orientalizing the Orient,"* identifies this stance as "a fixed, more or less total geographical position" taken "towards a wide variety of social, linguistic, political and historical realities" – in this case, "a full half" of the globe.[36] Said has been critiqued for his lack of historicity when considering Western European attitudes towards the East (a malleable term covering biblical lands, Islamic polities, and Asia as defined by the ancient Greeks), especially during a time when, as Nabil Matar asserts in *Turks, Moors, and Englishmen in the Age of Discovery*, "England was not a colonial power – not in the imperial sense that followed in the eighteenth century."[37] Likewise, Wroth's representations of Asians – Tartars, Persians, and residents of the regions ruled by the Ottomans – cannot be confined to the East-West dichotomy characterizing the nineteenth-century peak of Western European imperialism that primarily concerns Said. Nonetheless, Said's theorization of "imaginative geography" as "a set of representative figure, or tropes" constituting "the Western approach to the Orient" remains useful when assessing Wroth's romance, which took shape during the period Richmond Barbour, in *Before Orientalism: London's Theatre of the East, 1576–1626*, defines in terms of "proto-orientalism."[38] The "precolonial engagements" of the English with the "East," especially the empires of the Ottomans, Safavids, and Mughals, involved "more pliant, polyvalent attitudes toward various 'others.'"[39] These attitudes were premised on a mixture of admiration and fear, with England's marginal position within the early modern/colonial world system at the turn of the seventeenth century not allowing for the scorn associated with full-fledged Orientalism. In Wroth's case, her encounter with these "others" was enabled by contemporary reports in influential collections such as Richard Hakluyt's *The Principal Navigations, Voyages, Traffiques and Discoveries of the English Nation* and histories such as Richard Knolles's *The Generall Historie of the Turkes*, both published around the turn of the seventeenth century, with her family having an unusually close connection to early ventures in Russia, Central Asia, and Persia, as documented above.

Neglecting this "proto-orientalist" context, some of the most astute interpreters of Wroth's oeuvre have deemed the marriage of Rodomandro, "the great King of Tartaria" (*U2* 42), to the Morean princess,

Pamphilia, puzzling and implausible. Moreover, Rodomandro himself is cast as an anomaly, even though Hakluyt and Knolles include ample praise for "Tartars" from the Mongols to Tamerlaine in their widely read tomes.[40] For instance, Sheila Cavanagh, in her landmark study *Cherished Torment: The Emotional Geography of Lady Mary Wroth's* Urania, draws on classical and medieval sources and their Renaissance redactions to link the Tartar king to an "inauspicious" region whose inhabitants "are said to be uncivil or savage." Cosmologically, Tartaria is "under the signs of Aquarius and Saturn," and therefore "black and evil."[41] Kim Hall in her equally groundbreaking book, *Things of Darkness: Economies of Race and Gender in Early Modern England*, sees him in terms of "blackness" as a "secondary status," which anticipates the transatlantic slave trade.[42] As I propose, this marriage should be considered not only in terms of cultural and racial difference, but also in terms of newly Protestant England's alliances (actual and attempted) with Islamic powers against the Catholic Habsburg Empire. In Daniel Goffman's terms, the Ottomans were an integral part of the "Greater Western World" of mercantile exchanges and diplomatic alliances, along with the independent Moroccan kingdom; the Safavid shah likewise sought alliances with Western European sovereigns to counter Ottoman expansionism.[43] This context becomes particularly important in assessing Rodomandro, who is endorsed as "an exquisitt man in all things, and a Christian" (*U2* 46). As such, his union with Pamphilia, which enables the consolidation of East and West under (Western) Christian hegemony, is a clear case of proto-orientalist wish-fulfilment.[44]

As noted above, the first mention of Persians in the *Urania* is coupled immediately with Tartaria when a forlorn lady identifies herself as "daughter to the King of Tartaria; my mother was a Persian" (*U2* 9). To reiterate, she is represented through the black or "browne, butt" beautiful formula associated with Central Asian and other non-European characters (*U2* 7). Moreover, it is through this character that we first learn about the King of Tartaria, as when she claims, "My brother is well and arming in defence of the most rare Queene Pamphilia, against the fierce Soldaine [Sultan] of Percia" (*U2* 10). Subsequent to this brief, albeit overdetermined, description, Rodomandro's first physical appearance at the Morean court, ruled by Pamphilia's father, initiates the romance's *translatio imperii* from East to West. The "great King of Tartaria" has travelled to this seat of Western power, as his messenger announces to the Morean king, "heering of your magnanimitie and the glory of your Court" (*U2* 42). As the messenger continues, the Tartar king "returning home ward" after "tow [two] yeers abroade" – an exotic variant of the newly instituted Grand Tour – desired "to be eye wittnes[s] of your [the King of Morea's] glory, and to see thos[e] brave Princes whos[e] fame hath filled the world with admiration, and to learne amongst them the rare and perfect exeercise of Chivalry" (*U2* 42).[45] (Foremost among these princes is Amphilanthus, king of Naples, king of the Romans, and Holy Roman Emperor.)[46] This admiration is reciprocated, as it turns out "the King [of Morea] had heard very much of this ex[c]ellent Prince," who is praised as "the brave stranger," "the great Tartar," and "[a] brave and Com[e]ly Gentleman" (*U2* 42). The classic East to West trajectory therefore commences its reversal from West to East without displacing the centre of power in Christian Europe.

Complicating this rapprochement, as Hall observes, is "a color/ race schema" associated with early modern racialism that "from the beginning marks ... [Rodomandro] as unfavored and in some ways peripheral even though he wins Pamphilia's hand."[47] In particular, the courtly appreciation of Rodomandro's "hands soe white as wowld have beecome a great Lady" is immediately coupled with an apology for "his face of curious and exact features, butt for the couler [color] of itt, itt plainely shewed the sunn had either liked itt to[o] much, and soe had too hard kissed itt, ore in fury of his delicasy, had made his beames to[o] strongly to burne him" (*U2* 42).[48] This dissonance continues with the blazon on "[h]is diamound eyes (though attired in black)" (*U2* 42), which brands him with the faint praise of the "black but beautiful" formula applied earlier to the Tartar-Persian princess.[49] Even the description that "[t]his brave Prince, entering the roome of Presence, came with soe brave a countenance and yett soe sivile [civil] a demeanor as made all eyes subject to his sweetnes[s]" is qualified (*U2* 42), with the ensuing simile depicting him "black as the stag [that Pamphilia and Amphilanthus hunt] and as humble" (*U2* 43).[50] Amphilanthus's antipathy when he notices "the Tartarians black eyes must needs incounter the true heaven of Pamphilias gray eyes and yeeld to them, as to the perfect sky, the rule of his and their thoughts" further undermines Rodomandro's full acceptance (*U2* 44). Indeed, Amphilanthus has reason to be jealous, as Pamphilia eventually marries the Tartar king, despite her former (albeit secret) vows to Amphilanthus (*U2* 45).[51] Hence, in assessing the imaginative geographies of Wroth's romance with an understanding that this positive, if tendentious, depiction was normative for this proto-orientalist transitional period, we must still account for the dissonance of Rodomandro's representation as a "stranger," albeit a "brave" one, through a racialized discourse that projects a range of negative connotations (*U2* 42).

Encoding these contradictions, the events leading up to the Tartar king's marriage to Pamphilia are rendered through tropes of blackness associated with death and danger in early modern English culture: "By this little shadow foreseeing her longe time of darckest night, which now grew on as the black curtains covering awhile the seane [scene], wher[e]in the blacker tragidy is to bee acted; and the blackest did itt prove that ever fairest beautie ore sweetest fairnes[s] cowld have inflicted on" (*U2* 107). The tragedy is the report, which Pamphilia later learns is false, that Amphilanthus had married another woman (the Princess of Slavonia), which impelled her to marry Rodomandro. While this discourse of blackness is not overtly racialized, its association with the Tartar king is unmistakable, as is the tendentious contrast with "fairest beautie" as exemplified by the Greek princess (*U2* 107). When Pamphilia marries Rodomandro "all in black" (*U2* 108) – as Hall observes, "ostensibly because she is in mourning for her brother when in truth she is mourning the loss of Amphilanthus" – the overdetermined colour of her garb signals her own "ambivalent agreement."[52]

Along these lines, it is significant that Pamphilia turns immediately after her nuptials to a threatening letter from the Sophy of Persia, who also seeks her hand in marriage. In a departure from her generally mild manner, she scorns this Asian despot, who "in demaunding such a princess for wife by way of threat[e]ning and force" egregiously breaches the etiquette of Western courts (*U2* 108).[53] In recompense, she determines to "prepare for warr" (*U2* 109). Dismissing the Sophy as a "barberous fellow," she ultimately responds, "Tell him that when I marry, itt shalbee to such an one as shall bring mee to a safe and justly settled title of honor, nott to a tiranisde [tyrannized] and userped [usurped] one as his is" (*U2* 109). This retort sounds a discordant note in the romance as it follows without pause from her marriage to Rodomandro, whose realm was adjacent to Persia. Still, Pamphilia's necessary alliance with the "Asian Princes" (*U2* 109) remains contingent on their regard for the Tartar king, with her tenuous position corresponding to the relative powerlessness of the English vis-à-vis the Islamic empires during Wroth's lifetime.

The next episode featuring Rodomandro and Pamphilia confirms their marriage as a political union essential for advancing "this Christned [Christian, christened] world" in the cause of "the delicate, distressed princess, rightfull Sophie of Persia" (*U2* 115–16), as noted above. To confirm this military alliance, Rodomandro asks for "the [Morean] King's consent for his daughter Pamphilia" (*U2* 270), meaning his leave to take her to Tartaria with him as his wife and implying their earlier marriage ceremony had not been consummated. Suggesting the obstacles to Othello and Desdemona's union, Rodomandro uses similar rhetoric, stating, "Devine Lady ... the Tartarians are noe Orators, butt plaine blunt men. Our harts are rich in truthe and loyalltie. Prowde indeed wee ar[e], butt onely of Ladys favours, knowing our sunn-burnt faces can butt rarely attaine to faire ladys likings" (*U2* 271; cf. *Othello* 1.3.76–94). Unlike the former couple's tragic end, Rodomandro and Pamphilia provide proof of their union in the form of a "brave boy" (*U2* 406). Yet, the death of this son "soon after his arrival" at the Tartarian court means their blended lineage has no future, anticipating the shift in the dominant understanding of "race" from "lineage or genealogy" to "paradigms of physical and phenotypical difference" that Margo Hendricks and Patricia Parker chart in *Women, "Race," and Writing in the Early Modern Period*.[54] After this episode, Rodomandro does not speak, and so also has no future in the world of the romance, despite surfacing posthumously as Pamphilia departs Asia for Cyprus (*U2* 406–7).[55]

As Mary Floyd-Wilson establishes in *English Ethnicity and Race in Early Modern Drama*, Christopher Marlowe's Tamburlaine (the eponymous hero of the two-part play published in 1590), with his Central Asian (Tartar, Scythian, Parthian) genealogy, is depicted through "blindingly white conceptions of beauty" that are "insistently and peculiarly 'northern.'"[56] As David Wallace confirms in discussing "Petrarch and Scythia; Spenser and Ireland," this barbarous connection was the source of much anxiety for Western Europeans, and for the English in particular, during the medieval and early modern eras.[57] Hence, just as Richard Knolles's Tamerlaine, whom he identifies as a "Tartar king," is distinguished by his hair, which "was of a dark colour, somewhat drawing toward a violet right beautifull to behold," Wroth's Tartar king is represented through shades of difference rather than a strict Self/Other binary.[58] These Central Asian characters, in sum, are not so much "black" as unsettlingly "white," from the "soe white" hands of Rodomandro to the "snowe" whiteness of the Tartar-Persian princess (*U2* 42, 168). Analogously, Hakluyt glosses the chapter, "Of their [the Mongols' or Tartars'] forme, habite, and manner of living," from the medieval account by Friar John de Plano Carpini, with the marginalia: "Like unto Frobishers men."[59] The narratives of Martin Frobisher's three voyages "for the search of the straight or passage to China" (1576, 1577, and 1578), which

I analyse in chapter 2, cover the earliest published English accounts of their encounters with the natives of what is now northern Canada. Following the inaugural English voyages in search of a northeast passage by twenty years, Frobisher's frame of reference when viewing the natives he encountered was Central Asian: "They be like to Tartars, with long blacke haire, broad faces, and flatte noses, and tawnie in colour." Yet, "their colour" is described as "not much unlike the Sunne burnt Countrie man, who laboureth daily in Sunne for his living."[60] The point of comparison, in other words, is the English labourer and not the African slave, which would be more plausible from a British perspective through the first half of the seventeenth century.[61] This combination of difference and similarity is what drives Rodomandro's arguably proto-imperialist and proto-orientalist characterization.

As such, without ignoring the racialized connotations Hall emphasizes, we must acknowledge that the closeness of these "Tartars" to the English, with both defined as "white" and "tawny" depending on the circumstance, creates as much dissonance in Wroth's romance, where the Tartar king marries "the eastern starr, the never-enough-admired Pamphilia" without comment (*U2* 417), as does his distance as a stranger marked by blackness. Indeed, it is the combination of blackness and whiteness that renders him symptomatic of early modern discourses of race during this transitional era. Moreover, while it would be anachronistic to label the idea of Asia in the *Urania* as orientalist in the sense Said defines for the height of Western imperialism two centuries later, it also may be insufficient to describe this idea or concept as proto-orientalist in the sense Barbour defines in the context of Englishmen's subaltern status in Eastern empires. Rather, Wroth's prose romance showcases shifting discourses of "black" and "white" around the union of Asia and Europe under the banner of a universal Christian empire. As I shall elaborate in the next section, these global imperialist designs are further localized in the form of the court masque, which enabled some Jacobean women – albeit of the highest ranks – to articulate their agency and arguably their "authorship" through identifications with and appropriations of the lives of girls and women from the Islamic world in early modern England and Scotland.

Performing Race and Gender in Rodomandro's Masque

As I have argued thus far, both parts of the *Urania* represent imperialist ventures through an increasingly "dual, *hierarchized*" opposition of white over black and the associated divisions of West/East and Christianity/Islam.[62] The Holy Roman Empire is imagined as a bulwark for Western expansionism, the Ottoman Empire is placed "under erasure," and English investments in the transatlantic slave trade are displaced onto cross-cultural couplings. To this "imaginative geography," the manuscript continuation adds a "brave stranger" – "the great King of Tartaria" (*U2* 42) – who hails from the farthest reaches of Central Asia, coveted by the competing empires of Wroth's era, including Islamic ones.[63] He is also an Eastern Christian (perhaps a convert) who helps advance the imperialist forces of the West.[64] Called the "King of Tartaria" throughout the romance, at the very end he is associated with the court "att Qinzaie [Quinsai]" ruled by "the Great Cham"; this title, adapted from the Mongol tradition, could refer to Rodomandro's father or to Rodomandro himself (*U2* 394).[65] The uncertainties of the romance genre and the unfinished state of the manuscript likely account for this confusion of identity. In any case, from the medieval era through the early modern period, Western Europeans conflated Mongols and Tartars (more properly, Tatars) making the latter designation central to Rodomandro's characterization.[66]

Among the individuals who unsettle the binary opposition of black and white in the *Urania*, Rodomandro certainly is the most complex. As we have seen, he is described from his first appearance at a European court as "black," especially his face and his eyes, with a cascade of qualifiers attesting to his "lovelines[s]" and "beauty" (*U1* 42). He endorses this description when he broaches marriage to Pamphilia, a Greek princess from Morea and a queen regnant in Asia Minor, with his proposal evoking Othello's speech to the Venetian senate defending his marriage to Desdemona (*U2* 271). Yet, Rodomandro's "hands soe white" (*U2* 42) set him apart from the more famous "brave Moor" (*Othello* 1.3.290).[67] As Hall posits, "It is conceivable that his hands function as a sign of rank, which then mitigates his race/color status," especially through the "joining of hands" in marriage.[68]

Adding to this amalgam of race and rank, Rodomandro embodies the proto-orientalist opposition of East and West based on a European centre, with the tension between expansionist Christianity and expansionist Islam implicit in his characterization. As Sheila Cavanagh elaborates,

> since the *Urania* is being composed during a time of extensive exploration,
> Rodomandro's Tartarian origins reveal Wroth's attempt to complete an

imaginative circle around the entire globe, with Tartaria serving as a route for circumnavigation ... Accordingly, as King of Tartaria, Rodomandro controls access to the pathway that could facilitate the Christian conversion of the entire world.[69]

Benedict Robinson, in *Islam and Early Modern English Literature: The Politics of Romance from Spenser to Milton*, asserts more broadly that "Christendom" as a paradigm for cultural and political identity "had dreamed itself as a potentially world-spanning unity, a reincarnated Roman Empire," in contradistinction to the emerging political structure of "Europe" defined by conflicting nation-states. Specifically, "[w]here Christendom dreamed of becoming coextensive with the world, of obliterating all difference, 'Europe' emerges as a claim to difference, and thus remains predicated on a withdrawal from the world, a distance or reserve that cannot be overcome."[70] As I add, just as Wroth's sonnet sequence in the 1620s perpetuates a belated Petrarchan counterdiscourse, her romance returns to the residual paradigm of a universal Christian empire extending into Central Asia.[71]

Rodomandro, straddling the dichotomies of black/white, East/West, and Islam/Christianity, consequently facilitates *and* unsettles the movements of the *Urania* as it maps this expansionist, if imaginary, geography through marital alliances as well as military interventions. As such, even with his conspicuous marks of otherness, this Tartarian must be incorporated into the Western European-led alliance through marriage with the romance's central female character, Pamphilia, whose thwarted union with Amphilanthus, elected Holy Roman Emperor in the published version (*U1* 441), bridges both parts. Named for her inherited kingdom on the western edge of Asia Minor, Pamphilia bears the epithet "easterne starr" in relation to the imperial territories Amphilanthus inherits (*U2* 117, 417).[72] However, as mentioned above, the universal Christian empire that is the aim of the *Urania* hinges on succouring "the delicate, distressed princess, the rightfull Sophie of Persia" (*U2* 115–16), an Eastern Christian opposed to her "fierce" uncle (*U2* 10). Condemned as the "usurping Sophye of Percia" (*U2* 54), he is implicitly categorized as Muslim through the titles "Sultan," "Soldaine," "Souldan," and "Soldan."[73] The subsequent campaign in the East that resolves this struggle therefore depends on the Tartar king and other Eastern princes who serve him. In other words, the realization of universal empire in the romance requires the consolidation, not simply of Asia and Europe, signified by "East" and "West," but also of the Near and Far East as represented by Pamphilia and Rodomandro.

To reprise an earlier scene, the *Urania*'s global imperial plot begins with Rodomandro's unexpected arrival at the Morean court on the Greek peninsula, where he is described as having "soe brave a countenance and yett so sivile [civil] a demeanor as made all eyes subject to his sweetnes[s]" (*U2* 42). Although this description foregrounds the Tartar king's adherence to Western European norms, it concludes with some unsettling qualifiers: "When as lately his very looks were dangerous, butt non[e] need fear him, for though as valliant and stout as any, yett was hee soe discreete, soe civile, and soe curtious as non[e] cowld (if nott infinite rude) finde a cause to quarrell with him" (*U2* 46). As Joan-Pau Rubiés establishes in "Late Medieval Ambassadors and the Practice of Cross-Cultural Encounters," pre-modern courts across Asia and Europe similarly understood the concept of civility, as in "what it was to be 'civilized,'" with the Chinese representing the highest ideal for all.[74] Yet, from the sixteenth century onwards, civility in the West was increasingly articulated through a discourse of empire that defined "brave" as "wild" and "savage," projected onto the Native Americans the English sought to conquer, rather than as a "gallant" warrior or soldier, which could be applied cross-culturally.[75] Images of Tartars likewise varied in the period, from the stereotype of "barbarous persons who display despicable habits" formulated by the thirteenth-century missionaries to the Mongol court and republished in early modern imperialist propaganda such as Hakluyt's *The Principal Navigations* to the overwhelming praise of Tamerlane as a "Tartar king" and potential Christian opposed to the Ottomans.[76] At the same time, costume books featured the emblematic "Tartar warrior" alongside the "Persian satrap" to suggest extremes in eastern decadence and violence. Tartars were likewise grouped with the classical Scythians, who, as John Michael Archer establishes in *Old Worlds*, "are not European, nor particularly Asian."[77]

The response to these tensions, as suggested earlier, is "in manner of a maske" (*U2* 46), which dramatic form Martin Butler in *The Stuart Court Masque and Political Culture* identifies as the main vehicle for an increasingly cosmopolitan Jacobean court to mark the boundaries of "'who's in" and "who's out."[78] The first masque at Hampton Court featured King James I's Scottish and English courtiers, some with Welsh connections, as "Indian and China knights." Prominent among these courtiers was William Herbert, who would become Lord Chamberlain and the third Earl of Pembroke; he was also Mary Wroth's first cousin and "first love" – and eventually father of her two illegitimate children.[79] As Butler explains, "Even in the absence of a text [for this performance], *The Masque of Indian and China Knights* shows how powerfully Stuart festivals could articulate the court's collective identity, their ability to signal dependence and identification, association and belonging, and forge a unity knitted together from Whitehall's competing interest-groups." Furthermore, while "the forms adopted by *The Masque of Indian and China Knights* ... foregrounded the masquers' exoticism and otherness, they validated them in terms of festive incorporation into the greater body of the court." As such, the generic features innovated in this inaugural masque – "the entry of outsiders, their exotic and chivalric disguises, their approach, gift-giving, homage, and social dancing" – became the benchmark for Jacobean and later Stuart performances.[80]

While actual non-Western European ambassadors, such as those from Morocco and Muscovy, attended these masques, no record exists for non-Western performers of an equivalent rank.[81] The Tartar king in Wroth's romance consequently goes a step further in appropriating Jacobean "strategies of exclusion and inclusion" when he stages his debut performance.[82] Conventionally, the masque in Wroth's romance showcases "the Tartarian fashion" (*U2* 46), in line with other masques of the era that featured costumes from non-English, but not necessarily non-European or even non-British, ethnic groups.[83] Yet, it exceeds expectations by having these Asian men mix with "the [European] ladies when they would honor them with dauncing with them" (*U2* 46).[84] As was customary, the dance ends with "an infinite rich banquett prepared purposely for Rodomandro and his companion maskers [masquers], who were all princes in his countrye butt his subjects" (*U2* 49). These Tartars are thereby drawn into the world of the Morean court, whose norms of chivalry and civility they share, even as they are marked by variable racial and ethnic differences in complexion and costume.[85]

Wroth (in)famously appeared in at least one masque for the Jacobean court: *The Masque of Blackness*, performed on 6 January 1604 (O.S.)/1605 (N.S.), the first of a series of masques in which Queen Anna, James I's consort, performed and arguably "authored."[86] Echoes of this masque, which critics have deemed particularly significant for the Jacobean's court's negotiation of cultural otherness, appear in both parts of the *Urania* to extend Wroth's involvement with the genre.[87] For instance, towards the end of the published first part of the romance, Wroth introduces a character whose tragic story of love and betrayal commences with similar court performances. Pamphilia's younger brother, Philarchos, encounters this lady in a boat, with "onely a Dogge," preparing to die through lack of food or by becoming the dog's food (*U1* 534). We learn as she relates her story that she had been sentenced to a cruel death for some undisclosed crime (*U1* 540). But the first stage in this tragic plot occurs when she "saw those sports the Court affects, and are necessary follies for that place, as Masques and Dauncings, and was an Actor lik[e]wise my selfe amongst them" (*U1* 536). With many of her female characters shadowing Wroth's betrayal by William Herbert, who jilted her for a more lucrative match, this episode points towards her firsthand experience with the cultural and political dynamics of court entertainments.

In *Pamphilia to Amphilanthus*, the sonnet sequence appended to the published romance, Wroth explores this fraught negotiation of otherness through masque imagery in the poem,

> Like to the Indians scorched with the sunne,
> The sunne which they do as theyr God adore
> Soe ame I us'd by love, for ever more
> I worship him, less favors have I wunn.[88]

This stanza echoes the central premise of *The Masque of Blackness*: "To prove that beauty best,/Which not the colour, but the feature/Assures unto the creature" and to show, referring to the "*twelve nymphs, negroes and the daughters of Niger*," that "in their black the perfect'st beauty grows."[89] As with the masque, where Queen Anna and her ladies played these fair, as in beautiful, "Negroes," Wroth retains even as she complicates the conventional hierarchy of white over black:

> Better are they who thus to blacknes[s] runn,
> And soe can onely whitenes[s] want deplore
> Then I who pale, and white ame with griefes store,
> Nor can have hope, butt to see hopes undunn.[90]

Her blackness, indelible in the masque performance, where the ladies scandalously painted their exposed skin instead of donning vizards, is here rendered metaphorical.[91] Yet, it is whiteness, not blackness, that encodes the disease of melancholy for Wroth.[92] As in the rest of the sonnet sequence, the core paradox of this poem interiorizes an allegorized "Love" to avoid the dangers Petrarchism posed for women as subjects *and* objects of desire. The final volta runs, "Then let mee weare the marke of Cupids might," suggesting a potentially erotic and racialized bruising reminiscent of Shakespeare's Egyptian queen.[93] The penultimate line specifies "[i]n hart as they in skin of Phoebus light," alluding to the "scorched cheeks" of the "Ethiop" women masquers, one of whom Wroth played.[94]

These references to masques in the first part of the *Urania* and in the sonnet sequence appended to the published romance nevertheless appear late in the narrative and are not numerous enough to constitute a motif. The last enchantment occurs in "a round building like a Theater" (*U1* 372), but otherwise the romance highlights sonnets and lyric poetry. The manuscript continuation shifts this balance, scattering references to courtly performances throughout the narrative. The first mention of masques in part two, as in part one, frames a tale of love and betrayal set in "the kingdome of Dacia, wher[e] the King gave all the Royall entertainment that might bee, ore could bee imagined: Justs [jousts] and all exersises of warr were ther[e] and brav[e]ly performed, att nights maskes, and dauncings, and such court sports" (*U2* 14). In this episode, courtly performances lead to civil war, foreshadowing the "flames" in Asia culminating the plot strand that began with Rodomandro's debut at the Morean court (*U2* 220, 258, 378).[95] Other than this brief mention, "Two complete masques are included [in *U2*]: the King of Tartaria's masque of Honor triumphing over Cupid ... and Melissea's masque in dispraise of love's idolatry."[96]

Framed with a reference to Amphilanthus's jealousy over Rodomandro's apparent desire for Pamphilia (*U2* 44), the Tartar king's masque features twelve noblemen of his party, including himself, with twenty-four torch-bearers of lesser rank. A decorously contained ferocity defines the noble Tartarians, starting with Rodomandro who, as noted above, is ambivalently described as "soe discreete, soe civile, and soe curtious as non[e] cowld (if nott infinite rude) finde a cause to quarrell with him" (*U2* 46). As for the torch-bearers, "visards they had non[e], the most of them having faces grimm and hard enough to bee counted visards" (*U2* 46). This description lauds their martial abilities even as it projects an unsettling inscrutability, thereby reinforcing both positive and negative stereotypes of Tartars. To distinguish them from their torch-bearers, the noble masquers "had a pretty kinde of visards or slight coverings of their faces" and "[t]heir apparell [was] after the Tartarian fashion," signified by "spurrs of pure golde, butt nott soe longe as their torchbearers were, butt convenient to daunce with and nott to be offencive to the ladys" (*U2* 46). Here, the Tartar noblemen and their king perform their otherness through the stereotype of the fierce steppe warrior of the costume books and maps that circulated in early modern Europe, even as they modify their attire for a Western court that included women as influential members of the audience, as well as potential authors and performers. By conforming to the mores of a foreign court, unlike the Sophy of Persia (*U2* 108) and the Western prince Licandro (*U2* 77), the Tartar king and his men effectively open themselves to the cross-cultural alliances necessary to fulfil the imperialist aims of the romance.

In the first part of the *Urania*, the Western gaze is interrogated when the title character's maidservant thinks she "sees her beloved, Allimarlus, embracing a black woman," who is "the first dark other in the text." As Kim Hall continues, "In a larger sense, Allimarlus's embrace of the black woman represents female fears of the foreign difference that heroes – and travelers – encounter on these romantic adventures," with this episode highlighting "a gendered difference key to romance: men desire conquest, whereas women desire men."[97] Rodomandro's masque extends this interrogation by enacting a reverse ethnography that renders Western women exotic. As a result, it closely follows the premise of *The Masque of Blackness*, with the first speech from Cupid rebuking the Tartar noblemen for having "rambled abroad" in search of "vanities and change of featur[e]s" (*U2* 46). This allegorical figure demands, "May nott the beauties of Tartaria for ever hate mee, revile my government, scorne my power, to see their deeres thus stray from them to gaze on other faces? May nott your own Ladys curse mee to my face that I was missing to stay [stop] your Journeys?" (*U2* 46). He closes by condemning these noblemen, in the name of "the beauties of Tartaria," as "straglers" and "run-aways" (*U2* 46–7). The women of the Morean court thereby become the suspect "others."

Nonetheless, this reversal is quickly and violently overthrown by the allegorical figure Honor, who orders Cupid to "first beeginn your supplications heere to thes[e] all Judging eyes, thes[e] Ladys of blessedness and truest honor," meaning those of the Morean court (*U2* 47). In keeping with their eventual role as defenders of Western interests against the usurping Sophy of Persia, the Tartarians' honour conforms to the traditionally masculine code of military valour and courage. By contrast, the ladies' honour, informed by the betrayals in the two previous episodes featuring masques, corresponds to their putative "blessedness" or honesty (cf. *U1* 538). As a parallel, Hamlet harangues Ophelia, "Ha, ha? Are you honest?" (*Hamlet* 3.1.105), with "honest" glossed in *The Norton Shakespeare* as "chaste; truthful."[98] In an even more relevant comparison, Iago insinuates that Desdemona is unchaste using the racially loaded logic, "If she had been blessed, she would never have loved the Moor" (*Othello* 2.1.244). The question of women's honour harkens back to a crucial incident that occurred between the first appearance of Rodomandro at the Morean court and the staging of his masque. At this point, after hundreds of pages of wavering, Amphilanthus's jealousy upon Rodomandro's arrival propels him to marry Pamphilia through "a simple, oral pronouncement rather than a formal ceremony" (i.e., a contract *per verba de praesenti*), which he later breaches by publicly marrying another woman.[99] With elaborate euphemisms about their "hapiness" (*U2* 45), the romance remains coy about whether Pamphilia and Amphilanthus consummated their union. Even though their lovemaking would have been licit in this context, women in such situations became vulnerable to men denying the ceremony ever took place, as Wroth knew firsthand.[100] Moreover, as the prior episodes in the romance featuring masques highlight, even when an intimate liaison remains unconsummated, the consequences for the female partner if the facts were deemed otherwise could be deadly. The Tartar king, who will eventually marry Pamphilia in a public ceremony and certainly consummates their bond, as the birth of their son proves, shows immense tact in concealing what he likely knows.[101]

Negotiating the intricacies of court politics by faithfully following the masque form, the "brave Tartarian, whos[e] witt and pleasant feator did give much pleasure and admiration to the beeholders" received "[m]any and great thanks" – "especially [from] the excellent Lady," Pamphilia (U2 49). Echoing *The Masque of Blackness*, "feator" in this passage could be glossed "feature" to follow the description of Rodomandro: "for though black yett hee had the true parfection of lov[e]liness, and in loveliness[s] the purest beauty. For what is fairnes[s] with out feature, even as a picture is with out the life peece itt self?" (U2 42).[102] However, "feator" may have a more specific meaning, resonating with the adjective "featous": "Of persons and their limbs: Well-formed, well-proportioned, handsome"; "Of things: Skilfully or artistically fashioned; hence, in wider sense, elegant, handsome, becoming. Often of dress" (*OED*). Following the formula for the Jacobean masque, this performance of inclusion within the imperialist dynasty at the centre of the romance culminates when, pulling off "the[i]r visards" after the closing song, and with the king of Morea's permission, the noble Tartarians "tooke the ladys forthe to dance" (U2 49), which leads into the customary banquet. Henceforth, their king is no longer seen as an alien outsider, but as a provisional insider who facilitates the Western Christian hegemony the romance advances as an imaginary resolution to the reality of Ottoman expansionism.[103]

Wroth, by negotiating discourses of race, religion, and empire through the cross-cultural coupling of Pamphilia and Rodomandro, earned little applause. Rather, she faced the ire of prominent Jacobean courtiers for her exposure of violent patriarchal practices in the published first part of the *Urania*. The second part of the romance, a manuscript she likely broke off in the early 1630s, arguably shifted to a more cautious embrace of monarchial absolutism, Christian triumphalism, and traditional marriage. But it continues her exploration of imperialist themes, layering the anachronistic dream of a universal Christian empire with the increasingly exclusionary model of race that marked English involvement with the transatlantic slave trade and the colonies it supported. The romance posits Rodomandro, the prototypical "brave stranger" (*U2* 42), as essential for achieving this dream, which requires the dynastic union of East and West. Nonetheless, as a Central Asian who is described as black *and* white, it links him explicitly with the marginalized "blackamoors" in the romance and implicitly with the Native Americans the English confused with Tatars. This aporia, characteristic of the proto-imperial era when the English were acutely conscious of their belated status, opens an uneasy space for the marriage of this Asian king to Pamphilia, who represents the pre-Ottoman Greek world. As a result, they unite East and West under a Christian imperial banner stretching from Central Asia to Central Europe (*U2* 417). For his part, Rodomandro disappears from the main plot line of the romance after helping to secure European Christian hegemony over Asia only to haunt its margins posthumously. The Tartar-Persian princess disappears earlier in the romance as a dream projected by masculine desire, including for empire. However, she signals the presence of women from the Islamic world in the British Isles during the sixteenth century, about whom she certainly heard and may have encountered. By refracting these historical subalterns through her Tartar and Persian characters, Wroth underscores how gendered subalterns such as Ipolita the Tartarian and Teresa Sampsonia Sherley informed her own negotiations and alienation as an early modern woman writer.

Signifying Gender and Islam in Early Shakespeare: *The Comedy of Errors* (1594) and the Gray's Inn Revels

This chapter returns to the "Tartar girl" from earlier chapters, along with figurations of Turks, Amazons, and Africans, to parse the "gender trouble" – Judith Butler's resonant term for the "performative construction" of identity – associated with the multivalent subject positions instantiated during England's proto-imperialist and proto-orientalist era.[1] In particular, I proceed through a tropological consideration of multiple and contradictory "Others" in Elizabethan drama, with further attention to the historical agency of gendered subalterns from the Islamic world in early modern England.[2] As I show, these girls and women were not only refracted in performances such as Shakespeare's plays and Elizabethan court masques, but they were in the audiences for both.[3] Conventionally, Shakespeare's theatre has been isolated as the locus for such gender trouble because boys and young men played the female roles.[4] However, this assessment ignores the variegated sites for theatre in the era, including the royal courts and country houses where women appeared in aristocratic entertainments, often alongside professional male actors playing female speaking roles.[5] The Inns of Court, while exclusively male, opened their performance spaces to women audience members during their revels; frequently, stage and audience blurred in this raucous setting, with women assuming unintended roles as performers. Moreover, while cross-dressing was confined to male actors on the public stage, both men and women confounded gendered norms on London's streets.[6] Their "mingle mangle of apparell," in the Puritan polemicist Philip Stubbes's view, dangerously confused ascriptions of status/rank and sex/gender, to which we could add shifting ascriptions of race, religion, and ethnicity.[7] The latter concatenation, as detailed in previous chapters, accrued from the inaugural voyages of

Englishmen to the Americas in the second half of the sixteenth century, in competition with the Spanish and other Europeans, and their concurrent voyages to the Safavid Persian and Ottoman Turkish empires, where they were received as subalterns.[8] Protestant England's position as a proto-imperial nation vis-à-vis these more powerful empires consequently induced what we might call "racial trouble" in its designations of Self and Other along a continuum of "fair" (increasingly white) beauty, with "blackness," an ambivalent, albeit ultimately unassimilable, signifier.[9]

The 1594–5 Christmas revels at Gray's Inn, one of four Inns of Court that functioned primarily as finishing schools for upper-class males, exemplifies this gender and racial trouble through an imbricated series of performances: the semi-parodic allegory of the Prince of Purpoole and a pseudo-Russian ambassador, enacted by the young gentlemen of the Inns of Court; the madcap premier of Shakespeare's *The Comedy of Errors*, considered one of his first ventures into this genre; and *The Masque of Proteus*, involving professional and court performers, with Queen Elizabeth I in the audience.[10] In his influential reading of Shakespeare's *Love's Labour's Lost*, performed the same year, John Michael Archer follows previous critics in connecting the obscure reference to "Negro-Tartars" in the Gray's Inn Revels to "the entry of blackamoor musicians with the disguised Lords in the Muscovite or Russian 'masque.'"[11] As he affirms, this ascription of "blackness," as in "Negro," applies not only to the blackamoors (i.e., Africans) in the play, but also to the Muscovites (i.e., Russians), who were likewise associated with burning, branding, and slavery in Elizabethan poetry and prose. In Archer's earlier rendition of this argument, he states that "Negro-Tartar" also connotes the "'Nogai' or 'Nagay Tartar,' terms given by Elizabethan [and earlier sixteenth-century] travellers in Russia to the inhabitants of the area around the lower Volga River, a warlike people who had recently made peace with the tsar." He adds that the reference to "Bigarian" in the Gray's Inn Revels "may similarly be a play on Boghar or Bokhara [Bukhara], a city beyond the Caspian Sea that was a principal market for the Persian trade in slaves from Russia and eastern Europe."[12] The aforementioned Anthony Jenkinson and his companions, Richard and Robert Johnson, were the first Englishmen to explore the whole of the Caspian Sea, traditionally considered the boundary between Europe and Asia to the north, which Jenkinson mapped.[13] The "Tartar girl" he acquired for Queen Elizabeth has been described as a Nagayan (Nogay) from Astrakhan, which Tsar Ivan IV ("the Terrible") had conquered using scorched earth tactics shortly before Jenkinson's arrival.[14]

While *The Comedy of Errors* was published separately in the 1623 First Folio of Shakespeare's plays, it was not until 1688 that an eyewitness record of the complete 1594–5 revels was published as the *Gesta Grayorum: or, The History of the High and Mighty Prince, Henry Prince of Purpoole ... Together with a Masque, as it was presented (by His Highness's Command) for the Entertainment of Q. Elizabeth; who, with the Nobles of both Courts, was present thereat*.[15] While literary critics and historians have mined the *Gesta Grayorum* when glossing Shakespeare's early comedies – as Archer does so astutely – few have explicated this series of performances as a whole, which is how they were received if not conceived.[16] As I propose, if we read the published account holistically and historically, the reiterated figures of Turks and Tartars immediately come to the fore as epitomizing what Louis Montrose calls a "radical and hostile Otherness."[17] In the "New World" context he considers, this means cannibals and Amazons, who haunt the emerging Western European discourse of global empire. For the revellers at Gray's Inn, more concerned with the "Old World" in their proto-imperial moment, this "Otherness" is located in the Islamic (north)east and is considered hostile to "all *Christendom*" (21).[18] As a result, Western and Eastern Christians – namely, the Protestant English and the Orthodox Russians – are able to ally as "proximate figures of Otherness," despite their religious, political, and cultural differences.[19]

To add another layer, these multivalent relationships between the upper-class young men of the Inns of Court and the multi-ethnic characters they played were materially and metaphorically subtended by the lives of Black women in Shakespeare's London, many of whom traced their origins to Islamic West Africa. The aforementioned "Tartar girl" in Queen Elizabeth's court, who hailed from the Islamicate regions of Central Asia, also resonates in these productions, albeit less explicitly. Linking "New World" projections and "Old World" mythologies, the figure of the Amazon resonates with these gendered subalterns on multiple levels. From antiquity, these legendary warrior women were located in the northern regions around the Black Sea, dominated by the Crimean Tatars and their Nogay tributaries during the sixteenth century. By the early modern/colonial period, they were also associated with Africa and the Americas, as Sir Walter Ralegh attests in *The Discoverie of the Large, Rich, and Bewtiful Empire of Guiana* (1596).[20] As Montrose expands in his influential reading of Ralegh's treatise, "[t]he matriarchal, gynocratic Amazons are the radical Other figured but not fully contained by the collective imagination of European patriarchy."[21] In assessing the patriarchal "web of empire" indexed by the *Gesta Grayorum*, I thereby extend and complicate readings of the gendered "discourse of discovery" in the era by foregrounding the fraught historical embodiment of subaltern women from the Islamic world (along with the projection of Amazons into this space) and their neglected, albeit constitutive role in its literature, including Shakespeare's plays.[22]

The Inns of Court, Lucy Negro, and the Amazons

As Margaret Knapp and Michal Kobialka explain, "[t]he ultimate purpose of the Inns [of Court] was to develop future statesmen [women were not admitted as students], justices, and scholars, and therefore the students' time was taken up not only with the study of legal subjects, but also with the development of such courtiers' skills as dancing, fencing, writing poetry, and acting in plays and masques." As such, "at least two, and possibly as many as six, of Shakespeare's plays were performed in the great halls of the Inns of Court during his lifetime."[23] Francis Bacon, later Attorney General and Lord Chancellor of England, sponsored several masques for his alma mater, Gray's Inn, including the lavish *Masque of Flowers* (1613/14). The central portion of the 1594–5 revel's allegory, "the Councillors' speeches and the Prince's reply," has been ascribed to him.[24] Hence, even though Bacon is often cited as a detractor of royal court masques, he participated in similar productions at the Inns of Court.[25]

In addition to the importance of mise-en-scène for these cultural performances, which centred on Gray's Inn with occasional progresses through London, the timing was significant. As Knapp and Kobialka specify, "[t]he Christmas Revels, a tradition of the Inns dating from the medieval Feast of Fools and the Lord of Misrule, was a period running from 20 December (the Eve of the Feast of St Thomas) to Shrovetide (the day before Ash Wednesday [which in 1595 fell on 5 March]) during which the students organized a series of events for their own entertainment."[26] The deaths of the famous explorer Martin Frobisher (1535–94) and the cartographer Gerard Mercator (1512–94) occurred the same year, marking a watershed in English discourses of empire: the passing generation was aligned with John Dee's dream of reaching Cathay (China) through the northern route for commercial gain, which I address in chapter 2. The newer generation, represented by Richard

Hakluyt, endorsed the westward turn to the Americas for a more properly colonial project.[27] As noted previously, Hakluyt, in the preface to his 1589 edition of *The Principall Navigations, Voyages, and Discoveries of the English Nation*, praises Jenkinson and William Burrough, who contributed to Jenkinson's famous map of Russia and Tartaria, as "gentlemen of great experience, and observations in the north Regions"; in the preface to the 1599 edition, he lauds Jenkinson as "that valiant, wise, and personable gentleman."[28] Jenkinson's trade and diplomatic missions to Russia, Central Asia, and Persia consequently underpin what nineteenth-century historian James Anthony Froude dubbed the "Prose Epic of the modern English nation."[29] As I have argued throughout this book, subaltern women from the Islamic world, though seemingly marginal to this "epic" and the English expansionism it promoted, were simultaneously constitutive in the sense Jacques Derrida has defined and Gayatri Chakravorty Spivak has elaborated for the "supplement": "[c]ompensatory ... and vicarious, the supplement is an adjunct, a subaltern instance which *takes-(the)-place*."[30] They, too, inform the emerging anglocentric discourse of empire and its concomitant "ideologies of racial difference" through their strategies of survival and resistance: what Gerald Vizenor terms "survivance."[31]

We can begin to limn the significance of these subaltern girls and women by explicating the allegory that sutures the performances constituting the Gray's Inn Revels for the Christmas season of 1594–5. Self-consciously enacting the "the power of display" that marked Renaissance class privilege, "the revellers strove to (re)produce," as Douglas Lanier details, "the ceremonial texture of courtly society, its oratorical style, visual spectacle, ritualized actions, and management of diplomatic challenges." The tone of the revels was playful, with Rabelaisian touches, but it was not meant "to undermine respect for authority or to demystify ceremony." Indeed, it constituted "a kind of cultural dress rehearsal" for the young men who expected to accede to this class privilege upon leaving Gray's Inn.[32] The festivities began "about the 12th. of *December*" with the selection of "a Prince of *Purpoole*, to govern our State for the time; which was intended to be for the Credit of *Grays Inn*, and rather to be performed by witty Inventions, than chargeable Expences" (2). As Knapp and Kobialka gloss, Purpoole, as an instance of the cautious parody characteristic of the revels, is a simple "corruption of Portpool, the parish in which Gray's Inn was located."[33] Most of the wordplay involves similarly jejune puns. The Prince of Purpoole chosen to preside over these revels was "one Mr. *Henry Helmes*, a

Norfolk-Gentleman, who was thought to be accomplished with all good Parts, fit for so great a Dignity" (2). Crucially, he was "also a very proper Man of Personage, and very active in Dancing and Revelling" (2).[34] The balance of the opening proceedings carries forward this mimesis of the apparatus of state, from the appointment of a Privy Council to the circulation of "Letters ... in nature of Privy Seals" to secure the funds that would ensure the remaining fun (2). After these internal affairs were set in order, "there was dispatched from our State [i.e. Gray's Inn] a Messenger to our ancient allied Friend, the *Inner Temple*," one of the four Inns of Court, requesting that they send a resident ambassador to Gray's Inn to take part in the revels (4). This invitation initiates a centrifugal set of foreign relations, which in subsequent performances will extend from the brothers of the Inner Temple to Russians, who are cast as "proximate figures of Otherness," to figures of "radical and hostile Otherness," such as Tartars, Turks, and Amazons.[35]

The first Grand Night, "[u]pon the 20[th.] Day of *December*, being St. *Thomas's* Eve" (9), which featured the Prince of Purpoole's investiture with his crown and coat of arms, introduces the mode of Arthurian romance linked later in the revels to English mercantile ventures in Central Asia (9–10; cf. 60).[36] As a further medievalism, it showcases several speeches confirming the "*Signiories, Lordships, Lands, Privileges, or Liberties*" of the prince's retainers (11). The first pronouncement plays up the chivalric theme "to right and relieve all Wants and Wrongs of all Ladies, Matrons and Maids" (11). However, as in the rest of the revels, this veneer of gentility wears thin as the young gentlemen's predilection for prostitution is revealed. A subsequent announcement foregrounds the sexual trafficking that pervades the revels when it grants "*Lucy Negro*, Abbess *de Clerkenwell* ... the Nunnery of *Clerkenwell*, with the Lands and Privileges thereunto belonging, of the Prince of *Purpoole* by Night-Service in *Cauda*, and to find a Choir of Nuns, with burning Lamps, to chaunt *Placebo* to the Gentleman of the Prince's Privy-Chamber, on the Day of His Excellency's Coronation" (12). The loosely coded language of "Nunnery" for a brothel was common, with Shakespeare subsequently using it for Hamlet's abusive address to Ophelia (*Hamlet* 3.1.123–30, 137–40, 148). Analogously, the "Abbess" and her "Nuns" signify "a woman in charge of a brothel; a madam" and her prostitutes (*OED*).[37]

Lucy Negro, also known as "Black Luce," ran a notorious establishment in Clerkenwell close to the Inns of Court. In court testimony, she was called "an arrant whore and a bawde"; she may even have been the "Dark Lady" to whom Shakespeare addressed over two dozen son-nets.[38] It is very likely, as I elaborate below, that she sat in the audience for the first Grand Night, which culminated in the premiere of Shake-speare's *The Comedy of Errors*, which also alludes to her.[39] Yet, as Imtiaz Habib contextualizes in *Black Lives in the English Archives, 1500–1677*, "[h]er sexual exploitation as a prostitute is the most vicious form of the performance of a negative pathology for black people, particularly young black women, in which the only use that destitute enslaved black females can have is as casual sexual conveniences for the male public at large."[40] While Habib discounts Lucy Negro's agency in negotiating the constraints of class, gender, and race in Elizabethan London, and he fails to acknowledge how she facilitated the exploitation of other women dis-advantaged by class and/or race, it is true, as Duncan Salkeld empha-sizes in *Shakespeare among the Courtesans*, that the lives of even the most celebrated courtesans (the highest status among early modern sex work-ers) was precarious at best and often ended in misery.[41]

Hence, the conflation in the revels of the ideology of "protecting" women, whether through chivalry or cloistering, and the reality of Lucy Negro's livelihood catering to upper-class male sexual demands exposes what Walter Mignolo calls the "darker side of the Renaissance" as it incorporated the global commercial sex trade.[42] In chapter 1, I made the same argument for the "Tartar girl" Jenkinson acquired in Central Asia and brought to Queen Elizabeth's court: while he displays what Daryl Palmer in *Writing Russia in the Age of Shakespeare* describes as "a kind of intercultural self-fashioning that continues, in our own day, to define the sophistication of multi-national existence," the "Tar-tar girl" functions as a synecdoche for the human trafficking intrin-sic to the global pattern of commodity exchange characteristic of the modern era from the turn of the sixteenth century onwards.[43] Although we do not have the same evidence for Lucy Negro's life prior to her designation as "Abbess of Clerkenwell," collateral evidence for other African women in Scotland and England suggests a similar trajectory. Like many of these women, this gendered subaltern (or her forebears) plausibly hailed from Islamic West Africa, possibly via Portugal, which I outline in chapter 1. Unsurprisingly, none of this history concerns the young gentlemen of Gray's Inn as they celebrate their Christmas revels. Yet, despite the neglect of her background and agency in her own time and since, Lucy Negro's documented role in the revels pro-foundly informs the tendentious references to Amazons, Turks, and Tartars therein.

The first of these references – in this case, to the Amazons – occurs shortly after the nod to Lucy Negro in the pseudo-feudal pronouncements from the allegorical performance of the first Grand Night. With a casual brutality conveyed through the language of chivalry, one of the prince's retainers promises "on the Day of His Excellency's Coronation one *Amazon*, with a Ring to be run at by the Knight's [*sic*] of the Prince's Band" (12). With "Amazon" a slang term for prostitute, this description is rife with sexual innuendo. In anticipating the subsequent "hot skirmish" in "the Straits of the Gulf of *Clerkenwell*" against "the Admiral of the *Amazons*" (49–50), whose extended allegory suggests anal rape, it also encodes the sexual aggression that informed most of these fratboy jests.[44] With the pronouncement signalling the Prince of Purpoole's "Voyage Royal against the *Amazons*, to subdue and bring them under" (12), the projection of male violence onto these palimpsestic figures anticipates the metaphorics of sexual assault in Ralegh's *Discoverie of ... Guiana*, as when he (in)famously intones: "*Guiana* is a Countrey that hath yet her Maydenhead," implying that it is there for the taking, no consent required.[45] The next reference to the Amazons reinforces this projection of male violence onto subaltern and subversive women as the Prince of Purpoole's newly invested knights pledge "never to bear Arms against His Highness's Sacred Person, nor his State; but to assist him in all his lawful Wars, and maintain all his just Pretences and Titles; especially, His Highness's Title to the Land of the *Amazons*, and the Cape of *Good Hope*" (27–8). Here, the Amazons signify Central Asia and Africa simultaneously, with an allusion to the Americas by means of circumnavigations of the globe – most recently, that of Francis Drake from 1577 to 1580.[46] The proto-imperialist reach of the "Prince of Purpoole," and hence of the English ruling class, is thereby mediated through a gendered and racialized figure – in this case, the Amazon linked to Asia, Africa, and the Americas – who signifies the global routes coveted by the English during the Elizabethan era.

In the performances for Twelfth Night (5 January), the gender and racial trouble endemic to empire again surfaces with "A Letter of Advertisement from *Knights-bridge*, to the Honourable Council" of the Prince of Purpoole (48). Condemning highwaymen who prey on local travellers, the letter depicts "*another sort of dangerous People, under the Name of poor Soldiers, that say they were ma[i]med, and lost their Limbs in His Honour's Service and Wars against the* Amazons" (48). This description signals the intensifying anxieties about traditional hierarchies in the post-Armada years, with unpaid soldiers increasingly turning to robbery.[47] These anxieties come to the fore in "Another Letter from Sea, directed to the Lord Admiral" (49), where they recall the reference to Lucy Negro that launched the revels. The Lord Admiral writes: "I gave your Honour to understand, that His Excellency's Merchants of *Purpoole* began to surcease their Traffic to *Clerkenwell*, *Newington* and *Bankside*, and such like Roads of Charge and Discharge, because they feared lest certain Rovers, which lay hovering about the Narrow Seas, should intercept them in their Voyages" (49). The streets, that is, are no longer safe for streetwalkers and their customers. The cause, the Lord Admiral reveals, is "an huge *Armado* of *French Amazons* ... which being dispersed into sundry Creeks, work daily much damage to all sorts of People, and Adventurers hold in durance; not suffering one Man to escape, till he have turned French" (49).

Unpacking the "nodal point" of this dream of empire and its gender trouble points towards neglected contexts that help us parse its concomitant racial trouble.[48] To start, France maintained a long-term relationship with the Ottoman Empire, with formal agreements established early in the sixteenth century (1528 and 1536). The Ottoman fleet, led by Barbarossa, even wintered for eight months at the port of Toulon (1543–4), with the cathedral transformed into a mosque for the duration. As a result of this perceived infidelity to Western Christian unity, the French were pilloried as "Turks" in the religio-political sense.[49] By the 1590s, however, England had joined the French as one of the major Western Christian trading, diplomatic, and even military partners of the Ottomans. Their merchant ships were venturing more frequently into the Mediterranean, where a significant number of British sailors were captured by Barbary pirates and compelled either to convert or remain in prison. Other Britons may have embraced Islam freely, either for piety or gain. As a number of critics have shown, the resultant anxiety over the malleability of religious identity, particularly conversion from Christianity to Islam, increasingly informed discourses of race and gender in the period.[50]

The response in the revels to this anxiety is particularly violent: "five hundred fifty five" of the Amazons were incinerated and "ninety nine" imprisoned, with none of the men hurt (50). Symptomatically, the obliteration of the Amazons, who are not granted proper names, is displaced onto the English ships, which bear the slightly exoticized ones of "*Catharina Dardana, Pecta de Lee* and *Maria de Routlis*" (50). These ships were carrying "Cochenella [Cochineal], Musk, Guaiacum, Tobaco and *Le grand Vezolle*" (50): the spoils of the East and

West Indies, including several treatments for syphilis or the "French disease."[51] The Amazons in the Gray's Inn Revels therefore embody a gendered and racialized Other that must be subdued not only to ensure Western patriarchy, but more so to guarantee Western imperialism as it expanded across the globe. The English were belated in this effort: as Hakluyt bemoans, his countrymen (and women) "of all others [among the competing Western European nations] for their sluggish security, and continual neglect of the like attempts" are "either ignominiously reported, or exceedingly condemned."[52] In the meanwhile, the realm's future statesmen were elaborating their imperialist aspirations through the figure of the Amazon – along with the Turk and Tartar – by imaginatively deploying earlier English trading voyages across Central Asia to advance the expansionist dreams of Elizabethans like Hakluyt and Ralegh.

Turks, "Negro Tartars," and *The Comedy of Errors*

The success of the former proceedings raised the stakes for the next Grand Night, scheduled to take place "upon *Innocents-Day*" (20), which fell on 28 December.[53] Relatively more has been written about this episode because a play thought to be *The Comedy of Errors* was staged that evening, albeit to a mixed response. With concerns about the tarnish the lower-class "Players" cast on the revels (22; cf. 57), the main show privileged "a great Presence of Lords, Ladies, and worshipful Personages, that did expect some notable Performance at that time" (20): not from Shakespeare and his paid actors, but from the gentleman of Gray's Inn and their aristocratic patrons.[54] This performance deepened the allegory initiated by the Prince of Purpoole's enthronement by adding a foreign element: "our Friend, the *Inner Temple*, determined to send their Ambassador to our Prince of State, as sent from *Frederick Templarius*, their Emperor, who was then busied in his Wars against the Turk" (20). After an elaborate ceremony mimicking European diplomatic protocols, the Templarian Ambassador,

> made a Speech to the Prince, wherein he declared how his excellent Renown and Fame was known throughout all the Whole World; and that the Report of his Greatness was not contained within the Bounds of the Ocean, but had come to the Ears of his noble Sovereign, *Frederick Templarius*, where he is now warring against the *Turks*, the known Enemies to all *Christendom* (21),

etcetera! The Prince of Purpoole returned an equally flatulent speech, which repeats the description of the Turks as "an Enemy to all *Christendom*" (21) and affirms that "the Glory of ... [the Emperor's] Actions tend to the Safety and Liberty of all Civility and Humanity" (22).[55] These "positive" aspects of the Western European discourse of empire – glory, safety, liberty, civility, and humanity – are thus associated with Christians as opposed to Muslims.

Although England was not a global empire in the Elizabethan era, it did seek to emulate established imperialists such as the Habsburgs, as in this allegory, and even the Ottomans, as Gerald MacLean has identified.[56] Here, the mantle of the Holy Roman Emperor is assumed by a fraternal Inn of Court, praised as an "ancient Friend" (20), with efforts focused on what is represented as the inveterate foe of all Christendom, the Muslim Turks. Paradoxically, the English were expanding their diplomatic relations with the Ottomans at this time, with Edward Barton serving as the second English ambassador at Constantinople (Istanbul).[57] Hence, while this episode primarily evokes the Inns of Courts's anachronistic crusading credentials to advance the early modern anglocentric dream of matching the Habsburgs' imperialist achievements, it may also be offering a veiled critique of the Elizabethan alliance with Muslim "infidels."

At this point in the proceedings a lavish entertainment, along the lines of the aristocratic devices and masques that characterized the revels, should have been "performed for the Delight of the Beholders" (22). Instead, "there arose such a disordered Tumult and Crowd upon the Stage," which was positioned in front of the dais where the Prince of Purpoole presided, that the ambassador from the Inner Temple left in a huff and the alternative of "Dancing and Revelling with Gentlewomen" filled the gap (22).[58] Only "after such Sports, a Comedy of Errors (like to *Plautus* his *Menechmus*) was played by the Players" (22). If the gentleman and ladies were paying any attention, they would have witnessed one of Shakespeare's first plays and perhaps his first comedy, which critics traditionally have dismissed as simple farce, with some more recently, such as Martine van Elk, lauding "the play's intermingling of genres." In van Elks's view, the play, while modelled on the Roman New Comedy, combines "romance and farce" to explore "identity's loss and recovery," to which Robert Miola adds Aristotlean comedy and elements of tragedy.[59]

Infusing its ancient form with present concerns, *The Comedy of Errors* elaborates an ingenious variation on the mapping of the emerging global discourse of empire onto a woman's body: in this case, the obese and sexually demanding kitchen maid, Nell.[60] Adding another layer, some critics have proposed that this "swart" (3.2.101) or swarthy "kitchen wench" (3.2.94), who could be the maid Luce, also alludes to Lucy Negro, who was probably in the audience.[61] Nell and Negro accordingly double in performances of the play; yet, this character never appears on stage.[62] Instead, we first learn about her when the servant twin, Dromio of Syracuse, whom Nell mistakes for her erstwhile lover, Dromio of Ephesus, complains to his master using suggestive double entendres that "she would have me as a beast – not that, I being a beast, she would have me, but that she, being a very beastly creature, lays claim to me" (3.2.86–8). Through copious puns at Nell's expense, we understand that "her name and three quarters – that's an ell and three-quarters – will not measure her from hip to hip" (3.2.108–10). (The English ell measured forty-five inches.)[63]

Drawing on the new geographical knowledge, which was harnessed to the Western European drive for empire, Dromio cleverly depicts Nell as "spherical, like a globe" (3.2.113). Deploying the "blazon's inventory of fragmented and reified [body] parts," ostensibly in praise of the conventional female beloved, he associates each with a European country roughly running from north to south (Ireland, Scotland, France, England, Spain) (3.2.115–30).[64] He ultimately dwells on "America, the Indies," which is represented by her nose "all o'er embellished with rubies, carbuncles, [and] sapphires" (3.2.131–3): more prosaically, it is reddened with blue veins. Punning on the literal meaning of Netherlands, he responds, "I did not look so low" (3.2.137), with "nether" "[i]n various compounds signifying the anus or vulva" (*OED*). While the register in this blazon is comical, even farcical, it points towards the violence implicit in the rhetorical figure, which from a feminist perspective inscribes "a battle between men that is first figuratively and then literally fought on the fields of woman's 'celebrated' body," to cite Nancy Vickers's influential formulation.[65] It also recalls the earlier battle in the Gray's Inn revels to "subdue" the Amazons and "bring them under" (12), which in turn evokes the metaphorics of rape of the land (and its inhabitants) that infuses the anglocentric discourse of empire as inscribed in Ralegh's *Discoverie* .

While *The Comedy of Errors* does not develop the connection between trade, empire, and gender to the degree the contemporaneous plays of Christopher Marlowe do, or even the later plays of Shakespeare such as *The Merchant of Venice* (1596/7), *Othello* (1603/4), and *The Tempest* (1611), it does gesture towards voyages to the East, with a minor character, the "Second Merchant," announcing he is "bound/To Persia, and want guilders for my voyage" (4.1.3–4; cf. 4.1.104).[66] This lone reference to Safavid Persia does not derive from classical antecedents, as was more common in plays from the period, but relates specifically to early modern trade.[67] While this demand propels the internal plot rather than expands the setting, by following immediately upon Dromio's blazon to the "globe" that is Nell it recalls the northeastern routes the English "discovered" from the mid-1550s to the 1570s to circumvent the Iberian monopoly on the western routes.

The final allusion in the play to a region beyond the Mediterranean *oecumene* is less pointed, albeit still linked to the play's gender politics. When Adriana, Antipholus of Ephesus's estranged wife, asks Dromio of Syracuse about the man she assumes is his master, he answers: "he's in Tartar limbo, worse than hell" (4.2.32). As the plot of the play continues to devolve into maddening confusions of identity and relationships, this layered allusion projects the proto-imperialist and proto-orientalist connotations that the *Gesta Grayorum* transcribes more fully. "Tartar" here, as *The Norton Shakespeare* glosses, "is short for 'Tartarus,' the classical hell, but it also suggests the Tartars, Central Asian people reputed by Elizabethans to be particularly savage."[68] In fact, as I have shown elsewhere, on balance the image of Tartars in early modern English travel narratives and histories – where they were frequently "portrayed as amenable and even assimilable" – was positive, despite the reproduction of medieval friars' polemics against the Mongols in collections such as Hakluyt's.[69] As I elaborate here, the *Gesta Grayorum* similarly dramatizes this ambivalence towards Tartars, who can either assimilate into the Elizabethan court or join the Turks as enemies of Christendom.

The investiture of "the Knighthood of the Helmet" (26), with its metonymic representation of the Amazon in relation to the continents the Western European imperialists coveted, correspondingly contains a critique, albeit a subtle one, of England's recent rapprochement with the Ottoman Turks. Proceeding through an argument *ad absurdum*, this critique is embedded in the parodic articles of the "Royal Order" (27):

No Knight of this Order shall put out any Money upon strange Returns or Performances to be made by his own Person; as, to hop up the stairs to the top of St. *Paul's*, without intermission; or any such like Agilities or Endurances, except it may appear, that the same Performances or Practices do enable him to some Service or Employment; as, if he do undertake to go a Journey backward, the same shall be thought to enable him to be an Ambassador into *Turk*[e]*y*. (29)

Broadly mocking the contortions of courtiership, this passage more specifically associates the Sublime Porte in Istanbul with cultural backwardness, with the Ottoman Empire epitomizing political despotism in influential treatises.[70] This biased assessment was supported by the belief that petitioners to the sultan's court had to retreat backwards or face the sultan's deadly ire.[71] "Backwardness" also signified sodomy, frequently associated with "Turks" from the early modern period onwards.[72] The next scene features speeches from six councillors to the prince, which gradually modulates from the first's militant advocacy for expansionist warfare to the others' promotion of Queen Elizabeth's "policy of peace."[73] This cautious critique of the queen's pacific policy, against which the war party in her cabinet (including Ralegh) chafed, reinforces the negative references to Turkey at a time when Elizabeth was ratifying trade and diplomatic alliances with the Ottomans.[74]

During the Twelfth Night performances that followed, whose overdetermined depictions of Amazons we have already examined, Tartars are cast as enemies of Christendom like the Turks, with the "Knights of the Helmet" allied with the "Emperor of *Russia*" against them (43). These stage Tartars, like the actual "Tartar girl," were brought forcibly to England. In this case, three Tartars (presumably male) were "led as Prisoners, and were attired like Monsters and Miscreants" (43). Hence, while the Turks remain abstract enemies, the Tartars are historically embodied even as they are dramatically dehumanized. Even worse, they are represented as state enemies, having been caught while "conspiring against His Highness and Dignity" (43). To contain this threat, they are replaced by the allegorical personae of "*Envy, Male-content* and *Folly*" (44). While we have no firm evidence of "Turkish" embassies at the English court during the sixteenth century – indeed, as a leading empire in relation to "marginal England," the Ottomans did not deign to send official envoys, although Morocco sent an ambassador in 1600 – we do have evidence of Central Asians at court and elsewhere in London.[75] This allegorical representation, based on the usurpation of "*Vertue* and *United Friendship*" (44), thus suggests Tartars could assimilate more easily into English culture than Turks, even as their marks of difference remained indelible.

The heightened anxiety about the enemy within continues in the speech of "an Ambassador from the mighty Emperor of *Russia* and *Moscovy*" to the Prince of Purpoole, wherein he praises "your Knights of the *Helmet*" for venturing to the "cold Climate" of Russia to war against the Tartars (44–5). As documented in chapter 2, it was merchants who ventured to Russia in the sixteenth century, with commerce not conquest as their goal. They witnessed the aftermath of Ivan the Terrible's subjugation of the Tatar khanates, Kazan and Astrakhan, but they neither aided his efforts nor intervened to stop them. Indeed, the Muscovy Company ordered its agents to avoid matters of religion or politics, which enabled Jenkinson to negotiate difficult and even dangerous situations in Eastern Orthodox and Muslim courts.[76] The story the "Russian" ambassador delivers in his speech about the conquest of the *"Bigarian Tartars"* and the *"Ne-gro-Tartars"* accordingly bears some relation to the history of Ivan's destruction of the khanates (46). The tsar, however, followed a more flexible policy of incorporating Tatar nobles into his empire as retainers and proxy rulers. Although forced conversions followed in subsequent reigns, he did not insist that his Tatar retainers convert to Christianity.[77] The unremitting denigration of "Tartars" in this speech – they are called "barbarous," "Runagate," and "Vermine" (46) – thus seems atypical for Ivan and for the English merchants who sought to trade with him.

The pseudo-Russian ambassador goes on to praise the Prince of Purpoole as "a Bulwark of *Christendom*," who "by raising continual Trophies of strength[e]ned Tartars" will "keep the Glory of your Vertue in everlasting Flourish" (46). The prince's reward, with another submerged reference to the merchants' trade, is "a Ship laden with divers of the best and fairest Fruits, and other richest Commodities, of our Country" (46–7). With a parting assertion of his imperial ambitions, the prince responds: *"Our Self, with Our chosen Knights, with an Army Royal, will make towards our Brother of* Russia, *with my Lord here, his Ambassador, presently to join with him against his Enemies, the* Negarian Tartars; *more dreadful, the* Barbarian Tartars" (52). Here is evidence of the ambivalent derivation of "Negro" and "Tartar" from the referent Nagayan (Nogay), as well as "Barbarian" from Bukhara, which anticipates the troubling conflation of "Ethiop" and "tawny Tartar" in Shakespeare's *A Midsummer Night's Dream* (1595/6).[78] The Prince of Purpoole continues: *"And if* Fortune *will not grace Our good Attempt, as I am rightful Prince, and true Sovereign of the honourable Order of the* Helmet, *and by all those Ladies whom, in Knightly Honour, I love and serve, I will make the Name of a* Grayan *Knight more dreadful to the* Barbarian Tartars, *than the* Macedonian *to the wearied* Persians, *the* Roman *to the dispersed* Britains, *or the* Castalian *to the weak[e]ned* Indians" (52). All three touchstones of classical and contemporary Western imperialism are highlighted in an analogy that is belated, with the Russian tsar having conquered Kazan and Astrakhan four decades prior. Yet, this multilayered discourse of empire is also suggestive of the "post-colonial" *and* proto-imperial position of the English evoking their own history as a colonized people under the Romans, which Shakespeare represents in *Cymbeline* (1609/10), and their putative future as colonizers along the lines of the Spanish or even the Ottomans.[79] As the crowning masque in the revels underscores, this layering of colonial and imperial histories continues to inform the subject position of real and imagined Tartars in Elizabethan England, who oscillated between assimilation and abjection as they sought to survive and even resist their displacement.

The Masque of Proteus *and the Tartar Girl*

Following the Prince of Purpoole's "Journey towards *Russia*" (53), which lasted "until *Candlemas*" (2 February) (53), and his return from what he calls "*a most tedious and hazardous Journey, though very honorable, into* Russia" (54), the revels shift to a final masque staged for Queen Elizabeth at Shrovetide.[80] *The Masque of Proteus*, held in the Banqueting House at Whitehall Palace, offers a more refined treatment of malleable identities than the earlier *Comedy of Errors*, which is referenced in the explanation as to why a masque was staged instead of a play: "In that regard, the Plot of those Sports were but small; the rather, that Tedious-ness might be avoided, and confused Disorder, a thing which might easily happen in a multitude of Actions" (57).[81] The plot of the masque is indeed small: beginning with praise of "Neptune's *Empire*," it mainly consists of "[a]n Esquire of the Princes Company" taking questions from "*Proteus*, the Sea-God" about his adventures abroad (57–8).[82] What is most interesting about this production, given the concatenation of Tartar, Turk, and Amazon excavated above, is the presence of a "*Tartar-ian* page" at the Esquire's side (57), along with this page's invisibility in studies of the *Gesta Grayorum* and *The Comedy of Errors*.[83]

While the Esquire rehearses at length "*the Victory of* Austrican [Astra-khan]," which "[*h*]*ad made an end of the* Tartarian *War, / And quite dispers'd our vanquish'd Enemies / Unto their Hoards, and huge vast Wilderness*" (60; cf. xiii), the page does not speak at all. As this mode of silent display was the norm for women in Elizabethan and Jacobean masques, it is plau-sible that the "Tartar girl" who graced Queen Elizabeth's court played the "Tartarian page," even though she would have been close to mid-dle age at the time.[84] Since pages were meant to be boys or young men, this role instantiates the gender trouble characteristic of Shakespeare's transvestite stage, albeit in reverse.[85] It is even more likely that the "Tartar girl" was in the audience, as was Lucy Negro for the first Grand Night of the revels. In any case, when juxtaposed with the Tartar prisoners from the earlier night's performance, this page "boy" signals the violence that haunted her acquisition in Astrakhan and conversion into "Ipolita the Tartarian" for the Elizabethan court. Her presence, whether literal or spectral, also recalls the queen's proto-imperialist self-fashioning, which was the subject of chapter 2.[86] With the masque closing in a paean ostensibly directed to Proteus, but actually meant for Queen Elizabeth, England's imagined empire ambitiously extends from "Russia, China, *and* Negellan's [Magellan's] *Strait*" (65; cf. xx): that is, from Eurasia to the Americas. It thereby encompasses the legendary Amazons and the historical Turks and Tartars figured in the *Gesta Grayorum* and Shakespeare's play.

Building on the case studies from chapter 1 and the close contextualized readings adduced thus far, this chapter has traced how the lives of Lucy Negro, whose origins most likely went back to Islamic West Africa, and the "Tartar girl," who indubitably came from the Islamicate regions of Central Asia, resonate in the elite and popular literature of Elizabethan England. Lucy Negro probably witnessed the premiere of *The Comedy of Errors* on the first Grand Night of the Gray's Inn Revels. Shakespeare may have referenced her; the speechifiers at Gray's Inn certainly did. The "Tartar girl," renamed Ipolita the Tartarian, may have been in the audience for *The Masque of Proteus* on the last Grand Night, which was held at Queen Elizabeth's court. At the very least, the reference to a Tartarian page in the masque recalls her role as the queen's "deare and welbeloved woman" from the Islamic world. With the narrative of her life, like Lucy Negro's, ultimately inconclusive, we might imagine that Hippolyta, the Amazon queen from Scythia (Tartaria) subdued and brought under by the end of Shakespeare's *A Midsummer Night's Dream*, also embodies the Tartar page-cum-girl and other subalterns who were shaped by and who shaped the gender, racial, and religious trouble of Elizabethan England.[87] The next chapter, on one of Shakespeare's last plays, continues this investigation by examining discourses of gender, race, and religion within a history of competing empires that includes the established Spanish and Ottomans and the emerging English and French.

Chapter Five

Signifying Gender and Islam in Late Shakespeare: *Henry VIII* or *All is True* (1613) and British "Masques of Blackness"

Whereas the previous chapter situated one of Shakespeare's first plays, *The Comedy of Errors*, within a tropological and topical "web of empire" anchored by the concatenation of Tartars, Turks, and Amazons, this chapter locates one of Shakespeare's last plays, *Henry VIII* or *All is True*, within a century of "masques of blackness" abridged for a Jacobean court weighing its investments in trans-Atlantic expansionism.[1] As detailed in the introduction, during this transitional period – labelled "proto-imperialist," "proto-orientalist," and even "para-colonial" – the English oscillated between anxieties about their status as "sluggish" imperialists, which term Richard Hakluyt applied at the end of the sixteenth century, and as supplicants to the more powerful empires of the "Greater Western World," which in Daniel Goffman's estimation included the Ottomans.[2] This tension imbues the play from its opening scene, which focuses on the Field of Cloth of Gold (*Le Camp du Drap d'Or*), a political spectacle staged in 1520 within the English pale of Calais, which was reclaimed by France in 1558.[3] Ostensibly, the Field of Cloth of Gold celebrated the detente between Henry VIII and the French king, Francis I, who would go on to forge an alliance with the Ottomans in the mid-1530s; Henry's daughter, Elizabeth, would do the same fifty years later.[4] As Garrett Mattingly in his landmark study, *Renaissance Diplomacy*, summarizes, "The meeting at the Field of Cloth of Gold of Henry VIII and Francis I was personal diplomacy at its most pompous and spectacular." By contrast, "The two interviews between Henry VIII and Charles V which bracketed and nullified the Anglo-French encounter were personal diplomacy at, perhaps, its most effective."[5] In truth, the Field of Cloth of Gold was a diplomatic failure, yielding little more than monarchical display.

As I contend given this context of competing empires, the French imperial display in Shakespeare's *Henry VIII*, having "[m]ade Britain India" (1.1.21), casts the marginal English realm as a potential colonizing power *and* as a potential colonial "other."[6] Ian Smith, in *Race and Rhetoric in the Renaissance*, makes a parallel case for "Elizabethan classicism," with "England as the colonized object" and incipient colonizer.[7] Barbara Fuchs, in her articulation of "Imperium Studies," likewise argues that "recent inquiries into the connections between nation and empire for early modern England" should address, although for the most part they have not, "the complexities of the Norman Conquest (which made England simultaneously colony and colonizing metropole)."[8] As I add, and as the opening lines of Shakespeare's play show, Britain as late as the sixteenth century could join in the race for imperial spoils or it could become the spoils. Reinforcing this ambiguity, the play continues with a masque showcasing "[a] noble troop of strangers" (1.4.54), coded as Turks and Moors by analogy with similar entertainments in which the historical Henry VIII appeared.[9] This masque segues into the multivalent and troubling representations of three queens – Katherine of Aragon (former), Anne Boleyn (current), and Elizabeth (future) – all of whom are represented as "blackened" by their fall from patriarchal dynastic imperatives as measured by their inability to bear a male heir and as represented through tropes that point towards regions associated with the contemporaneous Islamic world.[10]

In this final investigation of the multivalent subject positions produced during England's proto-imperialist and proto-orientalist era, I therefore adduce the lives of the girls and women from the Islamic world that I have documented throughout this book as inextricable from the always already "fallen" women surrounding Henry VIII, whether native born (Elizabeth and Anne, despite the latter's French manners) or immigrant (Katherine, with her suspect Spanish origins).[11] These connections may be less explicit than those in Shakespeare's early plays, such as *The Comedy of Errors*, but they continue to resonate in this late play through allusions to Henrician entertainments involving Turks and Moors mentioned in chapter 1 and detailed here. Given the global circuits that constitute the early modern/colonial world I have traced thus far, I further situate this play as a response to England's involvement from the mid-sixteenth century through the early seventeenth century with the Safavids and Ottomans, and later the Mughals. Of particular importance is the Anglo-Ottoman alliance, which emerged during the 1580s and 1590s – that is, the late Elizabethan era – as a counterpoint to Catholic Habsburg designs on Protestant England. As detailed in earlier chapters, Spain, at the centre of the Habsburg Empire during Charles V's tenure as Holy Roman Emperor (r. 1519–56), blocked English efforts at global trade and colonialism. By the end of the sixteenth century, Philip II (r. 1556–98) threatened to bring England under Spain's tutelage, either through marriage (Philip was Mary I's husband and co-ruler of England from 1554 to 1558) or occupation (a threat that did not end with the celebrated defeat of the Spanish Armada in 1588).[12] To set this scene, I turn to the multivalent representations of the Field of Cloth of Gold in English historical and literary texts, including Shakespeare's play, where the French ally with the Turks and the English king masquerades as a "stranger" – and, by extension, a Moor.

Henry VIII, French Turks, and the Field of Cloth of Gold

As J.J. Scarisbrick details in his authoritative biography of Henry VIII, Western European politics during the sixteenth century involved shifting and often duplicitous alliances between two traditional rivals with new global imperial ambitions: France, led by Francis I, and Spain, with the Holy Roman Emperor Charles V at the helm. Although England could not match these colossi, it sought "to act as a third party who would be prepared to upset that balance."[13] The Ottoman Empire under Süleiman the Magnificent also figured into this diplomatic calculus, with France actively seeking an alliance with Christendom's purported Islamic "other."[14] Ostensibly, the political spectacle of the Field of Cloth of Gold was meant to advance a universal peace within Western Christendom to make way for a new crusade against the Turks, who having recently conquered Syria, the Hijaz, and Egypt were turning their forces towards Central Europe.[15] Deploying imperialist and orientalist tropes, a contemporary French report describes this spectacle as "superior to 'les miracles des piramides egiptiennes et les amphiteatres romains'" [the miracles of the Egyptian pyramids and the Roman amphitheatres].[16] Yet, even an ardent advocate of a unified Christian front such as the continental humanist Desiderius Erasmus realized "this talk of peace was but a façade."[17] Henry VIII's surreptitious conference with the Holy Roman Emperor Charles V in Dover while on his way to meet the French King Francis I at Calais reinforced this hypocrisy. As Joycelyne G. Russell summarizes in her meticulous history of the Field of Cloth of Gold, "It would probably be fair to suggest that the intention of this 'memorable meeting' was to deceive. It was to embody and set forth, in most sumptuous and dramatic guise, an Anglo-French understanding which hardly existed."[18] Six weeks of masques, banquets, tournaments, and other chivalric displays accordingly ended in a stalemate.

In Shakespeare's play, we do not see this spectacle but only hear about it through proto-imperialist and proto-orientalist allusions, as befits England's marginal position vis-à-vis these great powers. As the Duke of Norfolk avers in his report, which has been compared to Enobarbus's paean to Cleopatra in Shakespeare's earlier production, "Today the French,/All clinquant all in gold, like heathen gods/Shone down the English; and tomorrow they/Made Britain India" (1.1.18–21; cf. *Antony and Cleopatra* [1606/7], 2.2.196–245).[19] A number of critics have analysed this passage in terms of the politics of spectacle; however, no one to my knowledge has focused on the competing discourses of empire that inform it.[20] These discourses, to reiterate, represent Britain as a potential colonizer *and* as potentially colonizable.[21] Establishing the context for English imperialist aspirations during the sixteenth century, Nabil Matar in *Turks, Moors and Englishmen in the Age of Discovery* maintains,

> Historians and critics who have inaccurately applied a postcolonial theory to a precolonial period in British history forget that in the Elizabethan and early Stuart periods, England was not a colonial power – not in the imperial sense that followed in the eighteenth century. Although England had colonized Wales and Scotland and was waging a colonial war in Ireland, at the time Queen Elizabeth died, England did not yet possess a single colonial inch in the Americas.[22]

In other words, the sixteenth-century English crown was not an expansionist power beyond the British Isles, even though Henry VIII and later Elizabeth I sought to promote the realm as a potential counterweight to Spanish, French, and even Ottoman designs. Rather, as Kenneth R. Andrews affirms in *Trade, Plunder and Settlement: Maritime Enterprise and the Genesis of the British Empire, 1480–1630*, "it was the reign of James that saw the effective beginnings of the British Empire," reminding us that Shakespeare is recasting this proto-imperialist and proto-orientalist scenario for a newly expansionist, albeit still tentative, era.[23]

As such, in the play's depiction of the Field of Cloth of Gold, Henry VIII and his courtiers participate in displays that anachronistically align them with the global imperialist project to which the English remained belated throughout the sixteenth century. Typical glosses of Norfolk's lines include "the English made Britain look as (fabulously) rich as India or the West Indies."[24] Yet, an equally valid reading suggests the English are threatened by the French, described as glittering "like heathen gods" (1.1.19), who sought to turn Britain into fiefdom-cum-colony through dynastic imperialism.[25] As Retha Warnicke documents in *The Rise and Fall of Anne Boleyn*, the fear of "a French annexation of England" formed a prominent part of Henry VIII and his countrymen's concern over the absence of a male heir.[26] This threat seems even more pronounced when we consider that most Western Europeans deemed the French "heathens" for their alliance with the Ottoman Turks.[27] As Sydney Anglo in his influential study, *Spectacle, Pageantry, and Early Tudor Policy*, concludes, "[Cardinal] Wolsey summed up the official position when he remarked that the real Turk was he with whom they were occupied, that is the King of France, and that he knew no other Turk."[28] The historical Catherine of Aragon also held that "[t]he King of France is the greatest Turk."[29] Shakespeare's play underscores this analogy when detailing the effect of French cultural imperialism on English courtiers: "Their clothes are after such a pagan cut to't/That sure they've worn out Christendom" (1.3.14–15). In this case, English anxieties about potential colonization also point towards the Islamic world, with the "pagan" Ottomans encroaching on Western Europe and threatening English interests in the Mediterranean throughout the sixteenth and into the seventeenth century.[30]

"India" in the opening lines (1.1.21), overdetermined in early modern discourses of empire as "East" and "West," thus links England to the promise of imperial spoils even as it suggests its potential spoiling as the empire (be)comes home.[31] On the one hand, the play's Tudoresque aristocrats' critique of the excesses that made and marred the Field of Cloth of Gold anticipates the mercantile empire King James I was attempting to establish at the beginning of the seventeenth century. On the other hand, it raises the haunting memory of England's potential absorption by the imperial powers of Europe, including the Ottomans, from the previous century. As we shall see, the play projects this threat onto the queens associated with Henry VIII's reign, including his eventual heir, Elizabeth, by blackening them as inevitably "fallen" women. They are thereby estranged from the patriarchal succession upon which Henry's epochal declaration – "England is an empire" – depended.[32] However, to situate the gendered and racialized contests of authority dramatized in Shakespeare's play within this longer durée, we must turn to a genealogy of "masques of blackness" and related performances that extend from Scotland to England from 1507/8 to 1604/5. This genealogy foregrounds an ambivalent Africanist – and, by extension, orientalist – cultural logic of elevation and denigration that the "fair" Jacobean queen and her ladies harnessed as a vehicle for resistance to patriarchal control. As such, Queen Anna's (in)famous first masque with Ben Jonson, *The Masque of Blackness* (1604/5), encodes, even as it effaces, the lives of gendered subalterns in sixteenth-century Scotland and England, including Elen More, Lucy Negro, and other less well known girls and women from the Islamic world.

Turks and Moors in Scottish and English Court Performances

As suggested above, Queen Anna's negotiation of authorship and performance in *The Masque of Blackness*, for which she unconventionally stained her face, arms, and legs with black paint, was prefigured by a century of performances involving "Blacks" – both people of African descent and Europeans in blackface – in the Scottish and English courts.[33] As Paul Edwards documents in his groundbreaking study, "The Early African Presence in the British Isles," while people of African descent shaped and subverted British culture from the Roman era onwards, a critical mass did not settle in Scotland and England until the turn of the sixteenth century.[34] Imtiaz Habib, in *Black Lives in the English Archives, 1500–1677*, adds that many of these individuals were seized by Scottish and English privateers from the rival Portuguese; some of them continued as slaves in the British Isles, while others became court retainers, servants, and dependents rather than chattel.[35] As detailed in chapter 1, most of these captives hailed from the Islamic world and many probably came from a Muslim background, including Elen More; some may even have been African Christians, which did not prevent their forced servitude (if not always legal enslavement) by Western European Christians. By the late sixteenth century, possibly second- or third-generation people of African descent such as Lucy Negro, adduced in chapter 4, played a salient if marginalized role in early modern British cultural productions. Black women functioned as ladies-in-waiting at the late medieval court of King James IV of Scotland; they served as dancers in the sixteenth-century courts of King Henry VIII and Queen Elizabeth I of England; and some worked as prostitutes in the streets and brothels of London. Peter Fryer suggested years ago that "there is, perhaps, supporting evidence in the fact that the part of the 'Abbess *de Clerkenwell*' – 'abbess', in this context, means brothel-keeper – in the Gray's Inn revels at Christmas

1594 was played by a woman called Lucy Negro (whom one authority identifies as Shakespeare's Dark Lady)," a conclusion Duncan Salkeld has recently confirmed.[36]

As I have argued elsewhere, Elen More's casting as the "Black Queen of Beauty" in the Scottish court entertainments of 1507/8 signals the contradictory logic of Africanist ambivalence that informed Queen Anna's subsequent spectacle of "black beauty" at the English court in 1604/5, even though the material conditions and historical contexts for these respective performances made for very different investments and consequences.[37] The Scottish court poet William Dunbar, introduced in chapter 1, exploits this difference in "Ane Blak Moir," a poem of double-edged praise that alternately memorializes Elen More's role in chivalric terms and bestializes her through an anti-blazon that compares her mouth to a monkey's, her skin to a toad's, and her nose to a cat's.[38] In this chapter, I extend this discussion into the question of her provisional agency in early sixteenth-century Scotland and the continuing resonance of her life as a gendered and racialized subaltern in Queen Anna's later "masques of blackness" for the Scottish and English courts. Not surprisingly, Dunbar fails to record her response to the original spectacle or his verse, nor do we have any other record of her views. However, in a related account, "Pocahontas at the Masque," one which allows us to conceptualize the relationship between this Afro-Scottish "masque of blackness" at the beginning of the sixteenth century and Queen Anna's at the beginning of the seventeenth, Karen Robertson insightfully addresses the question of the other(ed) woman's response to early modern British entertainments with attention to the "Indian Princess," Pocahontas (a.k.a. Matoaka/Rebecca Rolfe), who witnessed a court performance of Ben Jonson's *Vision of Delight* during the Christmas celebrations of 1617. Robertson concludes that "[t]he limitations of the documents do not allow the production of a narrative of a subject who viewed and judged the English but do allow the tracing of her shadow within European texts, disturbances that mark an alternative presence."[39] Similarly, Elen More's response may be limned not only within the original Scottish reception of her role as the "Black Queen of Beauty," but also between the lines of the Africanist discourse characterizing the spectacles that subsequently defined Queen Anna as wife, mother, and queen: her marriage ceremony in Norway, her coronation and her eldest son's baptism in Scotland, and her debut masque for the English court, which I survey below. As I propose, Elen More's original performance persists as "an informing, stabilizing, and disturbing element" – to affirm Nobel laureate Toni Morrison's definition of Africanist ambivalence – in Queen Anna's *Masque of Blackness* a century later.[40]

Almost fifteen years prior to this controversial masque, an anticipatory Africanist ambivalence informed the metaphoric and, more disturbingly, the material registers of the multiple performances of blackness and beauty staged for King James's elaborate marriage ceremonies to his "fair" queen.[41] Following a lavish wedding by proxy in Denmark on 20 August 1589, a standard practice for European monarchs, fifteen-year-old Anna set off to join her royal husband in Scotland.[42] Unexpectedly, Anna's ship was caught in the storms of the autumnal North Sea, which James suspected were the result of "black" magic; as a result, the ship was diverted from its course to the uninviting coast of Norway.[43] Here she endured "miserable" conditions, according to a messenger's report to the anxious groom, upon which news James resolved to play the gallant and rescue his stranded bride.[44] James's travel was no less arduous than Anna's for, as Ethel Carleton Williams stresses in her biography of the queen, "[t]he winter of 1589–90 was unusually severe, even for those northern regions. The fjords were frozen over early and so was the sea near the coast, while the roads were sheets of ice." Surmounting these obstacles, James finally joined hands, on 23 November 1589, with his bride, who in Williams's words "looked very young and appealing, with her golden hair and ivory complexion."[45] Following royal protocol, James arranged for an elaborate entertainment in honour of his new queen, which featured, according to some reports, "four young Negroes [who] danced naked in the snow in front of the royal carriage."[46] Shortly after this command performance, in which the dancers' blackness served both to highlight and elevate the queen's "whiteness and 'pure' beauty," the four youth succumbed to the effects of the bitter Norwegian cold and died.[47] Not coincidentally, around the same time as this deadly spectacle, John Hawkins launched his first slaving expedition into West Africa, thus anticipating the triangular trade in African slaves, American raw materials, and English manufactured goods that subtended the official beginnings of the British Empire a century later.[48] Given this history, I maintain that Queen Anna's "fair" whiteness at this inaugural moment in her reign cannot be seen apart from the literal denigration of Black men and women it both illuminates and underwrites.[49]

Following Queen Anna's Norwegian wedding, her reception as queen in Scotland on 1 May 1590 reinforced the Africanist ambivalence that reportedly cost "four young Negroes" their lives. In this "repetition with a difference," the people of Edinburgh greeted Anna with an elaborate pageant consisting of

> three score young men of the towne, lyke Moores, and clothed in cloth of silver, with chaines about their neckes, and bracelets about their armes, set with diamonds and other precious stones, very gorgeous to the eie, who went before the chariot, betwixt the horsemen and it, everie one with a white staffe in his hande, to keepe of[f] the throng of people.[50]

Although this time the queen was entertained with "blackface" – Scottish youth disguised as Moors – the result in both cases was to highlight her "fair" white beauty by means of the early modern European predilection for exploiting "Blacks" and other subalterns as exotic accoutrements. In his paean to the new queen on the occasion of her entry into Edinburgh, the Scottish court poet John Burel reinforces this Africanist logic of praise and debasement. He begins by lauding "fair ANNE" and her entourage of "bewties" or beauteous nymphs, whose "hair like threeds of gold did gleit,/Thair facis fragrant and formose:/White was thair hyd thocht it wes hid,/Thair corall lips like rosis rid."[51] He goes on to juxtapose these golden-haired, white-skinned, rose-lipped beauties with a team of noble yet "savage" Moors ("the Moirs," "Thir savagis") from India ("the ynds") who, just as in *The Masque of Blackness*, leave "thair land and dwelling place/For to do honour to hir Grace." Burel's praise of the rich attire of the Moors – "For cheins quhilk ouer thair shoulders hang:/Gold bracelets on thair chakils hings,/Thair fingers full of costly rings" – reiterates and anticipates the lethal appropriation of blackness and beauty against which, and within which, the new queen's beauty was highlighted.[52]

The baptism on 30 August 1594 of Anna's eldest son, Henry, underscores this tradition of Africanist ambivalence in early modern British entertainments, which informs not only Queen Anna's masques, but also (as I shall show) Shakespeare's late play. A tract reprinted upon the accession of James as king of England in 1603, *A True Report of the most tryumphant, and Royall accomplishments of the Baptisme of the most Excellent, right High, and mightie Prince Henry Frederick*, records days of lavish celebrations in honour of the infant prince. The centrepiece of these celebrations involved a chivalric tournament meant to pit "three Turkes, three Christian Knights of *Malta*, three *Amazones*, and three *Moores*" against each other over the course of two days; however, since "the three last Gentlemen, who should have sustained these person-ages" did not appear, this portion of the celebrations proceeded *sans* Moors.[53] The figure of the Moor in this spectacle consequently marks the sort of conspicuous and constitutive absence that Christopher Miller, in *Blank Darkness: Africanist Discourse in French*, theorizes as a "nullity ... key to understanding European conceptions of Black Africa."[54] As I add, this "notion of a nullity," which includes the effaced lives of the girls and women from the Islamic world I have sought to recover, simultaneously functions as a "dangerous supplement" constituting the proto-imperial-ist and proto-orientalist imaginary of the newly combined Scottish and English courts.[55]

This baptismal banquet foregrounds yet another disturbing specta-cle meant to highlight "fair" whiteness at the expense of "fair" black-ness, one figured through tropes that point towards the Islamic world. Recalling the earlier appearance of Turks and Moors, *A True Report ... of the Baptisme* showcases

> a *Black-Moore*, drawing (as it seemed to the beholders) a triumphall Char-iot (& before it, the melodious noise of Trumpets and Howboyes [oboes]) which Chariot ent[e]red the Hall, the motion of the whole frame (which was twelve foot long, and seven foot broad) was so artificial within itselfe, that it appeared to be drawne in, onely by the strength of a *Moore*, which was very richly attired, his traces were great chaines of pure gold.[56]

The substitution of a "Moor" for the lion that was to have drawn the cart inverts the previous image of "savage nobility" into the "noble savage." Yet both stereotypes, as Margaret Hodgen establishes in her foundational study, *Early Anthropology in the Sixteenth and Seventeenth Centuries*, were inextricably related.[57] The tract offers a tendentious explanation for this last minute change: "(but because his [the lion's] presence might have brought some feare, to the nearest, or that the sight of the lights and torches might have commoved his tamenes[s])[.] It was thought meete, that the *Moore* should supply that roome," a conceit reprised in Shakespeare's *A Midsummer Night's Dream* the same year or shortly thereafter.[58] This entertainment, then, just as with the entertain-ments in the Scottish court before it, positions bestialized and exoticized "blackness" within a cultural dynamic that suppresses African-descent people's agency *even as* it elicits their participation in the production of the increasingly hegemonic norm of "fair" white beauty. In conflating the racialized and religious connotations of the term "Moor," it also points towards the complex negotiations of Elen More and other subalterns from the Islamic world in the early sixteenth-century Scottish court, including their survival and resistance.

The history of "masques of blackness" in the English court during the same period is similarly problematic and involves similar conjunctions of "fair" blackness and "fair" whiteness in tension with an emerging hierarchical opposition that ranked whitened beauty over an increasingly denigrated blackness. It also incorporates the material and figural presence of women and men from the Islamic world as a means to project English ambitions into the competing discourses of empire that impinged on the era. As mentioned previously, during a Shrovetide performance at Westminster in 1510, King Henry VIII appeared as a Moor, a description that carries Africanist and orientalist connotations. According to Tudor chronicler Edward Hall, the king and the Earl of Essex apparelled themselves "after Turkey fashion," signified by copious gold cloth and matching scimitars; their "torchebearers were appareyled in Crymosyn satyne and grene, lyke Moreskoes, their faces blacke." In addition, at least two of the ladies impersonated Moors using cloth rather than pigment, with "their heads rouled in plesauntes and typpers lyke the Egipcians, embroudered with gold. Their faces, neckes, armes and handes, covered with fyne plesaunce blacke ... so that the same ladies seemed to be nigrost or blacke Mores."[59] At least six other masques and entertainments featuring Africanist and orientalist characters played by blackened courtiers, mostly men, were sponsored by the English court between 1510 and 1560. Dramatic productions, including Shakespeare's *Tragedy of Othello, the Moor of Venice* (1603/4), likewise appeared with increasing frequency on the English stage.[60] As I have argued elsewhere, set within this extended genealogy, *The Masque of Blackness*, staged two months after *Othello*, marks a distinct departure precisely because of Queen Anna's negotiation of her cultural agency through her Africanist performance of "black beauty."[61] Besides being a unique instance of noblewomen playing "black-moors" in the Jacobean era, it was, in Anthony Barthelemy's words, "the first court masque written by Jonson, the first collaboration between Jonson and Jones, the first recorded use of perspective scenery in England, and the first recorded use of blackening to actually darken the skin of the royal maskers."[62] Prior to this court production, the British tradition when masquing as a Moor involved donning a vizard and other such disguises: black-masked demons populated the medieval theatre; black-masked jesters accompanied court and civic pageants; and later court masques were characterized by their extravagant use of black velvet to signify aristocratic ladies' "blackness."[63]

Not surprisingly, Queen Anna's coupling of blackness with feminine authority produced startling effects on the stage and in the audience, especially because, as Stephen Orgel indicates, "The masque is a form of play, and includes its audience directly."[64] As Puritan William Prynne's notorious attack in *Histrio-mastix*: *The Players Scourge, or Actors Tragedie* (1633) on female masquers and men playing female roles on the public stage attests, the intermixing of aristocratic women playing female parts and professional male actors, who played both male and female parts, significantly troubled gender hierarchies and identities.[65] Even more disconcerting, Queen Anna's innovations produced considerable discomfort in a courtly audience unaccustomed to seeing blackness represented as beautiful, especially by a woman author(ity). As in the case of Mary Wroth, the focus of chapter 3, early modern English audiences tended to see metaphorically "blackened" women as having fallen from patriarchal cultural, religious, and social (double) standards. As Queen Anna may or may not have expected, a similar stigma was mapped onto her due to her assertion of authorial agency as a producer of court entertainments, a stigma compounded by her appropriation of "black beauty" as a form of resistance to Jacobean patriarchy. Summarizing the effect of *The Masque of Blackness* on its audience, her biographer Ethel Carleton Williams opines: "It was a magnificent sight. Queen Anne hoped to show her English subjects that she could be as regal as Queen Elizabeth and yet at the same time unconventional and *avant-garde*"; yet, "[n]ever did she make a greater mistake. In spite of the brilliance of the *Masque of Blackness*, it was disastrous for her reputation, for it damaged the public image she was trying to establish."[66]

The negative response to the queen's debut masque with Jonson may be gauged by the diplomat Dudley Carleton's critique in his letter to Ralph Winwood, clerk of the Privy Council and later Secretary of State:

> Their Apparell was rich, but too light and Curtizan-like for such great ones. Instead of Vizzards, their Faces, and Arms up to the Elbows, were painted black, which was Disguise sufficient, for they were hard to be known; *but it became them nothing so well as their red and white, and you cannot imagine a more ugly Sight, then a Troop of lean-cheek'd Moors*. (emphasis in original)[67]

From Carleton's perspective, the ladies are metaphorically blackened – he views them as whores – because they are materially blackened as

Moors. The connection to the Islamic world is clear, as Jonson's gloss to Leo Africanus in his published version of the masque attests.[68] Concluding his letter to Winwood by rehearsing the revels, or general dancing and feasting following the stage performance, Carleton underscores his distaste at the indelible trace of blackness he sees in the royal women, a trace that threatens to mark the entire court. The gentlemen remain in constant peril of impressing the mark of blackness on their lips when kissing the ladies' hands, which they could not avoid and maintain court decorum. Scandalized by this indecorous double bind, Carleton bemoans that the Spanish ambassador "took out the Queen, and forgot not to kiss her Hand, though there was Danger it would have left a Mark on his Lips."[69] The ladies' blackness, invoking dis-ease in this courtly audience, consequently becomes an embodied site of sexually and racially charged cultural fantasies and fears, one that resonates with the lives of those subaltern girls and women I have limned throughout this book. They, too, can assimilate, especially Tartars and Persians, and at the same time they remain marked by cultural, racialized, and religious differences.[70]

As an antidote to this gender and racial trouble, Carleton, in his correspondence with the maven John Chamberlain, furthers his critique of Queen Anna's debut performance by depicting attempts to reassert Jacobean patriarchal control:

> The presentation of the mask at the first drawing of the traverse was very fair and their apparel rich, but too light and courtesanlike. Their black faces and hands, which were painted and bare up to the elbows, was a very loathsome sight and I am sorry that strangers should see our court so strangely disguised. The Spanish and Venetian ambassadors were both there and most of the French about the town. The confusion in getting in was so great that some ladies lie by it and complain of the fury of the white staffs. In the passages through the galleries they were shut up in several heaps betwixt doors and there stayed till all was ended; and in the coming out, a banquet which was prepared for the king in the great chamber was overturned, table and all, before it was scarce touched. It were infinite to tell you what losses there were of chains, jewels, purses, and suchlike loose ware, and one woman amongst the rest lost her honesty, for which she was carried to the porter's lodge, being surprised at her business on the top of the terrace.[71]

Notoriously, Carleton not only insists on labelling the masquing women "courtesanlike" for their bare arms, but he condemns the "loathsome" black paint adorning their skin. He also hints at the use of sexual violence to contain unruly women. Ultimately, he rejects the queen's representation of blackness as beauty, which, as I have been arguing, she deployed as part of her resistance to aristocratic patriarchal norms of "fair" whiteness. The masque thus registers its contest of authority at the levels of production and reception as Carleton, like Jonson, attempts to undermine the queen in gendered and racialized terms.

The conclusion of the masque nevertheless challenges this patriarchal closure by exposing the king's failure to contain the queen and her ladies' subversive and appropriative performance of "black beauty." After all, they retain their painted faces and arms well into the revels, proving that the king cannot really, as *The Masque of Blackness* promises, "blanch an Ethiop and revive a corse."[72] Indeed, it will take several years for the ladies to return in *The Masque of Beauty* as suitably white(ned) beauties.[73] Yet, even this companion masque, rather than simply endorsing the king's unilateral ability to "salve the rude defects of every creature," as proclaimed in *The Masque of Blackness*, continues to enact the troubling relationship between Africanist ambivalence and female authorship and authority that characterized the earlier production.[74] As we shall see, this potential for resistance on the part of the Jacobean queen and her ladies, which hinges on the appropriation of the agency of African and other subaltern women residing in the British Isles, continues to inform the representation of the "blackened" queens in Shakespeare's *Henry VIII*.

Blackening Fallen Courtiers and Queens

To recap, the historical Henry VIII's reign was inaugurated with a 1510 entertainment in which the king and the Earl of Essex appeared in orientalist splendour, with their male attendants in blackface, "lyke Moreskoes," and the court ladies covered in fine black cloth, "so that the same ladies semed to be nigrost or blacke Mores."[75] This disguising arguably constitutes the first "masque of blackness" for the English court, with similar masques staged in Scotland during the same period.[76] It presents an array of proto-imperialist and proto-orientalist signifiers with its "Turkish" clothing, its "Egyptian" headgear, and its participants' darkened faces. Once again, these signifiers could cut two ways, as expressed in the papal nuncio Francesco Chieregato's assessment: "In short, the wealth and civilization of the world are here; and those who call the English barbarians appear to me to render themselves such."[77] The English of Henry VIII's era, that is, had to prove they were *not* barbarians or constitutive outsiders.[78] Complicating Anglo's claim in his influential study that early Tudor representation of Turks and Moors in masques and entertainments were "without malice," I proceed by linking these Henrician displays in Shakespeare's play to the more explicit imbrication of gender, race, and empire in Jacobean masques and entertainments as situated within a century-long genealogy of "masques of blackness" for the Scottish and English courts.[79]

Assessing "the discourses of religious and racial difference in the Renaissance empires" from the Ottomans through the Spanish to the English, Margaret Greer, Walter Mignolo, and Maureen Quilligan find that

> [b]lack skin, despite the symbolic linkage of black with death and evil, carried few generalized negative connotations for a medieval Europe with little contact with blacks [i.e., sub-Saharan Africans]. As the representation of one of the Magi as black and the legend of Prester John demonstrate, blackness was exotic and could be coded positively.[80]

Even though these positive connotations persisted into the early modern period, discourses of blackness in English literature and culture became, as Kim Hall asserts in *Things of Darkness: Economies of Race and Gender in Early Modern England*, "increasingly infused with concerns over skin color, economics, and gender politics."[81] As Ania Loomba and Jonathan Burton confirm in *Race in Early Modern England*, these "contradictory elements ... do not indicate that race is 'not yet formed' ... but that it is always an amalgam of contradictory, unstable, and evolving ideas."[82] I submit that a related amalgam of "blackness" and "beauty" is rehearsed in Shakespeare's play through the falls of the courtiers Buckingham and Wolsey and, more surprisingly, through the tribulations of the saintly Queen Katherine.[83] Only subsequently do its proto-imperialist and proto-orientalist valences become explicit in the descriptions of the overtly sexualized Anne Boleyn, Katherine's erstwhile replacement. Perhaps even more surprisingly, they persist in the description of the newborn Elizabeth, who will become England's celebrated Virgin Queen. This conflation of three queens – former, current, and future – consequently underscores the cultural logic that blackens all women from a patriarchal perspective and points towards the accelerated racialization of "fair" beauty during the seventeenth century.[84]

From the first scene of Shakespeare's play, this ambivalent cultural logic characterizes the fallen courtier, the Duke of Buckingham, who declares when arrested at Wolsey's behest, "It will help me nothing/To plead mine innocence, for that dye is on me/Which makes my whit'st part black" (1.1.207–9). Although "blackness" in these lines symbolizes moral decay, in Henry's subsequent indictment of Buckingham this tendentious signifier is not merely aligned with ugliness, monstrosity, and damnation, but "fair" whiteness is set as its positive foil (1.2.115–25; cf. 1.3.58, 2.1.86). It bears repeating that this dichotomy is not inevitable: as David Wallace observes, "[t]he discourse of beauty in blackness gets mislaid, or (better) overlaid" during the transition from the medieval era to the early modern period; however, "[i]t is never entirely lost, although a discursive overlay of uglification and vilification intensifies during the centuries preceding and accompanying the African slave trade," which was still peripheral to the English economy in the early seventeenth century.[85]

The king's ruminations in this scene are also significant in that they link blackness with femininity, both proper and improper, a nexus that informs the play's representation of all its queens, as I shall show. Arguing against the traditional interpretation of Shakespeare's Katherine as the iconic "good woman," feminist literary critics have emphasized how, even though Henry approves of his (first) wife as chaste and obedient (2.4.130–9), she is by no means silent.[86] She thereby functions as a new type of icon boldly asserting her regal female agency. Despite her stature as the daughter of two reigning sovereigns (Ferdinand of Aragon and Isabella of Castile), Henry rebukes her for defending the Duke of Buckingham's honour against Wolsey's aspersions, just as she had previously ranked herself against Wolsey's economic exploitation of the common people.[87] As the play continues, her outspoken interventions into those political and legal spheres reserved for men reveal how even a "good woman" could be threatened with a "blackened" reputation.

During her trial at Blackfriars, Katherine expresses this contradiction by pleading that she is "a most poor woman, and a stranger,/Born out of your dominions" (2.4.13–14; cf. 2.3.17) and by claiming that "Ferdinand/My father, King of Spain, was reckoned one/The wisest prince that there had reigned by many/A year before" (2.4.46).[88] Likewise, when after the trial Wolsey accosts the queen in her chamber using Latin, she positions herself as "a housewife" to dissociate herself from this "strange tongue," which has been labelled the "'father' tongue" of Renaissance humanism (3.1.24, 44); however, it is clear she understands it.[89] These contradictions culminate in Katherine's last-ditch defence of her "honour," which in the early modern period depended on a woman's reputation for chastity. As the scene in her chamber continues, the queen finds herself interpellated into the subject position of a "blackened" woman despite her protestations.[90] Wolsey, her antagonist, insinuates as much when he says, "We come not by the way of accusation,/To taint that honour every good tongue blesses,/Nor to betray you any way to sorrow" (3.1.53–5).[91] To his suggestion that she may be tainted, she retorts that she was "[n]ever yet branded with suspicion" (3.1.127). Yet, her self-defence buttresses Wolsey's design to "blacken" her reputation by reinforcing the phallocentric terms he imposes on their confrontation.[92]

Ironically, this conflation of femininity and blackness also marks the moment when Wolsey falls from the king's favour, which reinforces the broad reach of this cultural logic. Henry's envoy, the Earl of Surrey, presages his indictment with the taunt, "I'll startle you/Worse than the sacring-bell when the brown wench/Lay kissing in your arms, lord Cardinal" (3.2.295–7). *The Norton Shakespeare*, like most other editions, glosses "brown" primarily in terms of class; however, it also stresses the misogyny encoded in the slur: "Surrey imagines Wolsey surprised with a country girl ('brown' because tanned or dirty from working, or perhaps ugly or promiscuous) when he should have been at mass."[93] R.A. Foakes in his influential edition likewise highlights this conflation when he glosses "brown wench" as "probably implying a slut, or an ill-favoured girl." But he also cites a passage that supports Kim Hall's analysis of "economies of race and gender in early modern England," despite the lack of critical attention to this facet: "(*Lydia*) so mote I thee thou art not faire,/A plaine brownetta when thou art at best."[94] A "brownetta" or brunette could signify "a girl or woman of a dark complexion" (*OED*), which by the late sixteenth century began to imply not "fair" in the sense of physical beauty, feminine propriety, moral rectitude, and whiteness.

Katherine's concern with her honour in Shakespeare's play persists until the moment of her death, when she is described as simultaneously "pale" (4.2.98) and "of an earthy colour" (4.2.99).[95] The possibility that her corpse, like her reputation, will be blackened accordingly impels her to deliver detailed instructions about her burial:

When I am dead, good wench,
Let me be used with honour. Strew me over
With maiden flowers, that all the world may know
I was a chaste wife to my grave.   (4.2.168–71)[96]

The historical Catherine of Aragon was not so honoured, with Henry VIII ignoring her final bequests.[97] Rather, Shakespeare's Katherine, *contra* those critics who claim her as either a traditional or a feminist icon, exemplifies how "blackness" as an overdetermined signifier colours all the females in the play.

Slinging Mud at Anne Boleyn

In critical discussions of the queens in Shakespeare's *Henry VIII*, Anne Boleyn has long taken centre stage, despite Katherine's significance as the female character who speaks the most lines and Elizabeth's importance as the prophesied queen who will consolidate England as a prospective empire. Anne's role in Shakespeare's play, by contrast to the historical record, remains primarily spectacular.[98] While she speaks far less than Katherine, she is showcased in most of the banquets, masques, and processions that characterized the Renaissance theatricalization of politics. Anne first appears as one of the ladies embellishing Cardinal Wolsey's much-touted banquet. Recalling the indictment of the cardinal's conspicuous consumption, registered most prominently by the Duke of Buckingham and Queen Katherine at the beginning of the play, the Lord Chamberlain enthuses, "This night he makes a supper, and a great one,/To many lords and ladies. There will be/The beauty of this kingdom, I'll assure you" (1.3.52–4). Portentously, the ladies are grouped with the other consumables at the banquet, implying that Henry VIII's appetites will propel Anne's career.

The historical Wolsey was known for his lavish banquets, one of which was described by the Venetian ambassador, Sebastian Giustinian, as surpassing those "either by Cleopatra or Caligula." As the ambassador adds, "the whole banqueting hall being so decorated with huge vases of gold and silver, that I fancied myself in the tower of Chosroes [6th c. Persian "shah of shahs"], where that monarch caused divine honours to be paid him."[99] Although this event predates Anne Boleyn's rise to the throne by eight years, it epitomizes the excess observers associated with the cardinal's household, which was often described in orientalist terms. Evoking this association, the banquet Shakespeare stages segues into a masque of exotic strangers, which Meg Twycross and Sarah Carpenter in *Masks and Masking in Medieval and Early Tudor England* equate with the entertainments commencing Henry VIII's reign.[100] In Shakespeare's play, dual anachronisms position Anne within the nexus of racialized blackness and gender that implicates all the play's queens (former, current, and future), including the seemingly saintly Katherine and the apparently innocent Elizabeth. Her "Frenchness," associated with the Ottoman Turks, further reinforces this feminization of "the foreign within" and connects her to the lives of girls and women from the Islamic world that I have traced throughout this book.

Following these descriptions of culinary and carnal excess, a series of double entendres from the randy Lord Sands frames the banquet scene. As Sands boasts, "had the Cardinal/But half my lay thoughts in him, some of these/Should find a running banquet, ere they rested" (1.4.10–12). A "running banquet," according to *The Norton Shakespeare*, shifts from "light refreshments" to "furtive, stolen pleasures." The gloss on "lay thoughts," defined as "secular," also encodes illicit sexual connotations.[101] This sexualized bantering between men continues until the ladies are invited to sit, with Lord Sands sandwiched between Anne and another lady. As this seating arrangement deliberately interrupts the ladies' solidarity, the now isolated Anne is increasingly interpellated into the patriarchal dichotomy "virgin/whore." This is a designation Lord Sands seals with a kiss (1.4.28–9), which presages Henry VIII's subsequent embrace of Anne.

Connected to the Africanist ambivalence that informed the court performances surveyed in the preceding section, this sexually charged scene contains the most frequent use of the term "fair," which oscillates with "black" as an index of what Kim Hall identifies as "the appearance or moral states of women."[102] Yet, as becomes clear from the excessive iteration of this term in relation to the denigrated ladies, the binary opposition between "fair" and "black" cannot but implode. These "fair ones" (1.4.14) find themselves anatomized into the "fair cheeks" (1.4.45) and other parts that constitute the Petrarchan blazon, which Nancy Vickers identifies as "a battle between men that is first figuratively and then literally fought on the fields of woman's 'celebrated' body."[103] After Henry declares Anne has "[t]he fairest hand I ever touched" (1.4.76), she confirms the de(con)struction of the dichotomy "fair/black" when she matches Lord Sands's smutty comments with her own knowing reference to his phallus as a titillating absent presence (1.4.48). Lord Sands's reference to the colour rising in the ladies' cheeks – "[t]he red wine first must rise/In their fair cheeks, my lord, then we shall have 'em/Talk us to silence" (1.4.44–6) – thereby positions Anne as the obverse of the "chaste, silent and obedient," and therefore proper, woman.[104] It also shows how "fair" was cast in an ambivalent, and not simply an opposing, relationship to "blackness."

As I submit, the masque of "[a] noble troop of strangers" (1.4.54) following this repartee reinforces this "blackening" through its allusions to the proto-imperialist and proto-orientalist entertainments of Henry VIII's era, despite its pastoral veneer. The stage directions for the entertainment embedded in Shakespeare's play instruct the dramatized king and his men to enter "as masquers habited like shepherds."[105] The audience additionally learns "they speak no English" (1.4.66), a provincial language in the period.[106] Rather, these aristocrats converse in French, an international language. As Twycross and Carpenter proffer, such courtly masquers strive for an "exotic familiarity," with the precedent for Shakespeare's masque – the aforementioned entertainment that inaugurated Henry VIII's reign in 1510 – showcasing the historical king and the Earl of Essex, "appareled after Turkey fashion ... girded with two swordes, called Cimiteries [scimitars]," a stereotypical orientalist accoutrement.[107] That the rest of the historical king's entourage consisted of ladies and gentlemen parading as "blackamoors" adds an Africanist aspect. While Shakespeare does not literally replicate this racialized (primal) scene, the "masque of strangers" in his late play recalls the historical king's appearance as a Turk with his entourage of blackamoors and anticipates the racialized and sexualized discourse of blackness that colours Anne's career.

This masque also resonates with the masque of strangers who appear "[l]ike Muscovites or Russians" in Shakespeare's earlier play, *Love's Labour's Lost* (5.2.122), which I assess in chapter 4 in relation to the "Tartar girl." Here, I extend my analysis by focusing on the racialized components of the play's impersonated Muscovites, who are accompanied by "blackamoor" musicians.[108] Explicating the rhetoric of blackness and beauty in this play, Kim Hall concludes that "[t]he 'painted' woman is threatening because her cosmetics reveal the 'artifice' of the politics of colour and thereby explode the contest of contraries set up by male discourse." Focusing on the "'blackamoors with music'" (5.2) who accompany the Muscovite masquers, she stresses that "their blackness was integral to their performance."[109] As John Michael Archer determines, the English in the early modern period considered Russians slavish and projected connotations associated with blackness onto them. He adduces "the 'Ne-gro-Tartars' of the Gray's Inn Revels of Christmas 1594–95," a term I unpack in chapter 4, and "a device of 1510 in which two lords appeared at Henry VIII's court in Muscovite costume along with two other lords and six ladies dressed as 'Nigers, or blacke Mores.'" Additionally, he asserts that the play represents its heroine "Rosaline's black beauty" as "not so much black as a mixture of shades: 'Of all complexions the cull'd sovereignty/Do meet, as at a fair, in her fair cheek' (4.3.231–2)." In other words, "Rosaline is 'fair' in that like a fair she unites contrasting principles for common profit."[110] As I add, Shakespeare's Tudoresque spectacles in *Henry VIII* similarly pun on the term "fair" to highlight the feminized consumer promoted by early English ideologies of empire.

These significations come to the fore during Anne's coronation procession when a gentleman remarks, "Our King has all the Indies in his arms,/And more, and richer, when he strains that lady" (4.1.45–6).[111] Here the new queen remains completely silent and does not appear in subsequent scenes. Presaging her fall shortly after her coronation, which is not represented in the play, the last time Anne speaks consists of an off-colour conversation in Act 2, scene 3 with an "Old Lady," who is a unique addition.[112] In this tête-à-tête, which critics have likened to the exchange between Desdemona and Emilia in *The Tragedy of Othello* (4.3.58–103), Anne expresses her sympathy for the discarded Katherine.[113] This *de casibus* set piece culminates with her declaration, "By my troth and maidenhead,/I would not be a queen" (2.3.23–4). In a play also titled, *All is True*, such assertions of "troth" are immediately ironized, as with Henry VIII's tendentious reflections on conscience (2.2.142–3).[114] Moreover, as the double entendres structuring the initial banquet scene suggest, Anne's maidenhead remains an uncertain commodity. Hence, whereas Desdemona's words with the worldly Emilia serve to highlight her virtue, Anne's conversation with the Old Lady results in her condemnation as a hypocrite (2.3.24–6).

The continuing parallel with Desdemona and Emilia's exchange is striking:

> OLD LADY: Yes, troth and troth. You would not be a queen?
> ANNE: No, not for all the riches under heaven.
> OLD LADY: 'Tis strange. A threepence bowed would hire me,
>   Old as I am, to queen it.   (2.3.34–7)

In a footnote, *The Norton Shakespeare* offers a paraphrase of these lines: "A bent ('bowed') and hence worthless coin would convince me to be a Queen. Sexual puns ('queen'–'quean,' or whore; 'bowed'–bawd) continue through the scene."[115] "Yet," as Walter Cohen observes, "Anne does become queen, without an explanation of her supposed change of heart but with a suggestive pun on 'quean' (whore) characteristic of

the entire sexualized exchange and of Anne's earlier banter [1.4.46–9]."
As he concludes, "The scene with the Old Lady, apparently invented by
Shakespeare, thus sullies Anne before she becomes a purely ceremonial
figure reduced to bearing royal children."[116] This denigration – in the
dual sense of "to blacken" and "to defame" (*OED*) – intensifies as the
Old Lady slings one double entendre after another at Anne.

When she is named Marchioness of Pembroke by the Lord Chamberlain, an honour which signalled Henry's official embrace, the Old Lady
launches into a parable that clinches her assessment of Anne's complic-
ity in the "blackening" of her reputation: "There was a lady once – 'tis
an old story –/That would not be a queen, that she would not,/For
all the mud in Egypt" (2.3.91–3), a locale redolent with orientalist connotations.[117] Despite Anne's protests to the contrary, it is precisely this
racialized and sexualized "mud" that sticks to her as she marries Henry,
bears Elizabeth, and prepares for her execution on charges of incest,
adultery, and treason. That she is likened to the riches of "the Indies"
(4.1.45) during her subsequent coronation only strengthens this sense of
her spoil(ing). Moreover, it is as a scandalously "[g]reat-bellied" woman
that the visibly pregnant Anne is anointed queen of England, even
though this well-known historical fact is displaced in Shakespeare's play
onto the raucous common women who greet her procession (4.1.78).
These "common" women, while they certainly connote fertility as critics have argued, simultaneously symbolize the chaotic female sexuality
that confounds patriarchal control: "No man living/Could say 'This is
my wife' there, all were woven/So strangely in one piece" (4.1.81–3).[118]
Ominously, Anne's coronation feast is held at the fallen Wolsey's former
palace, renamed Whitehall (4.1.99). This was also the banqueting hall
where the aforementioned *Masque of Blackness* (1604/5) was performed,
as well as *The Masque of Proteus* featuring a Tartar page discussed in
chapter 4.[119] Hence, as Jacobean imperialistic ambitions become increasingly salient by the end of the play, this overdetermined space propels
not only Anne Boleyn's interpellation as a "blackened" woman, but also
her daughter Elizabeth's.

The Elizabethan Queen of Sheba

Shakespeare's play draws to a close by juxtaposing King Henry's assertion of his absolute power as he promises to defend Cranmer, the Arch-
bishop of Canterbury, from his Privy Council (5.1.88–158) with the Old
Lady's announcement of Anne's safe delivery of Henry's unlikely heir,

Elizabeth (5.1.159–77).[120] Despite the Protestant triumphalism of this ending, the same Old Lady who confirmed the "blackening" of Elizabeth's mother's reputation re-emerges to announce Elizabeth's birth. Using the double-edged language associated with the play's fallen courtiers, the Old Lady responds to the king's hope that the child is the promised boy with a "yes" that means "no": "Ay, ay, my liege,/And of a lovely boy. The God of heaven/Both now and ever bless her! 'Tis a girl/Promises boys hereafter" (5.1.164–7). In the play, Henry does not overtly voice his displeasure at this news; still, the Old Lady complains that his gratuity of "[a]n hundred marks" hardly sufficed for the occasion (5.1.172).[121] When the king next appears, having enforced his hold over his Council, he remembers that he has "a fair young maid that yet wants baptism" (5.2.195) and reiterates that "I long/To have this young one made a Christian" (5.2.211–12). In this liminal space between birth and christening, Elizabeth remains little better than a "Turk" or a "Moor"; in this sense, she evokes the girls and women from the Islamic world I have examined throughout this study.

This "blackening" of the newborn Elizabeth is reinforced in the next scene, which does not feature the christening itself but focuses on the raucous commoners outside the doors, with the head porter instructing his men:

> What should you do, but knock 'em down by th' dozens? Is this Moorfields to muster in? Or have we some strange Indian with the great tool come to court, the women so besiege us? Bless me, what a fry of fornication is at door! On my Christian conscience, this one christening will beget a thousand. Here will be father, godfather, and all together. (5.3.30–6)[122]

This reference to a hyper-masculinized and hyper-racialized "strange Indian" echoes the earlier lines in which Elizabeth's mother, Anne, is conflated with booty from the Indies desired by her father, Henry; it also recalls the opening lines that likened England to the Indies, making the realm potential booty for expansionist empires, including the Ottomans. Ultimately, the promiscuity of this scene recalls the taint of incest that troubled Elizabeth throughout her long life.[123]

Reinforcing this gendered and racialized blackening, while Shakespeare's play concludes by providentially elevating the infant Elizabeth as England's future ruler, she is ultimately associated with the Queen of Sheba or "Saba" (5.4.23), who hailed from the region of Arabia Felix (modern Yemen, with the port of Aden an important stop for the nascent East India Company).[124] The allegorical figure of Sheba, as William Tate stresses, stood as the counterpart to James I's preferred representation of himself as Solomon.[125] Tate situates this Jacobean coupling in imperialistic terms by quoting Linda Levy Peck, who usefully "summarized the Jacobean ideal of empire as combining union of the kingdoms at home with a developing English colonial enterprise"; in Peck's words, "[i]n the Jacobean era new attitudes toward empire were spelled out which shaped the colonization of Ireland and laid the basis for English expansion across the Atlantic."[126] As Tate concludes, "James's desire for a union of the British Isles and his desire for American gold express the same attitude, and as a matter of convenience I will refer to these complementary notions collectively as 'imperial.'"[127] Although its North American settlements were still tentative, England from 1607 (the founding of Jamestown) can no longer be called proto-imperial or para-colonial.

As such, the conclusion of Cranmer's foretelling (actually, remembering) of Elizabeth's English Protestant and proto-imperialist reign endorses King James's pan-European Christian ecumenism with its expansionist turn:

> Peace, plenty, love, truth, terror,
> That were the servants to this chosen infant,
> Shall then be his, and, like a vine, grow to him.
> Wherever the bright sun of heaven shall shine,
> His honour and the greatness of his name
> Shall be, and make new nations.   (5.4.47–52)[128]

As *The Norton Shakespeare* glosses, this passage does not simply elaborate Genesis 17: 4, "A father of many nations have I made thee"; rather, it "compliments James on the 'new nation' he has established in America, appropriately named Virginia after the 'virgin' Queen Elizabeth."[129] Shakespeare's play thus embeds the proto-imperialist and proto-orientalist performances of the Tudor era within the global expansionist project that took off during the Jacobean period, which Kenneth Andrews explains "saw the effective beginnings of the British Empire: the establishment of colonies in North America, the development of direct trade with the East, and even the first annexation of territory in a recognized Spanish sphere of influence – the West Indies."[130] At the same time, as a late iteration of the genealogy of "masques of blackness" in the Scottish and English courts epitomized by *The Masque of*

Blackness, with its resistant assertion of female authorship and authority and its appropriation of the historical role of the "Black Queen of Beauty," Shakespeare's play dramatizes both the gendering of the emerging anglocentric discourse of empire and the effacement of girls and women from the Islamic world that underwrites it.

Chapter Six

The Intersecting Paths of Two Women from the Islamic World: Teresa Sampsonia, Mariam Khanim, and the East India Company

As I have argued throughout this study of the "presences" of girls and women from the Islamic world in early modern British literature and culture, the relatively more documented life of Teresa Sampsonia Sherley, a Circassian subject of the Safavid shah who travelled to England with her Persianized husband Robert, reverberates in numerous accounts from the period, including Mary Wroth's groundbreaking prose romance, *The Countesse of Mountgomeries Urania*, whose second part features Tartar and Persian princesses.[1] Less well known is Teresa Sampsonia's connection to Mariam Khanim, an Armenian subject of the Mughal emperor, whose links through marriage to two successive East India Company operatives (William Hawkins and Gabriel Towerson) brought her to England at approximately the same time.[2] As Alison Games explains in *The Web of Empire: English Cosmopolitans in an Age of Expansion, 1560–1660*, "English overseas companies [including the East India Company] generally forbid merchants to travel with their [English] wives."[3] However, this policy did not apply to foreign women married to Englishmen abroad, who generally did not travel with their husbands in any case.[4] Hence, Mariam may be the exception that proves the rule of women's exclusion from East India Company ships.[5] While most of the documentation for Mariam's life was deposited in the unpublished archives of the East India Company, the seventeenth-century English poet laureate John Dryden drew on these references to craft his first play set in Southeast Asia, *Amboyna, or the Cruelties of the Dutch to the English Merchants* (1673).[6] As Bindu Malieckal confirms, in Dryden's play "the Indonesian princess Ysabinda is an almost unidentifiable re-creation of a historical figure named Mariam Khan, wife of the English trader Gabriel Towerson."[7] Rather than advancing another reading of this tendentious characterization, which literary critics Carmen Nocentelli, Siraj Ahmed, Ayanna Thompson, Robert Markley, and Shankar Rahman have so ably analysed, I wish to focus on the intersecting paths of these two women as a coda to my investigation of the impact of the lives of gendered subalterns from the Islamic world during this proto-imperialist and proto-orientalist era.[8] Both Mariam Khanim and Teresa Sampsonia resided in England for extended periods during the first part of the seventeenth century, albeit not at the same time; however, they may have met when the East India Company ships on which they travelled around the Cape of Good Hope carried them in opposite directions. Whether they met or not – and it is likely they did – broaching these intersections reveals how the emerging anglocentric imperial project was secured through the traffic in women from the Islamic world, which propelled the global movements of dependent wives, servants, and slaves.[9]

While Teresa Sampsonia's journeys with her husband were widely chronicled, as I establish in chapter 1, Mariam Khanim, who travelled from the Mughal Empire to the British Isles during the same period the Sherleys were crisscrossing Europe, has received less attention. As Michael H. Fisher remarks in *Counterflows to Colonialism: Indian Travellers and Settlers in Britain, 1600–1857*, she was the daughter of the Armenian nobleman Mubarak Khan, who "reportedly served [the Mughal emperor] Akbar [r. 1556–1605] as a high-ranked courtier."[10] In 1609, Akbar's heir, Jahangir [r. 1605–27], bestowed Mariam on William Hawkins, who was known (to quote Robert Coverte, a fellow East India Company agent) "by the name of a Can [Khan], which is a knight, and keepeth company with the greatest Noblemen belonging to the King [i.e., the emperor or padishah]."[11] Hawkins himself narrates how Jahangir, seeking to keep him at the Mughal court, "was very earnest with me to take a white Mayden out of his Palace, who would give her all things necessary with slaves, and he would promise mee shee should turne Christian."[12] As Coverte explains, "the word Mogoll [Mughal] in their language is as much to say, the great white King; for he is a white man and of the Race of the Tartares"; hence, this "white maiden" conceivably could come from a Muslim background.[13] Hawkins, who sought to leave court, parlayed the padishah's move by refusing to marry "a *Moore* [Muslim] ... but if so bee there could bee a Christian found, I would accept it"; he assumed that a suitable "Christians Daughter" could not be found in the padishah's household. Jahangir prevailed, however, granting him "one *Mubarique Sha* [Mubarak Shah or Khan] his Daughter, who was a Christian *Armenian*, and of the Race of the most ancient Christians, who was a Captaine, and in great favour with *Ekber Padasha* [Akbar Padishah], this Kings Father." Clearly, this was an offer Hawkins could not refuse: he immediately married the unnamed woman "before Christian Witnesses" and subsequently in front of "a Preacher that came with Sir *Henry Middleton*." While Hawkins uses pronouns ("her," "she") to refer to his wife, other sources confirm her name was Mariam.[14] Similar to Teresa Sampsonia, then, Mariam Khanim occupied an ambivalent position in the Islamic empire of the Mughals and in the British Isles, where she resided for two years.

Although her natal family sought to keep her in India, on 5 March 1612 Mariam left for the British Isles with one English husband and landed almost a year and a half later with another. Hawkins records their departure on a Portuguese ship to the Red Sea, where they arrived on 3 April 1612; from thence, they sailed with the English fleet led by John Saris to Sumatra and Bantam, where the East India Company had established its inaugural base in Southeast Asia. On 30 January 1613, they sailed for the Bay of Saldania at the Cape of Good Hope, arriving on 21 April 1613. Hawkins's last words in his account are "[w]e departed from *Saldania* the one and twentieth of May, 1613."[15] He died shortly thereafter. After Hawkins's untimely death, Mariam was left without any family support, becoming what Karen Robertson in her deft analysis calls a "stranger widow."[16] Mariam arrived bereft at Waterford, Ireland, in early September 1613. After burying Hawkins there, she travelled to London and married Gabriel Towerson, in Robert Markley's words a "middle-aged and corpulent" captain of the East India Company fleet that had sailed from Bantam. As Markley elaborates in *The Far East and the English Imagination, 1600–1730*, "It is impossible to say to what extent her [Mariam's] actions were voluntary once Hawkins had died, but her story is revealing both for what it suggests about the choices facing women in the small, dispersed community of Christian merchants in the East and for what it reveals about Dryden's ideological imperatives in recasting his sources."[17] Even with these constraints, her petitions to the East India Company for redress as Hawkins's widow document her active negotiation of her cross-cultural, albeit vulnerable, status.[18] She lived with her second husband in England for two years from 1614 to 1616, after which the couple returned to India. Towerson abandoned her in 1618 to become a hero-martyr at Amboyna, as represented in John Skinner and Dudley Digges's *A True Relation of the Unjust, Cruell, and Barbarous Proceedings against the*

English at Amboyna in the East-Indies, by the Neatherlandish Governour and Councel there (1624).[19] While Mariam vanishes from the written record after 1619, Fisher affirms that "[t]oday's Armenian community claims ... [her] with pride."[20]

As I have posited, Mariam Khanim and Teresa Sampsonia, two relatively privileged women from the Islamic world who resided in England during the early seventeenth century, crossed paths, and may have met, when the East India Company ships on which they travelled carried them in opposite directions: Mariam Khanim was sailing from the Mughal Empire to the British Isles on the *Thomas* around the same time Teresa Sampsonia sailed on the *Expedition* towards the Mughal Empire and into Safavid domains. The encounter between Mariam and Teresa is especially significant as it marks the moment when the East India Company entered the established "web of empire" that stretched from India to Iran.[21] Yet, the copious secondary sources on the Sherley brothers and on the men who inaugurated the East India Company neglect this conjuncture. Such an erasure is not warranted, as documentation exists, however slight, for the meeting of these two women. Rather, its effacement in the scholarly literature derives from what feminist scholars challenging "patriarchal canonicity" have identified as the "inoculating critique of ... [a discipline's] own blind spots, so as to allow business to proceed as usual."[22] This erasure also derives from the English patriarchal practice of ascribing the husband's name to his wife (or wives in a serial sense), which has obscured married women's contributions whether they came from the Islamic world or were born in Britain.[23] This case study underscores why "micro-history" must be set in the broader field of "women's history," as I theorize in the introduction.

To start with the first leg of this two-pronged journey: Teresa Sampsonia and her husband, Robert, having concluded their diplomatic mission on behalf of Shah 'Abbas to King James I of England and other Western Christian rulers, sailed on 7 January 1613, "from Gravesend [a town in northwest Kent on the south bank of the Thames] on the East India Company's ship *Expedition*." Thomas Powell, Robert's companion during his eleven years in Iran, "had come up from his native Herefordshire with his Persian wife, and his brother Morgan," to return with him, along with "several Persians of both sexes, among whom was Robert's body servant Nazer Beg."[24] In the meantime, Mariam Khanim and her first husband, William Hawkins, had departed from Bantam for the British Isles on the East India Company ship the *Thomas*, captained by John Saris.[25] The East India Company customarily followed the route around the Cape of Good Hope, and this is where the ships that carried Teresa Sampsonia and Mariam Khanim met. As Boies Penrose explains in his influential study of the Sherley brothers, "Here they [Robert *and* Teresa] stayed above a fortnight watering and victualling, and keeping company with the *Hector* [*sic*], on which was William Hawkins [*and* Mariam], the first English agent at the Mogul's court, the *Thomas*, and the *Peppercorn* (Captain Downton) all homeward bound from India."[26] In a symptomatic omission, Penrose does not mention the two women, whose names I have inserted in brackets.

Fortuitously, given the muting in the East India Company records of female travellers and traders, evidence of the intersecting trajectories of these two women from the Islamic world was preserved in a letter addressed to Robert Sherley by Captain Nicholas Downton of the *Peppercorn*, who "the previous winter had given the Portuguese fleet a sound beating off Surat."[27] The letter was delivered in 1615 by the East India Company operative Richard Steel, who reconnoitered with Robert in Persia "and obtained through him licences to trade in certain ports."[28] Downton begins his letter by establishing the geographical coordinates of his earlier encounter with the Sherleys: "When in the *Peppercorn* I parted from you att Saldania, my poor means for so long a passage considered, I little thought from this place ever to have written to your Honour into Persia."[29] As Penrose glosses, "Here the writer refers to Robert's escapes at Gwadar and Laribandar [on the Arabian Sea], his sojourn with [the Mughal emperor] Jahangir at Agra and the subject of Persian trade."[30] Other sources, such as *A Chronicle of the Carmelites in Persia*, detail how Teresa, who is praised as "a true Amazon," participated in these journeys and facilitated Robert's escapes.[31] Continuing with East India Company business, Downton briefly digresses: "It gladdeth me to hear that my Lady Sherlye [Lady Sherley, Teresa Sampsonia] hath so well overcome her sea travell, and departed Agra in health." He adds, thereby establishing a tangible connection between the two women: "William Hawkins died homewards; so did most of the people in that ship. He was buried in Ireland, and his wife is married to Gabriell Towerson; Mrs. Towerson [Mariam Khanim] did visit your son [Henry, who was born and lived in England], and informed me of his health." William Foster, in his collection of *Letters Received by the East India Company from its Servants in the East*, transcribes the subject of the last sentence as "Mr. Towerson." Penrose, in *The Sherleian Odyssey*, transcribes it as "Mrs. Towerson." My reading of the manuscript letter supports Penrose. In either case, it is likely that Mariam Khanim, perhaps with her second husband Gabriel Towerson, visited Teresa and Robert's child while in England.

The Sherleys' son, Henry, was born the beginning of November 1611 and was still alive in 1622, when his English grandmother passed away, as confirmed by the annuity she bequeathed him.[32] In the absence of additional records, it appears that this "interesting Anglo-Persian perished at an early age" several years later. As Penrose concludes, "[t]his letter is of great interest as one of the few notices of the child Henry Sherley, whom his parents had very thoughtfully left at home at [the family seat of] Wiston."[33] Yet, as I have established, this short document also signals the impact of Teresa Sampsonia's and Mariam Khanim's lives beyond the tendentious discourse that was produced about them. It offers rare evidence of the camaraderie of women from the Islamic world who landed in England during this transitional period and who faced common challenges, from exoticized and even racialized depictions to the fraught combination of motherhood and global travel. At the very least, the two women knew of each other, as Mariam visited Teresa's son, who remained in England when the Sherleys returned to Safavid Persia. As such, they were able to forge bonds between women, however limited, beyond the "exchange of women" between men that otherwise determined their lives.

As specified in chapter 1, dependent wives such as Teresa Sampsonia and Mariam Khanim cannot be considered completely "voluntary" travellers in the sense Thomas Palmer outlines in his popular guidebook, *An Essay of the Meanes how to make our Travailes, into forraine Countries, the more profitable and honorable* (1606). However, neither can they be considered "involuntary" travellers, as were other women from the Islamic world who circulated within the early modern/colonial world system as servants or even chattel. Indeed, Teresa Sampsonia and Mariam Khanim brought several female servants with them as they sailed back-and-forth between the British Isles and the Islamic empires of the Safavids and Mughals. In shipmate Walter Payton's words, the second trip from London towards Persia on an East India Company vessel included "Sir *Robert Sherley*, the Ambassadour. *Teresha*, his Ladie, a *Circasian*. Sir *Thomas Powell*. *Tomasin* his Ladie. *Leylye*, a *Persian* Woman," along with other English, Armenian, and Persian men.[34] Mariam Khanim's entourage included, in Fisher's list, "'a gentle [or "well born" (*OED*)] waiting woman,' Mrs Frances Webb; a female companion, Mrs Hudson; and several servants," who may have been of South Asian origin.[35] As Penrose indicates, Mrs. Webb[e]'s child was "the second

English baby born in India"; Mrs Powell bore the first.[36] Unsurprisingly, the lives of these lower status women register even more ephemerally in the documentary record, although scholars such as Amrita Sen have recently excavated their agency.[37]

Finally, it is crucial that Teresa Sampsonia and Mariam Khanim's lives intersected due to the activities of the newly chartered East India Company at a time when England, along with Scotland, could not be considered an empire beyond the British Isles. The Sherleys' efforts to establish Anglo-Safavid trade and perhaps a military alliance against the Ottomans were certainly a failure. The East India Company remained a tenuous enterprise in both Asia and England until the 1660s.[38] The tendentious characterization of Mariam as Ysabinda in Dryden's *Amboyna*, staged and published in the late 1670s, nevertheless marks the moment when the East India Company secured England's reach into the Indian Ocean through strategic victories over the Portuguese and Dutch. Hence, if Mariam Khanim's path at the beginning of the seventeenth century was shaped by "marginal" England's proto-imperialist and proto-orientalist engagement with the vastly more powerful Mughal Empire, her effaced presence in English culture at the end of the seventeenth century signals the transition to a more fully realized anglocentric imperial project on a global scale.

Notes

Introduction: Can the Subaltern Signify? Tracing the Lives of Girls and Women from the Islamic World in British Literature and Culture, c. 1500–1630

1 For the term "proto-imperial," see Baldwin, "Colonial Cartography," 1754; for "proto-orientalist," see Barbour, *Before Orientalism*, 5–6, 15–16. "Proto" is a Latin prefix that means "earliest, original; at an early stage of development, primitive; incipient, potential" (*Oxford English Dictionary* [*OED*] Online, 2nd ed., 1989, s.v. "proto," 1a). For an astute study of the pre-colonial medieval era (1245–1510), with connections to the subsequent proto-colonial early modern era, see Phillips, *Before Orientalism*.

2 *Dar al-Islam*, literally "the house or abode of Islam," is traditionally defined as "a geopolitical unit, in which Islam is established as the religion of the state" (Kelsay, "Dar al-Islam"). Classical Islamic law allowed Jews and Christians to inhabit the *Dar al-Islam* as *dhimmis*, or protected minorities, albeit with lack of civic equality and other liabilities (Brodeur, "Islam and Other Religions"). The term "Islamic world" as I use it encompasses these minority groups.

3 Vizenor, *Native Liberty*, 24.

4 Ginzburg, *Threads and Traces*, 1–6; for more on "Microhistory," see ibid., 7–24. On "connected histories," see Subrahmanyam, *Explorations in Connected History* (2 vols.) and "Connected Histories." Said defines his "contrapuntal" approach, in *Culture and Imperialism*, "as making up a set of ... intertwined and overlapping histories" (18). Burton, in *Traffic and Turning*, modulates Said's approach into a comparative analysis using translated texts from synchronous Ottoman and Arabic sources (40–6). I follow Said more closely in "reading a predominantly Western archive"

against the grain, to paraphrase Burton (39, 47). As I propose, reading strategies that aim to recognize and recover traces of subaltern agency *within* the proto-imperialist and proto-orientalist archive should not be so glibly dismissed, especially when they involve gendered subalterns. I concur with Burton when he observes "that English discourse was not only permeable, but also permeated and influenced by Muslim voices" (52). However, I focus on the "voices" of girls and women from the Islamic world who resided in the British Isles for extended periods rather than those of Englishmen encountering their Ottoman counterparts abroad.

5 Anderson, *Subaltern Lives*, 1. For a comparative study of early modern "discourses of empire," see Pagden, *Lords of All the World*. I have also been influenced by Cohen, "The Discourse of Empire" and "The Literature of Empire." For the similar but not equivalent term, "colonial discourse," see Hulme, *Colonial Encounters*. For an important intervention, see Amer and Doyle, "Introduction: Reframing Postcolonial and Global Studies in the Longer *Durée*." See also Ogborn, *Global Lives*.

6 Ferguson, *Dido's Daughters*, 1. For a more recent assessment, see Wiesner-Hanks, "Early Modern Gender and the Global Turn."

7 I am referencing the landmark study by Ashcroft, Griffiths, and Tiffin, *The Empire Writes Back*. In focusing on the post-colonial, this study privileges the nineteenth and twentieth centuries; in focusing on literary production, it privileges post-colonial writers rather than the subalterns I consider, who did not have access to advanced literacy and opportunities for publishing but who nevertheless inscribed their agency, including their survival and resistance, within the colonial archive.

8 Distiller, Review of *A Companion to the Global Renaissance*, 600–1.

9 Greer, Mignolo, and Quilligan, in their introduction to *Rereading the Black Legend*, question whether the word "empire" (*imperum*) with its Roman roots should be applied to the Ottomans, with "Sultanate" more appropriate for an Islamic polity (23). They make a similar point about the Incans and the Russians. However, as Mignolo notes in his afterword, "Moscow as the Third Rome competes with and complements Istanbul (the Second Rome) and Rome proper" (322). With both the tsar and the sultan claiming the title "Caesar," it is appropriate to refer to both polities as empires in the early modern era. See also Matthee, "Was Safavid Iran an Empire?" He responds "in the affirmative, albeit with some qualifications" (238).

10 Stallybrass, "Marginal England, 31.

11 Cormack, *Charting an Empire*, 12. Cormack continues, "By the mid-seventeenth century, England had begun to develop as a true imperial power, portraying itself as the preeminent Protestant nation and preparing

to do battle with other European powers for rights to mercantile, colonial, and imperial ascendancy" (12).

12 Colley, *Captives*, 4.

13 For the designation "early modern/colonial period," see Mignolo, *The Darker Side of the Renaissance*, vii–viii. For a focus on England, see Vitkus, "The New Globalism." For more, see Loomba, "Early Modern or Early Colonial?"

14 Armitage, *The Ideological Origins*, explains that the Scottish monarchy during the sixteenth and seventeenth centuries, "like the English monarchy ... could be described anachronistically as 'colonialist' in that it used settlement, acculturation and economic dependency as a means to 'civilise' its territorial margins and their inhabitants. It would also be colonialist in that it chartered and encouraged overseas ventures and settlements in the Atlantic world during the early seventeenth century" (26). On the "Greater Western World," which encompassed "Christian Europe and the Muslim Ottoman Empire," see Goffman, *The Ottoman Empire and Early Modern Europe*, 8.

15 For a foundational study, see Davis and Farge, *A History of Women in the West*, first published as an English edition in 1993 (Italian ed., 1991). Ginzburg, in his "Preface to the English Edition" of *The Cheese and the Worms*, acknowledges the influence of Davis's groundbreaking work in early modern women's history on his approach to microhistory (xvii), as does Muir in "Introduction: Observing Trifles," ix. Also foundational is Wiesner-Hanks, *Women and Gender in Early Modern Europe*, first published in 1993. For more on methodology, see Chaudhuri, Katz, and Perry, *Contesting Archives*.

16 On the "subaltern," see the two iterations of Spivak's landmark essay in Morris, *Can the Subaltern Speak?* 21–78 and 237–91. On the "supplement," see Derrida, *Of Grammatology*, 141–64.

17 Morton, *Gayatri Spivak*, 121 (ellipsis in original), citing Spivak, "Subaltern Talk," 292. For a related assessment, see Maggio, "'Can the Subaltern Be Heard?'"

18 Malieckal advances this useful heuristic in her incisive study of "Mariam Khan," 116. For a related investigation of subaltern women's lives during the Mughal era, both in terms of sources and methodology, see Harris, *The First Firangis*, 150–84.

19 Coldiron, "Women in Early English Print Culture," 61, and *Printers without Borders*, 35–106.

20 "A letter written by the most high and mighty Empresse the wife of the Grand Signior *Sultan Murad Can* to the Queenes Majesty of *England*, in the

yeere of our Lord, 1594," in Hakluyt, *The Principal Navigations*, 2:311–12. For more on Safiye's letter, see Andrea, *Women and Islam*, 20–9. Some Ottoman women did travel to the sixteenth-century French court, on which see Skilliter, "Catherine de' Medici's Turkish Ladies-in-Waiting."

21 I follow Armitage, *The Ideological Origins*, in using "Britain" (and its associated adjective) as "a geographical expression, to refer to the island encompassing England, Wales and Scotland," with Ireland designated under the "Three Kingdoms" prior to the establishment of the United Kingdom of Great Britain in 1707 (3n8).

22 For a comparative study of nascent English nationalism in relationship to the "Turks," Irish, and others, see Suranyi, *The Genius of the English Nation*.

23 For the supplement "[a]s a *'subaltern instance,'*" that "stands as a limit, or a condition of possibility," see Morton, *Gayatri Spivak*, 104 (emphasis added). As Morton explains, "To counter the problem of speaking for the subaltern woman, and thus constituting her as a passive object of imperialist knowledge and power, Spivak develops an ethical strategy for reading the *clandestine presence* of the subaltern woman in the archives of imperialism and anti-colonial insurgency" (112; emphasis added). For other important terms, especially "culture" and "literature," see Williams, *Keywords*, 87–93 and 183–8.

24 For Henry VIII's title, see Brigden, *New Worlds, Lost Worlds*, 13. Elton, *England under the Tudors*, clarifies that "in December 1540, Henry adopted the title of king of Ireland" (180). For the complete document beginning, "Where by divers sundry old authentic histories and chronicles it is manifestly declared and expressed that this realm of England is an empire," see "Act in Restraint of Appeals, 1533 (24 Henry VII, c. 12), in Bray, *Documents of the English Reformation*, 78–83. While the wording was Thomas Cromwell's, the intent was Henry's, on which see Elton, *England under the Tudors*, 133, 483. For an astute analysis of the Henrician idea of empire, see Mottram, *Empire and Nation*, 37–101.

25 According to Burbank and Cooper, *Empires in World History*, "It was in 1773 that reference was first made to 'this vast empire on which the sun never sets'" as pertains to the British empire (238). According to Pagden, *Lords of All the World*, the Italian poet Ludovico Ariosto (1474–1533) earlier used this phrase to describe the Spanish empire (116).

26 Elton, "The Reformation in England," 234, and *England under the Tudors*, 160–2. Ferguson, *Dido's Daughters*, departs from this consensus, offering a pointed critique of Elton (141–3).

27 Pagden, *Lords of All the World*, 12.

28 Fuchs, "Imperium Studies," 72. Burbank and Cooper, *Empires in World
    History*, add: "In Rome, *imperium* first referred to the king's power
    to impose execution or beatings, to draft citizens into armies, and to
    command armies on campaigns ... Imperium meant the power to condemn
    people to death or to make them fight" (28). By the time of Augustus, "the
    emperor possessed *imperium maius*, meaning 'power greater than that
    of the man who should govern any province he should enter'" (32). For
    details, see Armitage, *Theories of Empire*.
29 As Scarisbrick, *Henry VIII*, indicates, the aborted proposals during the
    1520s to launch colonial expeditions across the Atlantic were largely
    "[Cardinal] Wolsey's bold design" (124). For more on Henry VIII and
    Western voyaging, see Quinn, *England and the Discovery of America*, 160–91.
30 As Scarisbrick, *Henry VIII*, explains, the new King Henry "had looked,
    albeit fitfully, to the new world which Spanish ships were opening up
    across the Atlantic." The choice before him "was, therefore, not just
    between being a quiet working monarch and a martial hero, not just
    between peace and war, but, in a real way, between new and old." In
    sum, "Henry VIII would lead England back into her past, into Europe
    and its endless squabbles, into another round of that conflict misleadingly
    defined as merely a Hundred Years War"; he "would pay so little
    attention to the Americas and Asia that, when overseas exploration was
    resumed over forty years later, his country would find that Iberian ships
    had meanwhile gained an advantage which it would take her [England]
    generations to rival" (21). See also Elton, *England under the Tudors*, 54 and
    476, and Loades, *Henry VIII*, 10–34. The capture of Calais on 7 January
    1558 occurred at the end of Mary Tudor's reign, on which see Loades,
    Mary Tudor, 294–7. For more on Calais, see Wallace, *Premodern Places*,
    22–90.
31 Scarisbrick, *Henry VIII*, 507; Scarisbrick adds that in the 1520s "one Robert
    Thorne, a Bristol merchant then in Seville, had urged Henry to return to
    the search for the North-West Passage, but his words drew no response"
    (124; cf. 508). Mayers, in *North-East Passage*, cites Thorne's letter of 1527 to
    Henry VIII (16); he also reproduces Thorne's 1527 map of the world, which
    he claims Thorne "secretly sneaked from some Spanish source" (43).
32 Canny, "The Origins of Empire," 1.
33 Armitage, *The Ideological Origins*, 9, 7, 1–3.
34 Burbank and Cooper, *Empires in World History*, 117–48.
35 Brigden, *New Worlds, Lost Worlds*, xi.
36 Andrews, *Trade, Plunder and Settlement*, 11. As Andrews stresses, "it was
    the reign of James [1603–25] that saw the effective beginnings of the British

Empire" (13), which was not fully realized until the end of the eighteenth century. See also Loades, *England's Maritime Empire*.

37 Sherman, *John Dee*, 171.

38 Scarisbrick, *Henry VIII*, 81; Wheatcroft, *The Habsburgs*, 103–40.

39 Jardine and Brotton, *Global Interests*, 54.

40 Brotton, *The Renaissance Bazaar*, 54, 115–16.

41 Fuller, "Where was Iceland in 1600?" 151. Quinn, *England and the Discovery of America*, documents Icelandic slaves in England during the 1480s (49–51).

42 As MacMillan states, in "Introduction: Discourse on History, Geography, and Law," this treatise "must be given pride of place for being the earliest justification for the expansion of the British Empire to be offered in Elizabethan England" (8). As such, it "was a tangible contribution to England's first, uncertain, permanent forays into the New World" (19). For more, see MacMillan, *Sovereignty and Possession*, 48–78.

43 As Foster explains, Queen Mary Tudor and her husband, King Philip of Spain, originally chartered this joint-stock company as "The Marchant Adventurers of England for the Discovery of Lands, Territories, Iles, Dominions, and Seigniories unknowen and not before that late adventure or enterprise by sea or navigation commonly frequented" (*England's Quest* 11). He adds that "[t]his cumbrous title was soon ousted in common parlance by the more convenient term 'Russia' or 'Muscovy' Company" (11n1).

44 Dimmock, *New Turkes*, 1–2, and "Guns and Gawds, 207–22.

45 Dale, *The Muslim Empires*, 200; Das, "'Apes of Imitation,'" 114–28.

46 MacLean and Matar, *Britain and the Islamic World*, 77. Also significant is Mitchell, *Sir Thomas Roe and the Mughal Empire*.

47 As MacMillan points out, in "Introduction: Discourse on History, Geography, and Law," "Most writers accept that Dee brought the term 'British Empire' into common usage" (2). Sherman, *John Dee*, concurs: "In a series of maps, treatise, and conferences from the 1550s and 1590s, Dee developed an expansionist program which he called 'this British discovery and recovery enterprise'" (149), as does Armitage, *The Ideological Origins*, 47, with this qualification: "Though Dee was certainly not the first to use the concept of the British Empire ... he was the first to theorise the maritime conception of the British Empire" (105). For more, see Cormack, "Britannia Rules the Waves?"

   On Hakluyt's promotion from the beginning of the 1580s of "an aggressive effort to colonize North America," see Mancall, *Hakluyt's Promise*, 70, 128–55. However, as Armitage, *The Ideological Origins*, clarifies, "Hakluyt's works remained thoroughly English and not British (let alone,

British and Irish) in scope. His aim was to chronicle the voyages, traffics and navigations of the English nation alone" (80). For more, see Carey and Jowitt, *Richard Hakluyt and Travel Writing*.

48 Burbank and Cooper, *Empires in World History*, 170. As they continue, "The notion of 'British' meant little before the Union with Scotland in 1707 and the world 'empire' in the sixteenth and seventeenth centuries referred to England being 'entire of itself,' independent of any superior authority" (170).

49 Baldwin, "Colonial Cartography," 1755. Sherman, *John Dee*, concurs: "In the sixteenth century the hands of textual experts ... did most to shape England's embryonic empire. They conjured with a considerable imagination a vision of sea power and global colonization from the pages of books and manuscripts ... as long as Elizabeth reigned – and for some time after – the British Empire remained a textual affair" (152).

50 Archer, *Old Worlds*, 16–17. Archer prefers "the Greek prefix [*para*]," which "means 'alongside of' without precluding either 'before' or 'beyond,' and can suggest both 'closely related to' and 'aside from,' as well" (17).

51 Jardine and Brotton, *Global Interests*, 16; cf. 14. For more on Spenser's conception of the British Empire, see Armitage, *The Ideological Origins*, 52–6.

52 On "the locus of enunciation in colonial situations," see Mignolo, *The Darker Side of the Renaissance*, 5–6.

53 Dolan, *True Relations*, 20. For a related case study, see Lynch, "Whatever."

54 Edwards, "The Early African Presence," 16.

55 Fradenburg, *City, Marriage, Tournament*, 225–64; Edwards, "The Early African Presence," 21–23.

56 Salkeld, *Shakespeare among the Courtesans*, 119–50.

57 My usage throughout this book concurs with Tharps's assessment in "The Case for Black with a Capital B": "When speaking of a culture, ethnicity or group of people, the name should be capitalized. Black with a capital B refers to people of the African diaspora. Lowercase black is simply a color." I acknowledge that this definition is culturally and historically specific.

58 Andrea, "Islamic Communities." Perhaps the earliest example immediately prior to the reign of Queen Victoria (1837–1901) is Mariam Begum ("Princess Moulvee"), who was associated with Nasir al-Din's 1834 embassy to England. For details, see Fisher, *Counterflows to Colonialism*, 265, 268–71; however, for women from the Islamic world who married Englishmen or who worked as servants in English families, conversion was the rule (182–9, 221–5).

59 Morgan and Coote, *Early Voyages*, 1:107–9; Hakluyt, *The Principal Navigations*, 1:305. I refer to the 1599–1600 edition, from which the controversial "Cadiz leaves" of the 1598 edition were removed; for details, see Payne, "Richard Hakluyt's *Divers Voyages* (1582) & *Principal Navigations* (1589; 1598/9 to 1600): A Census of Surviving Copies."

As Vásáry explains in *Turks, Tatars and Russians*, "Tatar" refers to the "Turco-Mongol overlords" of "the Kazan and Crimean Khanates," which were successor states of the Golden Horde (the western part of the empire founded by Chingis Khan "extending from the Aral Sea to the Lower Danube") (vii). On the Nogays in particular, see ibid., 27–34, and Khodarkovsky, *Russia's Steppe Frontier*, 76–130. On the origins of the European misnomer "Tartar" for the more correct term "Tatar," see Cogley, "'The Most Vile and Barbarous Nation.'" In the balance of this book, I use "Tartar" when referring to literary and other representations and "Tatar" when referring to historical individuals and groups.

60 Arnold, *Queen Elizabeth's Wardrobe*, 106–7. On human "pets" in early modern European courts, including finely dressed black boys, see Tuan, *Dominance and Affection*, 5, 132–61. For a late seventeenth-century elaboration, see Aravamudan, *Tropicopolitans*, 29–70.

61 Euben, *Journeys to the Other Shore*, 140.

62 Hendricks, "Feminist Historiography," 374.

63 Arnold, *Queen Elizabeth's Wardrobe*, 107.

64 See Bennett, *The Author*, for "a history of authorship" that runs from the medieval period through the postmodern era (6). Ben Jonson, who praised Wroth in his poetry and dedicated his play *The Alchemist* to her, heralded the "propriety author" in England, on which see Loewenstein, *Ben Jonson and Possessive Authorship*.

65 Hodgson introduced the term "Islamicate" for "the social and cultural complex historically associated with Islam and the Muslims, both among Muslims themselves and even when found among non-Muslims" (*The Venture of Islam* 1:59). I use this term for liminal regions such as Central Asia, Eastern Europe, and West Africa, where various Islamic and Christian empires competed without establishing a clear hegemony. The cultures of these regions were not limited to these dominant religious-cultural complexes, but were fundamentally informed by indigenous practices and beliefs. For more on terminology, see Hodgson, *The Venture of Islam*, 1:45–62. For a counterview, see Ahmed, *What is Islam?* 157–75.

66 Sturtevant and Quinn, "This New Prey," 68.

67 For the definition of "catachresis" as "abuse or perversion of a trope or metaphor," see Spivak, *A Critique*, 14. Vizenor, *Native Liberty*, likewise

stresses that "[t]he *indian*, of course, has no real referent, no actual native ancestors. The simulation of that name is a colonial enactment. The *indian* is the absence of natives. The name is an ironic noun, a simulation of dominance that transposes native memories, imagic moments, and stories of survivance" (162).

68 Dandelet, *The Renaissance of Empire*, 3.
69 Wroth, *The Second Part*, 271, 42. As Gossett and Mueller indicate in their "Textual Introduction," "The printed first part of the *Urania* is divided into four books comprised of approximately 350,000 words" and "the second part contains approximately 240,000 words" (xviii). On the early modern "drive to universal Christian empire," see Headley, "The Habsburg World Empire," 46.
70 Said, *Orientalism*, 49, 50, and *Culture and Imperialism*, 1–14.
71 Arnold, *Queen Elizabeth's Wardrobe*, 107.
72 Lanier, "'Stigmatical in Making,'" 303, citing Stubbes, *The Anatomie of Abuses*.
73 *Gesta Grayorum*, 44. Unless otherwise indicated, I refer to Greg's facsimile edition.
74 Montrose, "The Work of Gender," 25.
75 *Gesta Grayorum*, 21.
76 Montrose, "The Work of Gender," 18; Palmer, *Writing Russia*, xvii, 21, 32.
77 Although she does not dwell on his plays, Sedgwick includes a chapter on Shakespeare's sonnets (*Between Men* 28–48).
78 Hakluyt, *The Principall Navigations*, sig. *2. I retain the differences in spelling between the first and second editions (*Principal–Principall*) to distinguish between the two.
79 Unless otherwise indicated, all quotations from Shakespeare's plays come from *The Norton Shakespeare*. Parenthetical citations refer to act, scene, and lines. When listing dates for the plays, I draw on this edition.
80 Miller, *Blank Darkness*, 17; Williams, *Marxism and Literature*, 121–7.
81 Lindesay, *The Historie and Cronicles of Scotland*, 242–3; Hall, *The Lives of the Kings*, 15–17; Jonson, *The Characters of Two royall Masques*, sig. A3–C2ᵛ.
82 Ferguson, *Dido's Daughters*, 6. For an important study that shows how the "insistence on 'empirical evidence' of a black presence" in early modern England has hampered analyses of the history of race and racism in the period, see Hall, "Reading What Isn't There," 25.
83 As Malieckal explains, "Since Mariam Khan was the daughter of a 'Khan' [Mubarak Khan] in good standing with the emperors [Akbar (r. 1556–1605) and Jahangir (1605–27)], she might have been known as 'Begam' before and after marriage, since Hawkins, like her father, held the title of 'Khan'

[granted by Jahangir]" ("Mariam Khan" 103). I prefer the term "Khanim" [*Hanım*] to "Khan," as it still resonates as an honorific for women. Variants include Khanum or Khanoum.

84 Markley, *The Far East and the English Imagination*, 19. First staged in 1672, Dryden's *Amboyna* was published the following year. The expanded title, *Amboyna, or the Cruelties of the Dutch to the English Merchants*, is listed on page 1.

85 Matar, *Britain and Barbary*, 92–110; Colley, *Captives*, 23–134.

1. The "Presences of Women" from the Islamic World in Late Medieval Scotland and Early Modern England

1 Rosenthal, "Al-Mubashshir ibn Fâtik," states: "The English translation of [Anthony Woodville, 2nd] Earl Rivers, published by Caxton in 1477, was the first book in the English language to be printed in England, and it has been claimed to be the first book printed in England in any language" (134). Coldiron, "Women in Early English Print Culture," modifies this claim: this translation "was long thought to be the first book in English printed in England and is now called the second or third" (60). See also Hellinga, *Caxton in Focus*, "Dating the *Dictes*" (77–80) and "Earl Rivers and the *Dictes*" (84–6). For a preliminary discussion, see Andrea, "The 'Presences of Women' from the Islamic World."

2 Rosenthal, "Al-Mubashshir ibn Fâtik," 133–4. The Islamic calendar dates from the immigration of the Prophet Muhammad and his followers from Mecca to Medina in 622 C.E., on which see Faizer, "Hijra," and Dallal, "Hijri Calendar."

3 Rosenthal, "Al-Mubashshir ibn Fâtik," 140, 148. For more, see Rosenthal, *The Classical Heritage in Islam*, 28–9, 33–6, 124–44, and Hodgson, *The Venture of Islam*, 1:410–43.

4 Ahmed, *Women and Gender in Islam*, 29.

5 Coldiron, "Women in Early English Print Culture," 62. "Empeshement" is a transliteration of the "Old French *empechement*, *empeschement*, modern French *empêchement*," meaning "[h]indrance, prevention, obstruction; impediment, obstacle" (*OED*, s.v. "impeachment"). "Long" means "lengthy, prolix, tedious ... of a speaker or writer" (*OED*).

6 Coldiron, "Women in Early English Print Culture," 60–1; on the *Dictes*'s "multi-culturalism," see ibid., 62.

7 Rosenthal, "Al-Mubashshir ibn Fâtik," 137–8.

8 For an overview of women scholars in the classical Islamic period, see Nadwi, *al-Muhaddithat*.

9 For the definition of *Dar al-Islam*, see 131n2 above.

10 Edwards and Walvin, "Africans in Britain," 173. For more on the "More lassis [lasses]" and other "Moors" in Scotland at the turn of the sixteenth century, see Edwards, "The Early African Presence," 17. For the documentary references in chronological order to "the More lasses," "the blak lady" of the 1507 and 1508 tournaments, and "Elen More," see Habib, *Black Lives*, 281–94, 31–2. Cognizant of the inevitable gaps in the records, I use the name "Elen More" to mark the place of this gendered subaltern's agency and not to foreclose further discussion of her name.

11 The Muscovy or Russia Company was chartered in 1555, even though its members initiated their venture several years earlier, on which see Willan, *The Muscovy Merchants* and *The Early History*.

12 The epitaph in the Church of Santa Maria della Scala in Trastevere (Rome), which I have examined, lists her name as "Theresia Sampsonia Amazonites Samphuffi Circassiae Principis Filia" [Theresia Sampsonia, native of the region of the Amazons, daughter of Samphuffus, Prince of Circassia]; for a partial photograph, see Davies, *Elizabethans Errant*, between pages 174 and 175. Other variants in the records include "Teresia," "Theresa," and "Teresa." Eskandari-Qajar, "Persian Ambassadors," charts what he dubs "[t]he 'Teresia-Teresa' confusion (254n10). However, for an era when the spelling of proper names was not standardized (for instance, "Shakespeare," "Shakespere," and "Shakespear" were the most common spellings during its famous bearer's lifetime), the most important point about Teresa's name, as I shall denote her, is that it is modelled on St Teresa of Ávila.

13 Middleton, *Sir Robert Sherley*, 13, and, in a modern edition, "Sir Robert Sherley," 677.

14 Malieckal, "Mariam Khan," 98. For the use of "Khanim," see 139n83 above.

15 Vizenor, *Native Liberty*, 24.

16 Malieckal, "Mariam Khan," 116.

17 Fradenburg, *City, Marriage, Tournament*, 256, 258. For more, see Fradenburg's chapters "The Wild Knight," 225–43 and "The Black Lady," 244–64. For the occasion of the tournament, see Dunbar, *The Poems*, ed. Kinsley, 308.

18 Fradenburg, *City, Marriage, Tournament*, xiv; cf. 67–9, 158–9, 172, 199.

19 Edwards, "The Early African Presence," 16. On medieval models of "black beauty," see Fradenburg, *City, Marriage, Tournament*, 245. In Fradenburg's view, "the black lady of James's tournament (and Dunbar's parodic blazon of 'My ladye with the mekle lippis')" attests to "the discarnation and incarnation of beauty" (210, 254–6).

20 Andrea, "Black Skin, The Queen's Masques," 260. *The Masque of Blackness* was performed on 6 January 1604 (O.S.)/1605 (N.S.).
21 McManus, *Women on the Renaissance Stage*, 75–8, 82–7, 96. See also Wade, "The Queen's Courts," 61–2.
22 Habib, *Black Lives*, 28. He concurs with Niebrzydowski, "The Sultana and Her Sisters," 188, 204. Macdougall, *James IV*, states without any evidence that this "black lady" was "presumably from Spain, like King James's Moorish drummers" (294). For more, see Levin, "Women in the Renaissance," who places this "black lady" in the broader context of slaves of Eastern European, African, and Native American origin in Western Europe from 1350 to 1600 (161–4).
23 Saunders, *A Social History*, 37. Zilfi, *Women and Slavery*, observes that, despite the ban in Islamic law on enslaving fellow Muslims, "many sub-Saharan African Muslims" were "swept up in the raids that enslaved their Christian and animist neighbors" (210).
24 Trimingham, *A History of Islam in West Africa*, 64; cf. 3, 28–9, 32–3, 142, 149, 152, 155, 160.
25 MacLean and Matar, *Britain and the Islamic World*, conclude their summary of Habib's findings in *Black Lives* with an assessment that accords with mine: "From between 1500 and 1677, there are records attesting to no fewer than 448 'Black lives' in the country; most if not all of them presumably Muslim" (20). They do not provide any sources for this claim nor do they mention Elen More; however, my separate argument, backed by an extended connected history, confirms that at least some of the individuals identified as "Black" in Scotland and England during this period were originally Muslim or at least from the Islamic world.
26 Vaughan, *Performing Blackness*, 93.
27 On Petir the More, see Habib, *Black Lives*, 28–9; on the christening of Margaret More and Elen More, see ibid., 31. Habib adds that the "two African friars or 'more freris'" who "first appear in the treasury records on 28 March 1508" may have come from the ancient Christian country of Ethiopia, which sent representatives to Western Europe during the fifteenth century (34–5). See also Saunders, *A Social History*, "Baptism and Slave Children" (90–2) and "Blacks and Christianity" (149–65).
28 Edwards, "The Early African Presence," argues that "[t]he impression given by the [Scottish] Lord Treasurer's Accounts of the life of the Black people at court in the early sixteenth century is one of benevolence, essentially no different from the treatment of other retainers at court, and certainly not one involving slavery" (20–1). Bawcutt, in her edition of *The Poems of William Dunbar*, concurs: "there is no evidence that they were

enslaved or badly treated" (2:350). For a similar assessment, see Habib, *Black Lives*, 5. By contrast, Kinsley, in his edition of *The Poems of William Dunbar*, references "negresses at court in 1504 and 1511–13 ... presumably enjoying in the royal service a benevolent form of the black slavery which became common and fashionable in southern Europe during the fifteenth century" (308). Citing Kinsley, Niebrzydowski, "The Sultana and Her Sisters," concludes: "the Africans had arrived in Edinburgh via being enslaved by the Portuguese and continued to be enslaved as the 'court curiosities'" (201).

29 Habib, *Black Lives*, 32–3; Andrea, "Black Skin, The Queen's Masques," 257–60.

30 I have modernized the following passages from the sixteenth-century chronicle of Robert Lindesay of Pitscottie, *The Historie and Cronicles of Scotland*: "the turnament of the black knicht and the black lady" (1:242); "the king iustit him selff dissaguysed onknawin and he was callit the blak knicht quha gave battell to all thame that wald fecht for thair ladyis saik and speciallie of the knichtis and gentilmen of france ingland and denmark" (1:243). Bawcutt, in her edition of *The Poems of William Dunbar*, considers this account "unreliable," as "it is by no means certain ... that James IV jousted in disguise, either as the Black Knight (Pittscottie) or the 'wyld knycht' (Leslie)" (2:351).

31 Paul, preface to *The Accounts*, 3:xlix. The Scotch "ell" equals 37.2 inches (*OED*). According to Measuring Worth.Com, "in 2010, the relative value of £88 0s 0d from 1507 ranges from £53,000.00 to £21,800,000.00."

32 Edwards, "The Early African Presence," 21, who also offers modern English glosses (21–2). For the poem in Middle Scots, see Dunbar, *The Poems*, ed. Bawcutt, 1:113. As Bawcutt clarifies, the colophon reads "Quod Dumbar of an blak moir."

33 On these terms, which are more nuanced than a modern translation suggests, see Dunbar, *The Poems*, ed. Bawcutt, 2:351–2; Niebrzydowski, "The Sultana and Her Sisters," 210n73; and Edwards, "The Early African Presence," 23, 27n42.

34 A "flyting" is "[a] verse contest in insults, practised in particular by the Scottish poets of the early 16th century but present in Old English and Old Norse literature. The most famous example is the 'Flyting of Dunbar and Kennedie'" (Birch and Hooper, *The Concise Oxford Companion*, 255). For the text of "The Flyting of Dunbar and Kennedie," see Dunbar, *The Poems*, ed. Kinsley, 76–95, 282–6. In this poem, "Turk" [Muslim] (line 522) and "Machomete" [Muhammad] (line 526) are terms of abuse.

35 Scott, *Dunbar*, provides an influential (if patronizing) assessment of the poem as representing "the cruel enslaving of a negress as an object of amusement"

and of its subject: "It needs little imagination to guess the inner feelings of this wretched creature torn out of her natural and proper environment where she might have fulfilled her life with some humanity and dignity, subjected to this type of treatment, and meeting God knows what kind of end" (69). Fleissner, "William Dunbar's Sultry Pre-Shakespearean Dark Lady," 90–1, critiques Scott, as does Edwards, "The Early African Presence," 22–3. Levin, "The Women in the Renaissance," 163–4, endorses Scott's reading. Niebrzydowski, "The Sultana and Her Sisters," 201–2, critiques Fleissner.

36 Habib, *Black Lives*, 31.

37 Niebrzydowski, "The Sultana and Her Sisters," presents a detailed genealogy of the term "Moor" as it emerged in "Middle English and late medieval Scottish vernaculars" (190–3). See also Saunders, *A Social History*, xiii.

38 Macdougall, *James IV*, 201. On the "Iberian and Andalusian black Moors" in "Catherine of Aragon's entourage," see Habib, *Black Lives*, 21, 27.

39 Hall, *The Lives of the Kings*, 1:15, 17. Specifically, two of the six ladies masqueraded as blackmoors (17). "[T]he lady Mary, syster unto the kyng," was one of the six ladies; it is not clear what costume she wore.

40 Andrea, "The Ghost of Leo Africanus," 200.

41 Loomba and Burton, introduction to *Race in Early Modern England*, 1. See also their discussion "Religion, Class, and Color" (12–16) and "Religious Conversion and Race" (16–17).

42 For other Tatars in sixteenth-century England, see Andrea, "Persia, Tartaria, and Pamphilia," 31–2, and Dimmock, "Converting and Not Converting 'Strangers,'" 458n4, 466.

43 Morgan and Coote, *Early Voyages*, 1:107–9; Hakluyt, *The Principal Navigations*, 1:305. Morgan and Coote's edition includes sources from Hakluyt and from "State documents" not included in Hakluyt (1:i). Meshkat, "The Journey of Master Anthony Jenkinson," cautions that Morgan, in particular, presents an unbalanced view of early modern Anglo-Russian relations as he was influenced by Anglo-Russian hostilities in Central Asia during the late nineteenth century (224–8).

44 Arnold, *Queen Elizabeth's Wardrobe*, 107; Andrea, "Elizabeth I and Persian Exchanges," 181–6.

45 Cf. Saunders, *A Social History*, who documents how in the sixteenth-century Portuguese court "[w]omen slaves in attendance upon the queen and the princesses were treated almost as if they were free maids of honour" (82).

46 Toledano, *Slavery and Abolition*, 7–13. For more, see Malieckal, "Slavery, Sex, and the Seraglio."

47 For the institutional role of the *valide sultan* ("mother of the sultan"), see Peirce, *The Imperial Harem*, 91–112. Lal, *Domesticity and Power*, emphasizes the differences between Ottoman, Safavid, and Mughal imperial harems (219–26).

48 On these *"faux* classical" names, see Habib, *Black Lives*, 99, 135, 244, 258.

49 Epstein, *Speaking of Slavery*, 25. For more on Tatar girls and Mediterranean slavery, see Wallace, *Premodern Places*, 188–90.

50 Arnold, *Queen Elizabeth's Wardrobe*, 107.

51 Jones and Stallybrass, *Renaissance Clothing*, 18, who record that Lady Cobham was one of "the Ladies and Gentleman of the Privy Chamber and Bedchamber," and among those who received "[t]he highest wages for women at court" (18).

52 Arnold, *Queen Elizabeth's Wardrobe*, 106–7. For more, see Van Den Berg, "Dwarf Aesthetics."

53 Arnold, *Queen Elizabeth's Wardrobe*, 107. In chapter 2, I discuss Ippolyta/ Ipolita's livery in terms of global exchange.

54 Tuan, *Dominance and Affection*, 139–41, 1.

55 Andrea, "Persia, Tartaria, and Pamphilia," 29–36. Weatherford, *Genghis Khan*, makes the same point for earlier centuries, citing Chaucer as his example (234, 239; cf. 254).

56 On the controversial "question of Temür's religious beliefs," see Manz, *The Rise and Rule*, 17–18.

57 On the intensifying denigration of the female "blackamoor" in seventeenth-century English drama, see Habib, "'Hel's Perfect Character.'" For a possible Persian (or perhaps two) by the name of "Jehan" living in London during the seventeenth century, see Habib, *Black Lives*, 255.

58 On the misleading translation of Persian diplomatic titles as "ambassador" in Western European sources, see Burton, "The Shah's Two Ambassadors," who focuses on Robert's elder brother, Anthony. Robert is described as an *"ilchi"* (translated as "an envoy and ambassador") in "the 'fiat' or 'farman' bearing the seals of 'Abbas I," on which see Chick, *A Chronicle*, 1:217. Mehdizadeh, "Translating Persia," further clarifies: "This position of 'ambassador' associated with Robert, and Anthony before him, carried a meaning that would imply social as well as geographical mobility for an English audience. The term, however, was a mistranslation of the Persian word *ilchi*, or 'messenger' – a post given to the most expendable of figures in the Persian court" (97).

59 For the subaltern status of Christians in the Safavid Empire, see Waterfield, *Christians in Persia*, 11–79. As a Roman Catholic, Teresa Sampsonia was also a religious minority in Protestant England. With respect to her subaltern

status as the wife of an Englishman, see Fisher, *Counterflows to Colonialism*, who makes the parallel observation that "British laws [of coverture] ... gave Indian men more control over property than they did to married British women – including to the British women that Indian men married. Thus, cultural constructions of gender often aligned Indian and British men of the same class against British women" (11).

60 Significant book-length studies devoted to the Sherley brothers include Ross, *Sir Anthony Sherley*; Penrose, *The Sherleian Odyssey*; and Davies, *Elizabethans Errant*. More recent studies include Hertel, "Ousting the Ottomans"; Subrahmanyam, *Three Ways to Be Alien*, 73–132; and Publicover, "Strangers at Home." Another important source is Masood, "From Cyrus to Abbas," 147–79.

61 Euben, *Journeys to the Other Shore*, 140.

62 Nezam-Mafi, "Persian Recreations," 24.

63 Herbert, *A Relation*, 124–5; Coryat, "A Letter," 593.

64 On these earlier efforts, see Flannery, *The Mission of the Portuguese Augustinians*.

65 Penrose reproduces this petition in *The Sherleian Odyssey*, 225–6. He also cites a letter "from Walsingham Gresley, a relative of [the] Sherleys, to Sir Thomas Pelman" (22 Jan. 1619) that attests to Lady Sherley's linguistic abilities: "She hath rather augmented than lost any of her English language, for she speaks it very well" (204–5). For an analysis of this petition, see Andrea, "The Tartar Girl, The Persian Princess," 270.

66 These are reproduced in Canby, *Shah 'Abbas*, 56–7, 59, and discussed in Arthur, "'You will say they are Persian." On travel narratives and visual evidence, see Brentjes, "Immediacy, Mediation, and Media."

67 As Nashat emphasizes in the introduction to *Women in Iran*, cultural norms discouraged mentioning even the most highly placed women in official documents from pre-modern Iran. For a productive meditation on terminology ("Persia or Iran"), see Mehdizadeh, "Translating Persia," 169-74.

68 Chick, *A Chronicle*, 1:144. Lockhart, "European Contacts," follows this source in identifying Teresa as "the daughter of a Christian Circassian named Isma'il Khan, who was said to have been a relative of one of the shah's wives" (390). On the name Sampsonia (Sanphluf), see Nocentelli, "Teresa."

69 Herbert, *Some Years Travels*, 213.

70 Herbert, *A Relation*, 125.

71 Natho, *Circassian History*, 17, 19.

72 Shami, "Circassians," 599.

73 Jaimoukha, *The Circassians*, 12.

74 On Hakluyt's republication of these medieval accounts, see Andrea, "Persia, Tartaria, and Pamphilia," 31–2, and "The Tartar Girl, The Persian

Princess," 266–7. For a collection of these accounts, see Beazley, *The Texts and Versions*. For an astute analysis, see Bridges, "The Reinvention of the Medieval Traveller," who mentions a few British women who travelled to the East, and specifically to Jerusalem, during late antiquity and the medieval crusading period.

75 Jaimoukha, *The Circassians*, 12, 168–9. For more on Circassians under the Safavids, see Manz and Handeda, "Čarkas [Circassians]."

76 Chick, *A Chronicle*, 1:143.

77 Chick, *A Chronicle*, 1:144.

78 Specifically, "in order to have it [his annual pension from the shah] unencumbered, as the Persians have it, he had himself enrolled as a 'slave' of the king" (Chick, *A Chronicle*, 1:144). For more, see Peirce, "An Imperial Caste," and Babaie et al., *Slaves of the Shah*, 20–48.

79 Herbert, *Some Years Travels*, 213; Chick, *A Chronicle*, 1:143, 145.

80 Jaimoukha, *The Circassians*, 149. For more on this layering of religious cultures, see Natho, *Circassian History*, 112–25.

81 Chick, *A Chronicle*, 1:293. For details, see Andrea, "The Cultural Biography."

82 For a record of Teresa's baptism, see Chick, *A Chronicle*, 1:145. After stating "[t]hat she was baptized by the Carmelites on 2.2.1608 is a definite fact," Chick wonders, "had she not been baptized by Orthodox rite in Circassia, then?" (291n2). To clarify, the Catholic Church prohibits re-baptism as per the *Code of Canon Law*, Canon 84.1, which provokes questions about whether Teresa Sampsonia was a Muslim prior to her conversion to Roman Catholicism. Provisions are listed for conditional baptism if the validity of the first is in doubt, on which see Canon 869.1.

83 Nixon, *The Three English Brothers*, sig. K4.

84 Chick, *A Chronicle*, 1:144.

85 Matthee, "Christians in Safavid Iran," 15.

86 Butler, in his edition of Herbert's 1677 *Travels*, 475n950. As he elaborates, "Tzarievna Marta" was the "daughter of Davit I, King of Kakheti (r. 1603–1604). Abbas married her in 1604 and they were divorced in 1614" (403n642). Cf. Szuppe, "Status, Knowledge, and Politics," on the Safavid princess "Pari-Khan Khanum II, whose mother was a Circassian" (153).

87 Peirce, *The Imperial Harem*, 139.

88 Nixon, *The Three English Brothers*, asserts that Robert and Teresa had two children in Persia prior to their trip to England (sig. K4v). However, the couple left for this journey the day after they were married (Chick, *A Chronicle*, 1:144), which makes the birth of prior children highly unlikely. Penrose, *The Sherleian Odyssey*, characterizes Nixon as an "unreliable writer" (167).

89 Chick, *A Chronicle*, 1:145.
90 Canby, *Shah 'Abbas*, 57n2, citing "[p]ersonal communication with Edward Faridany." Canby posits that the "jewelled pistol in her right hand and watch in her left ... may be allusions to Robert's role in advancing the import of European technology to Iran."
91 On the matriarchal roots of Circassian culture, see Jaimoukha, *The Circassians*, 164–6; celebrated female warriors include Tirghetau from the 4th century BCE and Lashin from the 13th century CE (44, 48–9).
92 Chick, *A Chronicle*, 1:291. Another possibility is that Robert was poisoned.
93 Herbert, *Some Years Travels*, 213.
94 Chick, *A Chronicle*, 1:292.
95 Compare the similar devotion the traveler Pietro della Valle expressed for his Chaldean wife, Ma'ani, who died in Persia in 1621. He carried her remains with him until he returned to Rome in 1626 (Chick, *A Chronicle*, 1:290). For more, see Baskins, "Lost in Translation." For the example of Sir Thomas Glover, the English ambassador to the Ottoman Empire who preserved his wife's remains and transported them to London around the same time, see MacLean, *The Rise of Oriental Travel*, 222–3.
96 Davies, *Elizabethans Errant*, between pages 174 and 175, with English translations.
97 Natho, *Circassian History*, 25, 104.
98 For an astute study of gender and space in relation to this titular church, see Jones, "Envisioning a Global Environment."
99 Davis, *Women on the Margins*, 210.
100 Davis, *Trickster Travels*, 4. Davis refers to "Leo Africanus" (his Latinate moniker) as "al-Hasan al-Wazzan" before his baptism in Rome and "Yuhanna al-Asad" (John the Lion or John Leo) afterwards (65).
101 Davis, *Trickster Travels*, 11.
102 As Fisher, *Counterflows to Colonialism*, specifies, "[i]n order to marry legally" in Britain, men from India "had to be Christians, or convert – at least nominally – to Christianity" (11). Moreover, "[f]ar more Muslims than Hindus went to Britain" between 1600 and 1857 (4; cf. 12); "[o]verall, many more Indian men than women entered Britain" (10). The few Indian women who travelled to Britain during this period were either Eastern Christians, like Mariam Khanim, or converted to Christianity (10; cf. 45–6).
103 Davis, *Trickster Travels*, 109–16, 188–90. For a related argument, see Andrea, "Assimilation or Dissimulation?"
104 Habib, "Reading Black Women Characters," 72, 74. He refers to *the persistent but spectral evidence* of African women maintained in Scotland in the court of James IV" (69; emphasis added).

105 Fradenburg, *City, Marriage, Tournament*, xiv.
106 Arnold, *Queen Elizabeth's Wardrobe*, 107; Morgan and Coote, *Early Voyages*, 1:58, from "The voyage of M. Anthony Jenkinson." Jenkinson claims he deferred purchasing a Tartar child, as he "had more need of victualles ["food or provisions of any kind" (*OED*)] at that time then of any such merchandize" (58); however, he likely purchased the "Tartar girl" for Queen Elizabeth under similar circumstances.
107 Loades, *Elizabeth I*, 316.
108 Palmer, *An Essay*, 16. Palmer lists women in general – along with "Infants," "Decrepite persons," "Fooles," "Madmen," and "Lunaticke" – under "*What persons* are inhibited travaile" or prohibited from travelling (sig. A4v). In an earlier and equally influential treatise, Turler intones that "the wide wandering of Weemen cannot want [lack] suspition, & bringeth some toke[n] of dishonestie. Whereupon the Tragicall and Comicall Poets, when they bringe in any far *traueiling Woman*, for the most parte they feine [fashion, form, shape] her to be incontinent [unchaste]" (*The Traveiler*, 9).

2. The Islamic World and the Construction of Early Modern Englishwomen's Authorship: Queen Elizabeth I, the Tartar Girl, and the Tartar-Indian Woman

1 On Elizabeth as "'king' or 'prince'" and "virgin queen," see Duncan, "The Two Virgin Queens," 78. On Queen Elizabeth's written corpus, see Bell, *Elizabeth I*, 8. Bell cites May, who in his edition, *Queen Elizabeth I*, states that the queen "qualifies as the most prolific author among English sovereigns since the reign of King Alfred" (xx). Harrison, in his edition of *The Letters of Queen Elizabeth*, persuasively argues for the queen's authorship of state letters, whether she personally penned them, dictated them to her secretaries, or reviewed them for her final signature (ix–x). As Allinson adds in *A Monarchy of Letters*, "authority and authorship had become inextricably linked in European court culture by the mid-to-late sixteenth century" (17), with specific gendered implications for Elizabeth (12–16, 17–35). Quilligan, *Incest and Agency*, addresses early modern women's negotiation of authorship and authority with specific reference to Elizabeth I (33–75) and Mary Wroth (164–212). For more on female authorship in early modern England, see Wall, *The Imprint of Gender*, 279–340.
2 Burton, *Traffic and Turning*, 15.

3 On the contentious issue of terminology for the First Peoples (aboriginal, indigenous, native) of the Americas, see Forte, "Introduction: 'Who is an Indian?'" and Patrick, "Inuitness and Territoriality in Canada." The term Inuit (sing. Inuk) applies to the First Peoples of the Arctic regions Frobisher explored, who view the term "Eskimo" negatively; for details, see Steckley, *White Lies*, 9, 19–21, 23.

4 Hendricks, "Feminist Historiography," 374.

5 On the "inoculating critique of its own blindspot so as to allow business to proceed as usual ... in contemporary political [and literary] criticism," see Callaghan, "Re-Reading," 163, who cites Modeleski, *Feminism without Women*, 6. For more, see Callaghan, *The Impact of Feminism*, 1–29.

6 In addition to Queen Elizabeth's and Mary Wroth's groundbreaking achievements, the era also saw the first original tragedy published by an Englishwoman: Cary's *The Tragedie of Mariam, the Faire Queene of Jewry*, which can be found in Weller and Ferguson's modern edition. On "Allegories of Imperial Subjection" in Cary's play, see Ferguson, *Dido's Daughters*, 265–332.

7 Hakluyt, *The Principal Navigations*, citing title page. Hakluyt's collection (first and second editions) features Queen Elizabeth's correspondence with Muslim sovereigns including "the Great Turk [Sultan Murad III]" (1589: 163–6, 171, 183–4, 199–200; 1599: vol. 1, 418; vol. 2, 137–40, 145–6, 158–9, 191–2); "the king of Cambaia [Alauddin Riayat Shah, Sultan of Aceh]" (1589: 207; 1599: vol. 2, 245); "the Emperour of Marocco [Ahmad I al-Mansur, Sultan of Morocco]" (1589: 239; 1599: vol. 2, 119–20); and "the great Sophie of Persia [Shah Tahmasp I]" (1589: 361–2; 1599: vol. 1, 340–1). For an analysis of "A letter written by the most high and mighty Empresse the wife of the Grand Signor *Sultan Murad Can* to the Queenes Majesty of *England*, in the year of our Lord, 1594" (1599: vol. 2, 311–12), see Andrea, *Women and Islam*, 20–9; for the letters to the Russian tsar and the Persian shah, see Andrea, "Elizabeth I and Persian Exchanges," 171–4, an analysis I expand upon here.

8 Jardine and Brotton, *Global Interests*, 54, 47–8. For important studies of Queen Elizabeth's strategies of self-representation, which nevertheless fail to take into account her interactions with various Muslim rulers, see Montrose, *The Subject of Elizabeth*; Hopkins, *Writing Renaissance Queens*; and Frye, *Elizabeth I.*

9 On the Muscovy Company, see 136n43 and 141n11 above. On the Levant Company, see Epstein, *The Early History*; Wood, *A History*; and Vitkus, "'The Common Market.'"

10 According to Strong, *Gloriana*, during Edward VI's reign Elizabeth was seen as "a slip of a girl, whose future role was to be the King's sister and

who would certainly be expected to marry a foreign prince" (9). She continued to be seen as such until her elder sister Mary's false pregnancy became certain and death imminent; on this relationship, see Loades, *Mary Tudor*, 274–314, and Duncan, *Mary I*, 165–82.

On the significance of Ivan's contested title, see Madariaga, *Ivan the Terrible*, 49–50, 98. For an astute analysis, see Bertolet, "The Tsar and the Queen."

11 "The newe Navigation and discoverie of the kingdome of *Muscovia, by the Northeast, in the yeere 1553: Enterprised* by Sir Hugh Willoughbie knight, and perfourmed by Richard Chanceler, Pilot major of the voyage. Translated out of the former Latine into English," in Hakluyt, *The Principall Navigations*, 280–92, citing 280. For a modernized version, see Berry and Crummey, *Rude and Barbarous Kingdom*, 3–41. They establish that "[t]he version of the work in this collection is the creation of two men, Chancellor and Clement Adams" (4). An important earlier source is Willes, "For. M. Cap. Furbyshers Passage by the Northwest." For more, see Arber, *The First Three English Books on America*, esp. the section "Of Moscovy, Cathay, and the Northern Regions, 1550–1555," 281–334.

12 Morgan and Coote, *Early Voyages*, 1:ii.

13 Willan, *The Early History*, 6.

14 For details, see "The voyage, wherein Osepp Napea, the Moscovite Ambassadour, returned home into his Countrey, with his entertainment at his arrival, at Colmogro; and a large description of the manners of the Countrey," in Hakluyt, *The Principall Navigations*, 338–47 and Morgan and Coote, *Early Voyages*, 2:355–77. Madariaga, *Ivan the Terrible*, refers to Napea as "a Russian envoy," not an ambassador (126). Variants of his first name, which Morgan and Coote transliterate as "Joseph" (1:26n1), include Osep and Osip. They proffer that Napea or Nepeya could be a variation of "Napier" and broach "the possibility of his having been Scotch by origin" (1:125n).

15 For the Protestant view that Elizabeth was "miraculously raised to the throne by the direct hand of Providence," see MacCaffrey, *Queen Elizabeth*, 31. MacCaffrey lists among the "high-placed patrons at court" of the more militant Protestant faction Lord Robert Dudley, Earl of Leicester, and Sir Francis Walsingham (56), both of whom were actively involved with this trade. For details, see Willan, *The Early History*, 155–6, 201–2 (on Leicester) and 201–5 (on Walsingham).

16 Hakluyt, *The Principall Navigations*, 82; Morgan and Coote, *Early Voyages*, 1:5–6.

17 Hakluyt, *The Principall Navigations*, 332; Morgan and Coote, *Early Voyages*, 1:7. For more on the correspondence between Ivan and Elizabeth, see Allinson, *A Monarchy of Letters*, 111–29.

18 Morgan and Coote, *Early Voyages*, 1:cxiv–cxv. On Jenkinson's famous map, see Wilson, "Visible Bullets, 51, 54.

19 In October 1562, Jenkinson arrived at Qazvin (Morgan and Coote, *Early Voyages*, 1:xxxn1), where Shah Tahmasp I had moved his capital "in the aftermath of the humiliating Amasya 1555 treaty with the Ottomans" (Newman, *Safavid Iran*, 32).

20 Morgan and Coote, *Early Voyages*, 2:343, from "The names of such countries as I, Anthonie Jenkinson, have travelled unto, from the second of October 1546, at which time I made my first voyage out of England, untill the yeere of our Lord 1572, when I returned last out of Russia." Jenkinson's Russian expeditions (round trips from London and back) ran from 1558 to 1560 (when he travelled as far as Bukhara), 1561 to 1564 (when he travelled as far as Qazvin), 1566 to 1567, and 1570 to 1572.

21 Hakluyt, *The Principall Navigations*, sig. *4v; Hakluyt, *The Principal Navigations*, sig. *4v.

22 Fuller, *Voyages in Print*, 158. In high imperial style, Froude writes in "England's Forgotten Worthies" that "those five volumes [published by the newly formed Hakluyt Society in 1811] may be called Prose Epic of the modern English nation" (361). For more, see Bridges, "The Legacy of Richard Hakluyt."

23 MacLean, "East by North-east," 168; Warner, *Albions England*, 282. This is the sixth successively enlarged edition, the others being issued in 1586, 1589, 1592, 1596, and 1597; a "continuance" was published in 1606. Wagner died in 1609; a posthumous edition was published in 1612. Morgan and Coote, *Early Voyages*, 1:cxlix–clii, include chapters 66 and 68.

24 Warner, *Albions England*, 283, 282; Morgan and Coote, *Early Voyages*, 1:cl.

25 Warner, *Albions England*, 283, 287; Morgan and Coote, *Early Voyages*, 1:cl, cli.

26 Hakluyt, *The Principall Navigations*, 365; the full title continues: "alias, Hircanum, sent and imployed therein by the right worshipfull Societie of the Merchants Adventurers, for the discoverie of Lands, Islands, &c. Being begunne the foureteenth day of May, Ann[o]. 1561: and in the third yeere of the raigne of the Queenes Majestie that now is: this present declaration being directed and written to the foresayd Societie."

27 Hakluyt, *The Principall Navigations*, 368; Morgan and Coote, *Early Voyages*, 1:134. As Burton details in *The Bukharans*, Abdullah Khan [Abdullah II, r. 1551–98] captured Bukhara in 1557 (8–16); for his encounter with Jenkinson, see ibid., 13–14; cf. 5–6.

28 Peirce, *The Imperial Harem*, 113–49.
29 Szuppe, "Status, Knowledge, and Politics," 142.
30 Grosrichard, *The Sultan's Court*, 146, 143. In this section, "The Women," or "Ladies of the seraglio" (141–6), Grosrichard adduces late seventeenth-century French travellers to "the Orient," including Jean Chardin (1643–1713) and Antoine Galland (1646–1715), whose works (a travelogue and a French translation of the *1001 Nights*, respectively) were immediately translated into English. The elements in these narratives were anticipated by earlier masculinist fantasies, to which I would add Warner's, even though England (and France) were marginal powers vis-à-vis the Islamic empires of the sixteenth century. For feminist perspectives, see Booth, *Harem Histories*.
31 Warner, *Albions England*, 283; Morgan and Coote, *Early Voyages*, 1:cl.
32 Cohen, introduction to *Antony and Cleopatra*, in *The Norton Shakespeare*, 2621; Warner, *Albions England*, 283; Morgan and Coote, *Early Voyages*, 1:cl.
33 Bell, *Elizabeth I*, 86; for some of the sexual slanders the queen faced, see ibid., 81–2.
34 Warner, *Albions England*, 289; Morgan and Coote, *Early Voyages*, 1:clii.
35 Hakluyt, *The Principall Navigations*, 361–2; Morgan and Coote, *Early Voyages*, 1:112–14. As Morgan and Coote explain in *Early Voyages*, "Sophi, Sufi or Safi was a philosophy [more precisely, a theory and practice of Islamic mysticism], and became the surname of a dynasty of Persian monarchs, who adopted the tenets of the 'Sufi'" (1:112n1). On the Sufi origins of the Safavid dynasty, see Savory, *Iran under the Safavids*, 1–26. Although Jenkinson uses this term, "the Sophie of *Persia*," throughout his account of his first journey to the Persian court (1:130), by 1566 the English merchants consistently use the correct title "Shaugh" [Shah] in their accounts, though they still transcribed Tahmasp's name as "Thomas" (2:387).
36 Hakluyt, *The Principall Navigations*, 362; Morgan and Coote, *Early Voyages*, 1:112–13.
37 For the Uzbek threat, see Newman, *Safavid Iran*, 26–7.
38 Hakluyt, *The Principall Navigations*, 362; Morgan and Coote, *Early Voyages*, 1:114. Nonetheless, by the late 1560s through the late 1570s "Londro, meaning thereby London" and its "mayden Queene" were well known at the Safavid court (2:415, 454).
39 Lithgow, *A Most Delectable and True Discourse*, sig. N3. For more on Lithgow, see Bosworth, *An Intrepid Scot*. Biddulph, in *The Travels of certaine Englishmen* also discusses "those whom they call Franks or Free-men" (82–5). For more on Biddulph, see MacLean, *The Rise of Oriental Travel*,

49–114. Timberlake, in *A True and strange discourse*, corroborates the status of the English as *personae non grata*, as when he was barred from entering Jerusalem because he insisted on identifying himself as a (Protestant) Englishman, "for the Turkes flatly denied, that they had ever heard either of my Queene or Countrey, or that she paied them any tribute" (6).

40 Hakluyt, *The Principall Navigations*, 362; Morgan and Coote, *Early Voyages*, 1:113. For the second letter to Shah Tahmasp, issued in 1579, see Hakluyt, *The Principal Navigations*, 1:418.

41 Hakluyt, *The Principall Navigations*, 370–1; Morgan and Coote, *Early Voyages*, 1:145–7. For a description of this custom from the English merchants who voyaged in the region from 1568 to 1574, see Morgan and Coote, *Early Voyages*, 2:433. Matthee, "Christians in Safavid Iran," conveys the Carmelite missionaries' view that "Muslim Iranians in general abhorred Christians and were inclined to shun anyone other than Shi 'i Muslims as ritually unclean (*najes*)" (16). As Blow, *Shah Abbas*, points out, "Tahmasp was a more orthodox Shi'a than his father ... anxious to observe Islamic law ... and issued two Edicts of Repentance in which he attempted to ban all practices considered sinful or contrary to Islamic law" (12).

42 Hakluyt, *The Principall Navigations*, 371; Morgan and Coote, *Early Voyages*, 1:148.

43 Cf. Arthur Edwards's welcome in Shah Tahmasp's court four years later, where he secured trading privileges for the English merchant company in Safavid territories, on which see Morgan and Coote, *Early Voyages*, 2:393–402.

44 "The answere of her Majestie to the aforesaid Letters of the Great Turke, sent the 25 of October 1579, in the Prudence of *London* by Master *Richard Stanley*," in Hakluyt, *The Principal Navigations*, 2:138–40. For more, see Allinson, *A Monarchy of Letters*, 130–50; Andrea, *Women and Islam*, 23–4; and Burton, *Traffic and Turning*, 57–68.

45 Hakluyt, *The Principal Navigations*, 2:139.

46 Andrea, *Women and Islam*, 20–9.

47 On cloth as central to the early Anglo-Russian trade, see Foster, *England's Quest*, 5–6; Willan, *The Early History*, 2–3. On the trade in human chattel, see Hellie, *Slavery in Russia*, who identifies "a Russian slave in England in 1569," who "could have been a Russian, a Tatar, a Finn, a Pole, or a member of any of several other ethnicities" (22n32).

48 Palmer, *Writing Russia*, 52.

49 Andrea, "Elizabeth I and Persian Exchanges," 177–81. Mignolo addresses each end of our current era of globalization in *The Darker Side of the Renaissance* and *Local Histories/Global Designs*, respectively. *The Darker Side*

of Western Modernity is the final volume in this triology. Also relevant is Tlostanova and Mignolo, *Learning to Unlearn*.

50 Palmer, *Writing Russia*, 70n94; Morton, *The Jenkinson Story*, 40; Morgan and Coote, *Early Voyages*, 1:52, drawing on "The voyage of M. Anthony Jenkinson, made from the citie of Mosco in Russia, to the citie of Boghar in Bactria, in the yere 1558: written by himself to the Merchants of London of the Moscovie companie," in Hakluyt, *The Principall Navigations*, 347–59. *Pace* Palmer, Morton's study offers a useful, if anecdotal, account of Jenkinson's entire life, adding to Morgan and Coote's narrower focus in *Early Voyages* on his northern career.

51 Morton, *The Jenkinson Story*, 41; Morgan and Coote, *Early Voyages*, 1:58.

52 Morton, *The Jenkinson Story*, 41. The *OED* records several definitions for "wench" current in Jenkinson's era: "a girl, maid, young woman; a female child"; "a girl of the rustic or working class"; "a wanton woman; a mistress." It could also serve as a term of endearment, which seems unlikely in this context.

53 Palmer, *Writing Russia*, xiv.

54 Morton, *Jenkinson Story*, 55.

55 Loades, *Elizabeth I*, 311, 316.

56 Jardine and Brotton, *Global Interests*, 133.

57 Loades, *Elizabeth I*, 316.

58 Loades, *Elizabeth I*, 311.

59 Arnold, *Queen Elizabeth's Wardrobe*, 107, with the first citation from the "warrant dormant." A "warrant dormant" is "one drawn out in blank to be filled up with a name or particulars, when required to be used" (*OED*, s.v. "dormant," 2b). On human "pets," see 138n60 above.

60 Arnold, *Queen Elizabeth's Wardrobe*, 107. The first item refers to "[a] linen fabric, originally called, from the province of Holland in the Netherlands, Holland cloth" (*OED*). On the latter two items, deemed particularly luxurious, see Jardine and Brotton, *Global Interests*, 83.

61 Arnold, *Queen Elizabeth's Wardrobe*, 214.

62 Strong, "'My Weepinge Stagg I Crowne,'" 106. Strong acknowledges Yates's earlier association of the painting with "Boissard's *Virgo Persica* in his *Habitus Variarum orbis Gentium*" (106), which she elaborates in *Astraea* (221). Strong, *Gloriana*, also points out Elizabeth's practice of wearing "dresses of the different nations," which in his view reflected "political alignment" rather than cultural appropriation (21). The cover of Andrea, *Women and Islam*, features this portrait.

63 As Moss proposes, "Strong's recent argument for Walsingham [i.e., Frances Walsingham, wife of the Earl of Essex, as the subject of the

portrait] is intriguing but barring additional evidence, it seems prudent
for her to remain 'An Unknown Woman,' which is the title by which
the painting is currently displayed." I thank Professor Moss for sharing
his conference paper, "'Are you now or have you ever been Queen of
England?'" For another reading of the portrait, see Brown, "A New Fable
of the Belly." See also Laoutaris and Arshad's forthcoming study, "'Still
renewing wronges.'"

64 For an overview, see Matthee, *The Politics of Trade in Safavid Iran*.

65 On the trade of English cloth to Russia into Persia, see Morgan and Coote,
Early Voyages, 1:115. For the trade of Persia silk, spices, and drugs back to
England, see ibid., 1:136. When efforts to establish Anglo-Persian trade
resumed in the first decades of the seventeenth century – this time through
the southern route via India – its focus remained "the hope of exchanging
English woolens for raw silk, which was much in demand in London,
owing to the efforts that were being made, under the patronage of King
James, to promote the silk-weaving industry" (Foster, *England's Quest*, 295).

66 Arnold, *Queen Elizabeth's Wardrobe*, 34.

67 Singh, "Introduction: The Global Renaissance," 1, citing Hearn, *Dynasties*.
The passage in Hearn continues: "indicating England's domination of
the seas and plans for imperialist expansion in the New World"; she
goes on to clarify that "[i]n terms of long-term damage to the Spanish
the destruction of the Armada actually achieved little, but at the time it
was fêted both by the English and the Dutch as a significant victory" (88).
Strong, *Gloriana*, marks 1579 as a benchmark in portraiture of Elizabeth,
"when the imperialistic and maritime aspirations of the *magus* Dr John
Dee were taken up by the government" (41). Prior portraits cannot be
seen as "vehicle[s] for native imperial aspirations. Those came only in
1579 in George Gower's awkward presentation of Elizabeth as a Roman
Vestal to whom, for the first time, the globe is given as an attribute" (42).
As such, "The portraits produced during this period [post-1579] take on
an impenetrable mask which looks back across the centuries to the holy
countenance of majesty of the Byzantine and the medieval emperors and
shares with them a common debt to sacred imperialism" (42–3).

68 Hodgson, *Rethinking World History*, 26; Jardine and Brotton, *Global Interests*, 54.

69 Goffman, *The Ottoman Empire and Early Modern Europe*, 8. For more, see
Skilliter, *William Harborne and the Trade with Turkey*.

70 Vizenor, *Native Liberty*, 24.

71 For primary sources on the Frobisher voyages, see Stefansson, *The Three
Voyages*, and Collinson, *The Three Voyages*. For archival, archeological,
and ethnographical research, see Alsford, *The Meta Incognita Project*, and

Symons, *Meta Incognita*. For a new historicist analysis of Frobisher's voyages focusing on "the issues of representation, exchange, and captivity," see Greenblatt, *Marvelous Possessions*, 109–18.

72 The first published text promoting the northwest route – Gilbert's *A Discourse of a Discoverie* – uses Columbus as a touchstone in an opening sonnet and in the closing argument. On Gilbert, see Probasco, "Cartography as a Tool" and "Sir Humphrey Gilbert." See also Regard, *The Quest for the Northwest Passage*, esp. Fuller, "Arctics of Empire"; Niayesh, "From Myth to Appropriation"; and Lemercier-Goddard, "George Best's Arctic Mirrors."

73 Sherman, *John Dee*, calls these voyages "the Cathay Campaign" (xiv, 172); see also Sherman, "John Dee's Role."

74 As Symons stresses in "The Significance," this northwest venture, while "a costly failure" in terms of resource extraction and a "false start" in terms of colonization, significantly impacted "England's awakening interest in an empire in North America" (1:xxi, xxvi). For the prior northeast venture, see Foster, *England's Quest*, 3–56.

75 For a list that includes the female investors in Frobisher's voyages, see Collinson, *The Three Voyages*, 164–5. For details, see McDermott, "The Company of Cathay," 157–65. Two English women were charter members of the Muscovy/Russia Company, on which see Willan, *The Muscovy Merchants*, 10.

76 Cheshire et al., "Frobisher's Eskimos," 24; English sources state that "the boy's name was 'Nutioc' and that he was aged about fourteen or fifteen months" (30). As Sturtevant and Quinn, "This New Prey," indicate, "[t]he first Eskimos who can be securely documented in Europe were brought to Zeeland [in the Netherlands] in 1567: a woman and child kidnapped some months earlier by French sailors, evidently in Labrador," displayed in "the Mill inn in the Hague," whose owners "charged admission" (61); their images circulated in several broadsides (65). For more, see Seaver, "How Strange is a Stranger?"

Callaghan, in her influential study *Shakespeare without Women*, perpetuates the false story that the Inuit boy was born in England (75). She cites Mullaney, *The Place of the Stage*, 65, who relies on faulty secondary sources rather than primary sources in making this claim.

77 For the designation "New World" or "American" natives for these captives, see Vaughan, *Transatlantic Encounters*, 1, 10.

78 For a revisionist history, see Gómez, *The Tropics of Empire*.

79 Sturtevant and Quinn, "This New Prey," 68.

80 For the definition of "catachresis" as "abuse or perversion of a trope or metaphor," see Spivak, *A Critique*, 14. For more, see 138n67.

81 Churchyard, *A Discourse*, sig. A4; Lyne, "Churchyard," 688. See also Oakley-Brown, "Churchyard," and "Taxonomies of Travel." For a book-length biography, see Woodcock, *Thomas Churchyard*.

82 For the first two titles, see Churchyard, *A Discourse*, sigs. B3 and H2. "A Prayse, and Reporte of Maister Martyne Forboishers [*sic*] Voyage to Meta Incognita," gathered with the other two in the Huntington Library volume I examined, was also published as a separate tract. On Queen Elizabeth's travels within England, see Cole, *The Portable Queen*. See also McRae, *Literature and Domestic Travel*, on Queen Elizabeth's progresses (145–73) and Churchyard's role as a "deviser" of these entertainments (154–5, 157–61). For more on "Elizabeth I and Travel Writing," see Jowitt, *Voyage Drama and Gender Politics*, 15–60.

83 Churchyard, *A Discourse*, sig. A4.

84 Arnold, *Queen Elizabeth's Wardrobe*, 107.

85 Stefansson, *Three Voyages*, 2:235–6. Variations on the woman's name include "Egnoge" (ibid., 2:235), "Egnock" (Cheshire et al., "Frobisher's Eskimos," 38), and "Arnaq" (Sturtevant and Quinn, "This New Prey," 84). Cf. Forbes, *The American Discovery of Europe*, who mentions "three Greenlanders called Calitgoch, his wife Egnocth, and child Nutiocth" whose kayaks were driven onto the shore of Holland in 1577 (81). For Inuit practices of naming and their significance, see Bennett and Rowley, *Uqalurait*, 3–10.

86 On the Inuit oral history related to the Frobisher voyages, as recorded by American Arctic explorer Charles Francis Hall during his first Arctic expedition on Baffin Island (1860–63), see Stefansson, *Three Voyages*, 2:240–7; for a connection to twentieth-century Inuit communities, see Rowley, "Inuit Oral History," and "Frobisher Miksanut." For the indispensability of oral narratives as a source for early English encounters with the natives of the Americas, see Kupperman, *Indians and English*, 1–15. For the importance of reading "a broad range of colonial documentation" for "native conceptions and metaphors" embedded therein, see Whitehead, introduction to Ralegh, *The Discoverie*, 26. For "an attempt to tell the story of the Roanoke ventures from the perspective of the Indians who confronted and attempted to make sense of Sir Walter's colonists," see Oberg, *The Head in Edward Nugent's Hand*, xii, and Caison, "Looking for Loss."

87 McRae, *Literature and Domestic Travel*, 14. For the broader critical debate about "what *counts as travel*" (44), with particular attention to whether "coerced journeys" should be included in this category (55), see Buzard, "What Isn't Travel?"

88 Loomba and Burton, introduction to *Race in Early Modern England*, 1.
On George Best's narrative of the Frobisher voyages, see ibid., 5, 15, 23;
for a selection from his treatise, see ibid., 108–10. For more on Best, see
Householder, *Inventing Americans*, 79–104; Brown, "Native Americans
and Early Modern Concepts of Race," 84–5, 94, 97; and Smith, "'For They
Are Naturally Born.'"

89 Elsner and Rubiés, *Voyages and Visions*, 7. For a related approach, see
Sherman, "Strirrings and Searchings," 17–36. For a more detailed
discussion, see Andrea, "'Travelling Bodyes,'" 138–42.

90 Elsner and Rubiés, *Voyages and Visions*, 8–9.

91 Cheshire et al., "Frobisher's Eskimos," 50. For the Renaissance
recuperation of Jason "to lend mythic aura to the discoverers of America,"
see Peyré, "Marlowe's Argonauts," 106.

92 Elsner and Rubiés, *Voyages and Visions*, 17–20.

93 Elsner and Rubiés, *Voyages and Visions*, 7. For a broader view, see Parker,
Global Interactions, 110–45. For local instances, see Fumerton, *Unsettled*,
and Woodbridge, *Vagrancy*.

94 Cheshire et al., "Frobisher's Eskimos," 42, 49n17, citing "Doctor Doddyngs
Report." For the Latin original, see Collinson, *Three Voyages*, 189–91.

95 Cheshire et al., "Frobisher's Eskimos," 41, citing "Doctor Doddyngs
Report." Watt and Savours, "The Captured 'Countrey People,'" 2:559. The
captives arrived in England "about" 1 October 1577 (Stefansson, *Three
Voyages*, cxv); the man was buried in Bristol on 8 November 1577, dying
from the injuries sustained during his capture; the woman was buried in
Bristol on 13 November 1577; the child died in London shortly thereafter
and was buried at St Olave Hart Street (Watt and Savours 560–1; Thrush,
Indigenous London, 222–5).

96 Cheshire et al., "Frobisher's Eskimos," 41; "a second time" refers "to the
fact that the previous Eskimo man, brought back on the 1576 expedition,
had also perished before he could be exhibited at court" (48n11).

97 Cheshire et al., "Frobisher's Eskimos," explains that "[t]he child is
referred to as 'him' because the information that it was a boy is contained
in one of the two other surviving references" (30).

98 Kupperman, *Indians and English*, x.

99 Said, *Culture and Imperialism*, 51 (emphasis in original).

100 For a facsimile edition that includes these illustrations, see Harriot, *A
Briefe and True Report of the New Found Land of Virginia: The Complete 1590
Edition*.

101 Mignolo, *Local Histories/Global Designs*, 58–9, 105; for more, see ibid., 13,
20–1, 93–111, 327–30. For a related study, which nevertheless does not

acknowledge Mignolo and the Latin American theorists he cites, see Makdisi, *Making England Western: Occidentalism, Race, and Imperial Culture*. Makdisi develops the claim that "England at the turn of the nineteenth century was not Western" in the sense of "opposed to the East," which he defines as "a cultural or civilizational opposition framed along a very specific moral and temporal or developmental matrix" that "was still very much in the process of formation" (xii). He designates "the set of cultural and political discourses underlying and sustaining the emergence of this new conception of the West as Occidentalism" (xiii). Makdisi therefore shares with Mignolo a critique of the transhistorical dichotomy between East and West, with "the West" always already dominant, that subtends Said's model.

102　Mignolo, *Local Histories/Global Designs*, 327. Mignolo goes on to explain that "Occidentalism ... is the overarching geopolitical imaginary of the modern/colonial world system, to which Orientalism was appended in its first radical transformation, when the center of the system moved from the Iberian Peninsula to the North Sea, between Holland and Britain" (59). Hence, "without Occidentalism, there is no Orientalism" (57).

103　Fabian, *Time and the Other*, x–xi; Mignolo, *Local Histories/Global Designs*, 283.

104　Vaughan, *Transatlantic Encounters*, 11, citing the manuscript record. For Hakluyt's published version, see "A note of Sebastian Cabotes voyage of discoverie." Quinn, *North America*, records that "three men were brought to the king's court, described as being dressed in skins and eating their meat raw (or perhaps half raw). They were seen there a year later dressed as Englishmen, but were not heard to speak" (126). He further specifies that "[t]he captives appear to have been Indians rather than Eskimo, and they are likely to have been Micmac or other mainland Algonkians" (126). The same year, a Portuguese voyage to the same region captured fifty natives ("[p]robably they were Micmac, though just possibly from a more southerly Algonkian tribe"), sending them to Lisbon as slaves (123). In 1509, French explorers brought natives from this region ("probably Micmac") to Rouen in Normandy (131). Thrush, *Indigenous London*, identifies the Cabots' captives as Inuit (2).

105　Cheshire et al., "Frobisher's Eskimos," claim that the Flemish painter Cornelis Ketel "did five paintings of Calichough in all: three in his native dress, one in English dress and one naked"; "two of his four pictures of 'the strainge woman' ... were intended from the start 'for

the Quene at new yeares day'" (34). These critics assume Calichough
was the man captured on Frobisher's second voyage, along with the
woman and child. However, Sturtevant and Quinn, "This New Prey,"
associate Calichough with the man Frobisher and his crew captured in
1576 (73).

106 For the cultural import of this false gold, see Montgomery, "'All that
glisters.'"

107 McDermott, *Martin Frobisher*, 190.

108 Quinn, "Frobisher," 1:17; Quinn, *North America*, adds: "The Frobisher
voyages in search of a Northwest Passage were the first English ventures
to attract publishers in any number" (554).

109 Settle, *A true reporte* , sig. Cv; Stefansson, *Three Voyages*, 2:17. Depictions
of this battle and of the captured Inuit man and woman are included
as full colour plates in Symons, *Meta Incognita*, 2:178–9 (inset). On the
pictorial record, see Cheshire et al., "Frobisher's Eskimos," 31–6; for
further details, see Sturtevant and Quinn, "This New Prey," 72–6, 78–9,
82–3, 86–7. Ellis, *A true report*, documents several encounters with the
indigenous people but does not mention the woman.

110 For Renaissance examples, see Yarnall, *Transformations of Circe*, 99–162;
for examples from the anglocentric discourse of empire, see Brookes, "A
Feminine 'Writing that Conquers,'" 229.

111 Hendricks, "Feminist Historiography," gives the parallel example of
"'a negress named Maria'"; Drake and his crew abducted her from
a Spanish ship in 1577 (368, citing Don Francisco de Zarate). After a
few months, Drake abandoned "[a] pregnant Maria ... on a deserted
island in the Indian Ocean" (368). As Hendricks concludes, "like Maria,
thousands of young women forcibly taken from Africa's west coast
became subject to sexual exploitation and rape by European sailors.
Some, in recognition of the limited power that might become available
to them, became the mistresses of European men such as Zarate or
Francis Drake" (368).

112 On the five missing Englishmen, see Settle, *A true reporte*, sigs. C2v–C5;
Stefansson, *Three Voyages*, 18–19; and Rowley, "Inuit Oral History," 212.
For accounts of the Inuit captives' attempts to escape, see Cheshire et al.,
"Frobisher's Eskimos," 28.

113 Stefansson, *Three Voyages*, 2:227.

114 Best, *A True Discourse*, 1:50; Stefansson, *Three Voyages*, 1:50. As Best's title
page conveys, his treatise is "Devided into three Bookes," which are
separately paginated.

115 Best, *A True Discourse*, 2:23; Stefansson, *Three Voyages*, 1:68.

116 Best, *A True Discourse*, 2:23–4; Stefansson, *Three Voyages*, 1:68. For an insightful reading of this passage, see Smith, "'For They Are Naturally Born,'" 241.

117 Bennett and Rowley, *Uqalurait*, 210. Watt and Savours, "The Captured 'Countrey People,'" observe of this incident that "[s]aliva may well have been more beneficial than the apothecary's salves, because it contains antimicrobial substances such as lysozymes which dissolve bacteria and factors which help the skin to grow" (555).

118 Best, *A True Discourse*, 2:25; Stefansson, *Three Voyages*, 1:69.

119 Bennett and Rowley, *Uqalurait*, 106, citing the elder Uqpingalik [Orpingalik], of the Arviligjuarmiut Inuit. On the "Seasonal Round of the Arviligjuarmiut," see ibid., 360–82.

120 Best, *A True Discourse*, 2:25; Stefansson, *Three Voyages*, 1:69.

121 Best, *A True Discourse*, 2:25; Stefansson, *Three Voyages*, 1:70.

122 Best, *A True Discourse*, 3:60–1; Stefansson, *Three Voyages*, 1:122–3. For other accounts that identify the natives encountered on Frobisher's northwest voyages as Tartars, see Hall, "The First Voyage," 153, and Lok, "Michael Lok's Account," 166. Wallace, *Premodern Places*, states that Tartars were "a subject of enduring interest to Hakluyt: for there remains the tantalizing possibility that 'Scythians and Tartarians' might 'haue [have] found the way to America, and entered the same'" (121). Almost fifty years later, John Smith, who travelled extensively in Ottoman lands as a soldier and captive prior to his colonizing role in Virginia and New England, compared "Indians to Tartars" (Kupperman, *Indians and English*, 168). For more on the links between Smith's Ottoman and Virginia ventures, see Kupperman, *The Jamestown Project*, 51–60.

123 Best, *A True Discourse*, 1:29; Smith, "'For They Are Naturally Born,'" 234; Vaughan, *Transatlantic Encounters*, 10.

124 Best, *A True Discourse*, 3:63; Stefansson, *Three Voyages*, 1:125.

125 Vizenor, *Manifest Manners*, 49; Craton, "Slavery and Slave Society," 108.

126 Cheshire et al., "Frobisher's Eskimos," 41, citing "Doctor Doddyngs Report." Cf. Best, *A True Discourse*, who also alludes to anthropophagism as he extends his association of the Inuit as "a kinde of Tartar" with the qualifier, "or rather a kind of Samowey [Samoyed, or the Nenets of Siberia]," whom the Russians considered "eaters of themselves" (2:61). Steckley, *White Lies*, clarifies that the stereotype of "Inuit cannibalism was popularized in Britain, in large measure to shift blame from English gentlemen" who resorted to this practice on their northern voyages from the sixteenth through the nineteenth centuries (22). For a report of early sixteenth-century English cannibalism, see "The voyage of master Hore

and divers other Gentlemen, to Newfound land, and Cape Breton, in the yeere 1536. and in the 28. yeere of King Henry the eight," in Hakluyt, *The Principall Navigations*, 517–19, and in a slightly but significantly extended version in Hakluyt, *The Principal Navigations*, 129–31. For other accounts, see Taylor, "Master Hore's Voyage." For an astute analysis of these records, see Levy, "Man-Eating." For a nineteenth-century episode, see Beattie and Geiger, *Frozen in Time*, 16–17, 74–5, 95, 111–17.

127 On this anxiety, see Lestringant, *Cannibals*.

128 Watt and Savours, "The Captured 'Countrey People,'" 560.

3. The Islamic World and the Construction of Early Modern Englishwomen's Authorship: Lady Mary Wroth, the Tartar-Persian Princess, and the Tartar King

1 Larson and Miller, *Re-Reading Mary Wroth*, features several essays that focus on Wroth as "author": most notably, Lewalski, "Authorship"; Van Note, "Performing 'fitter means'"; and Stapleton, "Measuring Authorship."

2 Specifically, Wroth published the first original *secular* sonnet sequence, as Anne Vaughan Locke (Lok) had previously "appended a sonnet sequence" based on Psalm 51 to her translation of *The Sermons of John Calvin* (1560), on which see Salzman, *Reading Early Modern Women's Writing*, 12. For modern editions, see Wroth, *The First Part of the Countess of Montgomery's Urania*, and Wroth, *The Second Part of the Countess of Montgomery's Urania*. All subsequent references to the *Urania* will be from these editions and will be abbreviated *U1* and *U2* respectively. For the sonnet sequence, which is not included in these editions, see Wroth, *The Poems*.

3 See the editions of Wroth's *Love's Victory* edited by Brennan (based on the Penshurst manuscript) and Cerasano and Wynne-Davies (collated Penshurst and Huntington manuscripts). For more on these manuscripts, see Salzman, *Reading Early Modern Women's Writing*, 60–89.

4 On Pamphilia as the "principal character" in the *Urania* and one of Wroth's most prominent "self-portraits within the work," see Roberts, "Critical Introduction," xxv, lxxi.

5 See Jonson, *The Cambridge Edition*, for "A Sonnet: To the Noble Lady, the Lady Mary Wroth" (7:142–3) and his two additional poems addressed to her (5:170–1). Jonson also dedicated his 1610 play *The Alchemist* to Wroth (3:557). For more on Jonson and Wroth, see Brennan, "Creating Female Authorship."

6 On Wroth's trip to Flushing as a nine-year-old girl, see Hannay, *Mary Sidney, Lady Wroth*, 63–6.

7 Wroth herself disambiguates the terms "fair" (beauty) and whiteness
for male characters (*U1* 39) and female characters (*U1* 33, 61); elsewhere,
she privileges the Petrarchan red-and-white ("snow and roses") beauty
standard (*U1* 263). On "Fair Beauty and Race" in early seventeenth-
century England, see Snook, *Women, Beauty and Power*, 38–61; for more on
Wroth, see ibid., 124–33.

8 For another instance of Wroth putting the Islamic world "under erasure," in
this case the contested island of Cyprus, see Andrea, *Women and Islam*, 36–42.
For a broader view, see Brummett, "Mapping Trans-Imperial Ottoman Space."

9 On Wroth's choice of genres, see Lewalski, *Writing Women*, 243–307. For an
analysis of Wroth's romance that complements my own, see Bearden, *The
Emblematics of the Self*, 158–95.

10 Dandelet, *The Renaissance of Empire*, 3. As Dandelet elaborates, "as an
intellectual, cultural, and political project," this "was nothing less than the
dominant master narrative that drove European political life for the entire
early modern period" (3). On "Britain as Late Renaissance Empire," see
ibid., 248–81. For a related analysis of *Urania* Part I, see Lockey, *Law and
Empire*, 187–218.

11 On "Wroth's topicality" as it relates to Wroth herself, see Roberts, "Critical
Introduction," lxxi–lxxv.

12 Headley, "The Habsburg World Empire," 94. Armitage, in his introduction
to *Theories of Empire*, xv–xxxiii, puts this imperial discourse, which Headley
analyses in terms of the Spanish king and Holy Roman Emperor Charles
V, in a broader temporal and geographic frame. For more, see Bosbach,
"The European Debate on Universal Monarchy," 81–98, and Pagden, *Lords
of All the World*, 29–62. Yates, *Astraea*, 29–121, discusses English aspirations
to universal monarchy in the sixteenth century. For the early seventeenth
century, see Patterson, *King James VI and I and the Reunion of Christendom*.

13 For the useful heuristic, "refracted representations," see Malieckal,
"Mariam Khan," 116.

14 Dandelet, *The Renaissance of Empire*, 248. Important studies of Wroth in
relationship to the "Sidney circle" include Alexander, *Writing After Sidney*;
Miller, *Changing The Subject*; Waller, *The Sidney Family Romance*; and Lamb,
Gender and Authorship. See also Quilligan, *Incest and Agency*, 164–212.

15 On Wroth's uncle's travels across Central Europe, including to the Holy
Roman Empire, see Duncan-Jones, *Sir Philip Sidney*, 63–85 and 113–40.
Philip Sidney also supported early ventures to the New World and even
sought to travel on one of Sir Francis Drake's ships, on which see Kuin,
"Querre-Muhau"; Greene, *Unrequited Conquests*, 171–94; and Maslen,
"Sidneian Geographies."

16 On Mary Sidney's representation of Cleopatra in *The Tragedie of Antonie*
and Mary Wroth's representation of a "Black-moore" woman in *Urania*
Part I, see Hall, *Things of Darkness*, 184, 188–9. For more on early modern
English representations of Egypt, see Archer, *Old Worlds*, 23–62.

17 *U1* 422; *U2* 31; Wroth, *The Poems*, 99. Other representations of Egypt
include the standard references to the Nile (*U1* 323) and the pyramids
(*U1* 588).

18 Skretkowicz, *European Erotic Romance*, 2. For the geopolitical valences of
this recuperation of Greek (Hellenistic) romance, see Stanivukovic, *Knights
in Arms*.

19 Hakluyt, *The Principall Navigations*, 280; Willan, *The Muscovy Merchants*,
46, 122. As Archer details in *Old Worlds*, "The Muscovy Company of
merchant adventurers was chartered by the Crown in 1555, two years
after its founders sponsored the first English voyage to Russia. An
account of the 1553 expedition based largely upon the observations of
Richard Chancellor, its surviving leader, appeared in Hakluyt's *Principall
Navigations Voiages and Discoveries of the English Nation* (1589) ... Chancellor
was raised in the Sidney household, and the narrative contains a long
speech attributed to Company member Henry Sidney, friend to Edward
VI and father of Philip Sidney, praising Chancellor upon his election"
(112). Archer adds: "The great map of Russia and Tartary that [Anthony]
Jenkinson produced in 1562" was "dedicated to Henry Sidney" (114).

20 Willan, *The Muscovy Merchants*, 10–11, 117.

21 Hannay, *Philip's Phoenix*, 38–42.

22 Hannay, *Mary Sidney, Lady Wroth*, 181.

23 As Roberts specifies, "In discussing Wroth's topicality, I use the term
'shadowing' because it accurately describes the intermittent nature of her
references" ("Critical Introduction" lxxi).

24 Middleton, *Sir Robert Sherley*, 13.

25 Andrea, "English Women's Writing and Islamic Empires," 290.

26 Hall, *Things of Darkness*, unpacks the formulation "'Nigra sum, sed
formosa' (I am black but beautiful)" (107–16), as does Iyengar, *Shades of
Difference*, 44–79. Epirus lies between Greece and Albania.

27 Andrea, *Women and Islam*, 47, citing Fuller, *The History of the Worthies of
England*.

28 Hall's *Things of Darkness* begins with the lines "'Away, you Ethiop!'
and 'Out, tawny Tartar' (3.2.257 and 263)" (1; cf. 22). Hall describes
Rodomandro as "almost literally 'the tawny Tartar,' who is black and out
of favor" (207). Cf. Archer, regarding Giles Fletcher's description in *Of the
Russe Common Wealth* of Tartars as "of a tanned colour into yellowe and

blacke" as it relates to Shakespeare's *Love's Labour's Lost* (*Old Worlds* 124). For more, see Salzman and Wynne-Davies, *Mary Wroth and Shakespeare*.

29 See Games, *The Web of Empire*, where she states: "My goal is to provide a vantage point on English expansion in these crucial years before an empire emerged by focusing on the overlapping and intersecting worlds of commercial and colonial enterprises and the transoceanic global perspectives that men derived through their travels from one ocean basin to another" (7). Games does deal with a few women travellers, such as Lady Catherine Whetenall, and the effect of men's travel on the women who stayed at home.

30 For the reverberations in Western Europe of the 1453 Ottoman conquest of Constantinople (Istanbul), see Meserve, *Empires of Islam*, especially her vivid description of Aeneas Sylvius Piccolomini's response. He became Pope Pius II in 1458. On the names for this city, see Finkel, *Osman's Dream*, 57.

31 Lewalski, *Writing Women*, also lists "[s]everal giants, griffons, and other monsters [that] serve villains who embody the Pagan (Muslim) threat" (289); she recognizes that "[b]ehind them and their allies we should probably recognize Christian Europe's fear of the Ottoman Turks" (290). For more, see McJannet, "Pirates, Merchants, and Kings," and Jowitt, "'Et in Arcadia Ego'."

32 For the marriage as "interracial," see Hall, *Things of Darkness*, 206, and as "intercultural," see Cavanagh, "Prisoners of Love," 97. Sanchez, in *Erotic Subjects*, productively and provocatively situates this marriage within "a much queerer *ménage à trois* between Pamphilia, Amphilanthus, and Rodomandro" (141).

33 For another reading of this scene, see Andrea, *Women and Islam*, 51.

34 On the "subaltern instance," see Morton, *Gayatri Spivak*, 104. For more, see 134n23 above.

35 Ferguson, *Dido's Daughters*, 316–29, discusses the imbrication of race and religion.

36 Said, *Orientalism*, 49–50, and "Empire, Geography, and Culture," in *Culture and Imperialism*, 1–14. Akbari, *Idols in the East*, offers an incisive engagement with Said's "imaginative geography" (13–15), as well as an apropos analysis of a "Saracen and Christian" romance hero (Feirefiz from Wolfram von Eschenbach's *Parzival*) whose "skin remains both black and white" (197).

37 Matar, *Turks, Moors, and Englishmen*, 10; for a similar view, see Goffman, *Britons in the Ottoman Empire*, 4.

38 Said, *Orientalism*, 71, 73; Barbour, *Before Orientalism*, 17.

39 Barbour, *Before Orientalism*, 5.
40 On these positive, if tendentious, representations of Tartars, see Andrea, "Persia, Tartaria, and Pamphilia," 29–36.
41 Cavanagh, *Cherished Torment*, 39–40. On these sources, see Hodgen, *Early Anthropology*, 111–61.
42 Hall, *Things of Darkness*, 206.
43 Goffman, *The Ottoman Empire and Early Modern Europe*, 8. See also Knobler, "Pseudo-Conversions and Patchwork Pedigrees" and "Missions, Mythologies." Knobler's book, *The Power of Distance*, is forthcoming from the University of Notre Dame Press.
44 As Barbour, *Before Orientalism*, concludes: "For if fictive exercises of display and containment could bespeak cultural strength and justify state power, they also tended to be wishful" (9). On wish-fulfillment as a characteristic of the genre, see Fuchs, *Romance*, 6.
45 On the pre-history of the Grand Tour, see Games, *The Web of Empire*, 17–46. On the travels of men from the Islamic world to the West prior to the eighteenth century, see Matar, *In the Land of the Christians*.
46 Wroth modelled Amphilanthus, Pamphilia's fickle lover, on William Herbert, Wroth's cousin, lover, and father of her two illegitimate children; for details, see Roberts, introduction to Wroth, *The Poems*, 24–6.
47 Hall, *Things of Darkness*, 206. See also Archer, *Old Worlds*, who discusses how "Russians were symbolically 'blackened' along with Africans because of the servile nature attributed to them in western European texts" during the sixteenth century; however, "by the seventeenth century ... Russians have become white, however dark their eyes or high-flown their complexions" (122, 132). A similar projection applied to Central Asians, such as the Tartar king, albeit in reverse, on which see Weatherford, *Genghis Khan*, 254–6.
48 The word "curious" in this description, to follow the usage in Wroth's era, means "made with care or art; skil[l]fully, elaborately or beautifully wrought" (*OED*). Hall, *Things of Darkness*, discusses the class, gender, and racialized connotations of "fair hands" for other male characters in the romance (208–10).
49 Cf. the minor character, Follietto, who is described as "a Very hansom black man, well-shaped for strength, well-featur[e]d of face, butt ill-complexioned; yett had hee exceeding white hands, and they showed a hope his skinn was answerable" (*U2* 61).
50 The "presence chamber" or "chamber of presence" is "a room, especially one in a palace, in which a monarch or other distinguished person receives visitors" (*OED*). For an incisive discussion of the discourse of civility as it

pertains to the Tartar and Persian characters in the romance, see Zurcher, "Civility and Extravagance."

51 On the validity of these vows, see Roberts, "'The Knott Never to Bee Untied.'" For a related analysis, see Kusunoki, *Gender and Representations*, 87–131.

52 Hall, *Things of Darkness*, 206. On "clothing, color, and disguise" in Wroth's romance, see Frye, *Pens and Needles*, 190–222.

53 From the beginning of the romance, Pamphilia is praised as "generally the most silent and discreetly retir'd of any Princesse" (*U1* 61).

54 Hendricks and Parker, introduction to *Women, "Race," and Writing*, 2.

55 Cavanagh, *Cherished Torment*, insightfully assesses "Rodomandro's apparent death and resurrection in the manuscript" (190–4).

56 Floyd-Wilson, *English Ethnicity*, 91.

57 Wallace, *Premodern Places*, 190–4.

58 Knolles, *The Generall Historie*, 235; for other examples, see Andrea, "Persia, Tartaria, and Pamphilia," 35–6.

59 Hakluyt, *The Principal Navigations*, 54.

60 Hakluyt, *The Principall Navigations*, 615, 621, 627.

61 According to Habib, *Black Lives*, while Catherine of Aragon brought "two slaves to attend on the maids of honour" when she arrived in England from Spain at the beginning of the sixteenth century (23), persons of African descent in the British Isles cannot be assumed to be slaves prior to the transfer of the monopoly over the transatlantic slave trade from the Iberians to the English at the end of the seventeenth century (57–8).

62 Cixous, "Sorties," 91; for another translation, see Cixous and Clement, *The Newly Born Woman*, 64.

63 For early modern maps representing Central Asia as Tartaria, see Brancaforte, *Visions of Persia*, 164–5. On the maps Wroth likely consulted, including Mercator's and Ortelius's, see Hannay, *Mary Sidney, Lady Wroth*, 244.

64 Connell, "Western Views of the Tartars," 24–8, adjudicates the shifting designations of "East" and "West" from the medieval through the early modern period. I use the term "the West" with his qualifications in mind. See also Connell, "Western Views of the Origin of the 'Tartars.'"

65 On Wroth's use of this title, see Cavanagh, "'The Great Cham.'" For historical Mongol titles and other terms, see Jackson, introduction to Rubruck; for more, see Hildinger, preface to Carpini. The name "Quinsai," for modern Hangzhou, was popularized by Marco Polo. For more on Polo's and related representations of "Farther Asia" and their impact on English literature, see Murrin, *Trade and Romance*, 9–61.

66 As Cogley, "'The Most Vile and Barbarous Nation,'" indicates, "Fletcher and many others in Tudor-Stuart England (1485–1714) viewed the Mongols, the Turks, the Tatars, and the Timurids simply as Tartars" (783).

67 Hannay, *Mary Sidney, Lady Wroth*, speculates that Wroth saw Shakespeare's *Othello* during the 1604/5 season (123).

68 Hall, *Things of Darkness*, 210, citing Shakespeare's *Othello* (3.4.46–7). Cf. Kusunoki, "Gender and Representations of Mixed-Race Relationships," who proposes that "Wroth seems to be quite conscious of the portrayal of mixed-race marriage in *Othello*, and deliberately revises Shakespeare's approach to the issues of both race and gender" (25).

69 Cavanagh, *Cherished Torment*, 41.

70 Robinson, *Islam and Early Modern English Literature*, 14.

71 Hannay, *Mary Sidney, Lady Wroth*, remarks that Wroth "wrote sonnets in an old-fashioned mode" (xiii; cf. 181–2). For Wroth in relation to Petrarchism, see Distiller, *Desire and Gender*, 80–97; Kennedy, *The Site of Petrarchism*, 163–250; Moore, *Desiring Voices*, 125–50; and Dubrow, *Echoes of Desire*, 99–162.

72 Hannay, *Mary Sidney, Lady Wroth*, proposes that, "[i]n addition to their more global designations, this may reflect [William Herbert, third earl of] Pembroke's home in Wiltshire to the west of London and the court, and [Mary] Wroth's home in Essex to the east" (244). Pamphilia is associated with Wroth; Amphilanthus with William Herbert. For more on Herbert in relation to Wroth, see Roberts, "Critical Introduction," lxxvi–lxxxix.

73 See the "Index of Characters in Part Two" (*U2* 568).

74 Rubiés, "Late Medieval Ambassadors," 40.

75 The etymology for "brave" in the *OED* lists as a source "Italian *bravo* brave, gallant, fine" and the association of "*bravo* (in Spanish also *bravio*) with Old Italian *braido*, *brado* wild, savage, which is also a sense of Spanish and Portuguese *bravo*." The first definition for the noun "brave" is "[a] brave man, a warrior, soldier: since 1800 applied chiefly to warriors among the North American Indians." For more, see Hodgen, *Early Anthropology*, 354–85.

76 For the former view, see Cavanagh, *Cherished Torment*, 39; for the latter, see Andrea, "Persia, Tartaria, and Pamphilia," 30–4.

77 Archer, *Old Worlds*, 108. On Tartars and Persians in costume books, see Brancaforte, *Visions of Persia*, 53–4.

78 Butler, *The Stuart Court Masque*, 36, and "The Court Masque." For a related analysis, see Campbell, "Masque Scenery."

79 Butler, *The Stuart Court Masque*, 63; on William Herbert's role in the masque, see ibid., 63–4.

80 Butler, *The Stuart Court Masque*, 66–7.
81 On the presence of the Moroccan and Russian ambassadors at the masques, see Butler, *The Stuart Court Masque*, 50, 53, 55. Hannay, *Mary Sidney, Lady Wroth*, speculates that Wroth may have seen both ambassadors at court entertainments (77); she may also have encountered Pocahontas at a masque performance (177–8). For more, consult Robertson's groundbreaking article, "Pocahontas at the Masque."
82 Butler, *The Stuart Court Masque*, 39. Unlike Henry VIII in the English court and James IV in the Scottish court, James I of England (VI of Scotland) did not perform in masques and other entertainments.
83 For a preliminary reading, see Andrea, "The Tartar King's Masque."
84 Iyengar, *Shades of Difference*, 80–100, examines Jacobean masques featuring Irish natives and Native Americans, as well as various masques of "blackness."
85 Cf. Cavanagh, *Cherished Torment*, 47, and "What is my nation?" 104.
86 On the "authorship" of this masque, see Andrea, "Black Skin, The Queen's Masques," 249–55, and McManus, "'Defacing the Carcass.'"
87 *The Masque of Blackness* in Jonson, *The Cambridge Edition*, 2:503–28. For other perspectives on Wroth's involvement in this masque, see Spiller, *Reading and the History of Race*, 153–201, and Bromley, *Intimacy and Sexuality*, 145–78.
88 Wroth, *The Poems*, 99, lines 1–4. Roberts retains the original spelling, but adjusts capitalization. In the 1621 published edition of *Pamphilia to Amphilanthus*, the word "Love" is capitalized. On the sonnet sequence and the masque form, see Hagerman, "'But Wroth pretends.'" For the view that "Wroth's crown of sonnets contained within *Pamphilia to Amphilanthus* is a masque rather than part of a traditional sonnet sequence," see O'Hara, "Sonnets as Theater," 59, and *The Theatricality of Mary Wroth's* Pamphilia to Amphilanthus, 56–103.
89 *The Masque of Blackness* in Jonson, *The Cambridge Edition*, 515, lines 70–2; 513, lines 34–5; 516, line 104.
90 Wroth, *The Poems*, 99, lines 1–4.
91 On Queen Anna and her ladies' subversive and appropriative use of "black face" paint, rather than masks (vizards) or cloth, see Andrea, "Black Skin, The Queen's Masques," 255–6, 264.
92 Wroth, *The Poems*, 99, lines 5–8.
93 Wroth, *The Poems*, 99, line 12; cf. Shakespeare, *Antony and Cleopatra* 1.5.27–9.
94 Wroth, *The Poems*, 99, line 13; *The Masque of Blackness* in Jonson, *The Cambridge Edition*, 518, line 135, 145; cf. line 123.

95 Cavanagh, *Cherished Torment*, 113–23. For an illuminating discussion of Dacia, which the early moderns identified with Transylvania and Wallachia (in modern Romania), see Matei-Chesnoiu, *Geoparsing*, 103–4.

96 Lewalski, *Writing* Women, 283. In Lewalski's estimation, "[a]s an embodiment of Rhodomandro's hopes, the masque stages the subordination of (Pamphilia's) desire" (296).

97 Hall, *Things of Darkness*, 188–9; *U1* 49–50.

98 *The Norton Shakespeare*, 1706.

99 Roberts, "'The Knott Never to Bee Untied,'" 115.

100 Roberts, "Critical Introduction," lxxiii.

101 Hannay, *Mary Sidney, Lady Wroth*, considers the possibility that Wroth was not a virgin upon her marriage to Robert Wroth due to a prior *"de praesenti* wedding pact" with William Herbert (107–8).

102 The *OED* lists the following forms for *"feature, n."*: Middle English "fetour(e), ... feture, feyture ... fetur, (fay(c)ture, fetture, fe(i)ter, feetour ... feuter, fewter ... feauture) ... feature."

103 Ravelhofer, in her innovative analysis "An English Masque at Constantinople," in *The Early Stuart Masque*, asserts that "[i]n the mid-seventeenth century, the Ottoman Empire represented a weakened but still formidable military and substantial economic power" (231). Finkel addresses the widespread misperception of Ottoman decline in "'The Treacherous Cleverness of Hindsight,'" 148–75, from a historical perspective.

4. Signifying Gender and Islam in Early Shakespeare: *The Comedy of Errors* (1594) and the Gray's Inn Revels

1 Butler, *Gender Trouble*, ix–xi; 24–5. For more, see Salih, "On Judith Butler and Performativity"; on "The Matter of Race," see Salih, *Judith Butler*, 92–5.

2 I use "tropological" in "[t]he predominant sense until the late 17th cent[ury]": "Relating to, involving, or of the nature of a trope or tropes; metaphorical, figurative" (*OED*). This sense connects with Hayden White's use of the term as defined in "Historicism, History, and the Figurative Imagination," in *Tropics of Discourse*, 115–16. For another framing of this argument, see Andrea, "Amazons, Turks, and Tartars."

3 On women in the audiences of Shakespeare's plays, see Howard, *Stage and Social Struggle*, 74–94. For a qualifier, see Callaghan, *Shakespeare Without Women*, 14–15, 139–65.

4 On Shakespeare's "all-male stage," see Garber, *Vested Interests*; Orgel, *Impersonations*; and Levine, *Men in Women's Clothing*.

5 On women in masques and other performances, see McManus, *Women on the Renaissance Stage*; Tomlinson, *Women on Stage*; and Findlay, *Playing Spaces*.

6 See Henderson and McManus, *Half Humankind*, 264–89, which reproduces two accounts of public cross-dressing from 1620: *Hic Mulier: Or, The Man-Woman* and *Haec Vir: Or, The Womanish-Man*.

7 Lanier, "'Stigmatical in Making,'" 303, citing Stubbes, *The Anatomie of Abuses*. Collinson, "Elizabethan and Jacobean Puritanism," qualifies the standard description of Stubbes as a "puritan" (34–5, 57).

8 For these shifting ascriptions, habits, or marks of identity, see Holmberg, "In the Company of Franks." In relation to *The Comedy of Errors*, see Akhimie, "Bruised with Adversity."

9 As Thompson notes in *Performing Race and Torture*, "to employ *white* as a racial signifier was not commonly used until the late seventeenth century" (60). For more, see 185n84 below.

10 On the Inns of Court, see Baker, "The Third University." On "what is putatively ... [Shakespeare's] first play," see Kinney, "Shakespeare's *Comedy of Errors*," 155.

11 Archer, "*Love's Labour's Lost*," 329. On these musicians, see Chapman, "The Appearance of Blacks," who argues that they are African-descent performers and not Englishmen in blackface. For an astute analysis of the "Muscovite" references in *Love's Labour's Lost* in relation to the *Gesta Grayorum*, see Shvarts, "Putting Russia on the Globe," 136–42. For similar connections, see Niayesh, "Muscovites and 'Black-amours.'"

12 Archer, *Old Worlds*, 124. Chapman, "The Appearance of Blacks," claims that the "Negro Tartars in the Gray's Inn revel" are also African performers (87). He consequently effaces their more direct Tatar (Central Asian) referent. Bukhara, on the ancient Silk Road, is currently the fifth largest city in Uzbekistan.

13 On Jenkinson's famous map, see Archer, *Old Worlds*, 114, and Wilson, "Visible Bullets," 51, 54.

14 The Crimean Tatars sacked and burned Moscow in 1571, killing "more than 150,000 persons, together with all the English, Flemings, Italians, and Germans who were resident in the city" (Palmer, *Writing Russia*, 69). For contemporary accounts, see Berry and Crummey, *Rude and Barbarous Kingdom*, 124, 191–3, and 271–4. While this incident may be in the background of the Gray's Inn Revels, the Crimeans are not mentioned directly.

15 Unless otherwise indicated, I refer to the facsimile edition of the *Gesta Grayorum*, ed. Greg, citing page numbers parenthetically. This tract follows

the Old Style English calendar, with the year beginning on 25 March. Bland, in his introduction to his modernized edition of *Gesta Grayorum*, discusses its publication history (ix–xii). Finkelpearl, *John Marston of the Middle Temple*, clarifies that "[t]he text is not strictly an account of what occurred; in part, it is what the young men had planned to present' (38n20). For manuscript sources, see Nelson and Elliott, *Inns of Court*, 2:435–85.

16 Godman, "'Plucking a Crow,'" observes that "[s]urprisingly little attention has been given to the *Gesta* as a dramatic piece in itself (editions and anthologies usually excerpt only the part relating to the performance of *Errors*)" (53). Rivlin, "Theatrical Literacy," surveys critics who make passing reference to the latter in their studies of the former (78n25). For focused treatments of the revels, see Leonidas, "Theatrical Experiment"; Rhatigan, "Audience, Actors, and 'Taking Part'"; and McCoy, "Law Sports and the Night of Errors."

17 Montrose, "The Work of Gender," 25. For a critique of Montrose's privileging of male heterosexist fantasies, see Brookes, "A Feminine 'Writing that Conquers.'"

18 McJannet, "Genre and Geography," establishes how the Eastern setting of these plays "suggests a paradoxical relation between humanist veneration for ancient Greek culture and Christian hostility to the Muslim Turks" (87). *The Comedy of Errors* is set in the ancient Greek city of Ephesus, which became part of the Ottoman Empire in 1390 and is now in the Republic of Turkey.

19 Montrose, "The Work of Gender," 18; Palmer, *Writing Russia*, xvii, 21, 32.

20 As Ralegh reports in *The Discoverie*, "The memories of the like women are verie ancient as well in *Africa* as in *Asia*" (23; ed. Whitehead, 146).

21 Montrose, "The Work of Gender," 25.

22 For these phrases, see the full titles of Games, *The Web of Empire* and Montrose, "The Work of Gender." Maguire, "The Girls from Ephesus," insightfully analyses the Amazonian subtext of *The Comedy of Errors*; for another reading, see Schwarz, *Tough Love*, 49–78. Sousa, *Shakespeare's Cross-Cultural Encounters*, 10–39, assesses representations of Amazons in Shakespeare's *A Midsummer Night's Dream* and *Two Noble Kinsmen*.

23 Knapp and Kobialka, "Shakespeare and the Prince of Purpoole," 432, 431, 443n2. For a related study, see Cormack, "Locating *The Comedy of Errors*." On the exclusion of women from the Inns of Court, see Green, *The Inns of Court*, 32.

24 Greg, introduction to *Gesta Grayorum*, vi. For more on Bacon as "a patron of the masque," see Schelling, *Elizabethan Drama*, 117–19. See also Nelson

and Elliott, *Inns of Court*, for "Bacon's Essay on Masques and Triumphs," 2:781–2.

25 For "Francis Bacon's famous denial of the value of court masques," see Butler, *The Stuart Court Masque*, 8. For more on his involvement in the *Masque of Flowers*, performed on 6 January 1613 (O.S.)/1614 (N.S.), see Shohet, *Reading Masques*, 110.

26 Knapp and Kobialka, "Shakespeare and the Prince of Purpoole," 435. As Greg indicates in his introduction to the *Gesta Grayorum*, the date of the final performance for *The Masque of Proteus* at Shrovetide would have been either Monday, 3 March, or Tuesday, 4 March (vi). On the "Christmas Celebration," see Green, *The Inns of Court*, 56–96, esp. 71–85. On Shakespeare's *Twelfth Night* (1601/2), which premiered at Middle Temple (one of the four Inns of Court), see Arlidge, *Shakespeare and the Prince of Love*, 8–20.

27 See Woolley, *The Queen's Conjurer*, on Dee's "ideas on imperialism" (75), which shaped the first English voyage to Russia in the sixteenth century (97–100; cf. 117). See Mancall, *Hakluyt's Promise*, on the "grammar of colonization" crafted by Hakluyt, meaning "the language and logic that would guide the English colonization of North America" (129).

28 Hakluyt, "To the Reader," in *The Principall Navigations*, sig. 4v; Hakluyt, "To the Reader," in *The Principal Navigations*, sig. *5v. For more, see Baron, "William Borough and the Jenkinson Map of Russia."

29 Froude, "England's Forgotten Worthies," 361. For more on Froude's oft-cited phrase, see Fuller, *Voyages in Print*, 158–62.

30 Derrida, *Of Grammatology*, 145 (emphasis in original); see also Spivak, "Translator's Preface," lxx–lxxii, lxxxiv–lxxxv.

31 Vizenor, *Native Liberty*, 24; Loomba and Burton, introduction to *Race in Early Modern England*, 1.

32 Lanier, "'Stigmatical in Making,'" 302, 319. In the *Gesta Grayorum* "the Right Honourable Sir *William Cecill*, K$^{t.}$ [Knight] Lord Treasurer of *England*" receives special mention as an alumni sponsor of these revels (4). For more on its membership, see Prest, *The Inns of Court*, 5–17, 21–46.

33 Knapp and Kobialka, "Shakespeare and the Prince of Purpoole," 435.

34 Nelson and Elliott mention in their introduction to *Inns of Court* that Helmes would have borne most of the costs for the revels (1:xx).

35 Montrose, "The Work of Gender," 18, 25.

36 On the connection between Arthurian mythology and the western "discourse on the other," see Godzich, "Forward," xiii.

37 On this slang, see Newman, *Cultural Capitals*, 134–47. "Cauda" is Latin for "tail" (*OED*), with phallic connotations. "Placebo" in "post-classical

Latin [was] used to denote the Office for the Dead (frequently *c*1220–1503 in British sources), from the first word of the first antiphon of vespers in the Office for the Dead (*Placebo Domino in regione vivorum*, Psalm 114:9 (Vulgate: Roman Psalter, Gallican Psalter)" (*OED*). With "to die" "in the late 16th and 17th cent[uries]" meaning "[t]o experience a sexual orgasm" (*OED*), the sexualized wordplay continues.

38 Salkeld, *Shakespeare among the Courtesans*, 120, 135, 129–30.

39 Salkeld, *Shakespeare among the Courtesans*, 22, 120, 128, 135.

40 Habib, *Black Lives*, 107.

41 Salkeld, *Shakespeare among the Courtesans*, 4–9, 20, 24.

42 For the early modern/colonial period, see Mignolo, *The Darker Side of the Renaissance*, though he does not deal with human trafficking per se; for our postmodern/postcolonial era, see *A Global Report on Trafficking in Persons*, issued by the United Nations Office on Drugs and Crime.

43 Palmer, *Writing Russia*, 52.

44 The passage continues: "wherein the Merchant having gained the Wind, came up with her in such close manner, that he brake his Boltsprite in her hinder Quarter" (*Gesta Grayorum* 50). Cf. Salkeld, *Shakespeare among the Courtesans*, 130–2.

45 Ralegh, *Discoverie*, 96; ed. Whitehead, 196. However, Ralegh elsewhere claims that he ordered his men not "to take from anie of the [native] nations so much as a *Pina* [pineapple], or a *Potato* roote, without giving them contentment, nor any man so much as to offer to touch any of their wives or daughters" (*Discoverie*, 52; ed. Whitehead, 165). In this way, he attempts to distinguish the English from the Spanish in order to form alliances with native leaders. Cf. Sanford, "A Room Not One's Own," who surveys "the abundance of sexual references in the literature of exploration, where the land is frequently figured as a woman to be ravished and the pun on the word *country* to refer to women's genitals (as in Hamlet's "country matters' [3.2.105]) was commonplace" (63).

46 Andrews, *Drake's Voyages*, 40–80, places Drake's circumnavigation of the globe (1577–80) in the context of the eastern trade from Russia to Persia.

47 MacCaffrey, *Elizabeth I*, 37.

48 On the "nodal point" of a dream, see Freud, *The Interpretation of Dreams*, 317; for an elaboration of "Freud's Tropology of Dreaming," see White, *Figural Realism*, 101–25.

49 On the sixteenth-century Franco-Ottoman alliance, see Isom-Verharren, *Allies with the Infidel*.

50 For an apropos analysis of *The Comedy of Errors*, see Degenhardt, *Islamic Conversion*, 40–9.

51 On the designation of syphilis as the "French disease," see McGough, *Gender, Sexuality, and Syphilis*, 1–16. On guaiacum and other "cures," see ibid., 72–3, 102–4. For an interesting discussion of syphilis, trade, and *The Comedy of Errors*, see Harris, *Sick Economies*, 29–51. Regarding "*Le grand Vezolle*," Bland, in his edition of *Gesta Grayorum*, admits he has "been unable to identify this reference' (103n29). I have had no better luck!

52 Hakluyt, "Epistle Dedicatorie," in *The Principall Navigations*, sigs. *2–*2v.

53 On the significance of this night, see Kinney, "Shakespeare's *Comedy of Errors*," 157–65.

54 For the debate over "whether the 'Errors and Confusions' of the grand night' of 28 December were staged or genuine," and therefore whether Shakespeare's play was part of this plan or whether it was "an improvised substitution or dismal flop," see McCoy, "Law Sports and the Night of Errors," 288–91.

55 Green, *The Inns of Court*, earlier (and aptly) applied the descriptor "flatulently" to these speeches (73).

56 MacLean, *Looking East*, 20–3.

57 Edward Barton, who served as Queen Elizabeth's ambassador to the Ottoman Empire from 1588 to 1596, succeeded William Harborne, who served from 1583 to 1588. According to Wood, *A History of the Levant Company*, Barton sought "to persuade the sultan to join England in the Spanish war, and to mediate peace between the Turks and the [Holy Roman] emperor" (81). As MacLean and Matar elaborate in *Britain and the Islamic World*, Barton also "help[ed] restore Protestantism to Moldavia, where a Jesuit takeover had occurred," "took part in the behind-the-scene negotiations that led to the appointment of the Orthodox Patriarch in Istanbul," and joined "Sultan Murad's military expedition into Hungary" (82).

58 On the position of the stage, see Knapp and Kobialka, "Shakespeare and the Prince of Purpoole," 436–8.

59 Van Elk, "'This sympathizèd one day's error,'" 47–8; Miola, "The Play and the Critics," 17–20.

60 For an incisive reading, see Tommaso, "'Th' receiving earth,'" 272–4. For more, see Parker, *Literary Fat Ladies*, 17–18, and *Shakespeare from the Margins*, 65–8.

61 The adjective "swart" denotes "[d]ark in colour; black or blackish; dusky, swarthy," with particular reference to "the skin or complexion" (*OED*). On the Luce/Nell/Lucy Negro nexus, see Salkeld, *Shakespeare among the Courtesans*, 133–4; he posits the unnamed courtesan in the play as yet another double for Lucy Negro. For an editorial approach to the names "Luce" and "Nell," see Whitworth, "Rectifying Shakespeare's *Errors*,"

243–4. For a feminist analysis, see Maguire, "The Girls from Ephesus," 357, 367, 369–70, 384 n13.

62 Elliott, "Weirdness in *The Comedy of Errors*," early on observed that "Shakespeare refrains from bringing Nell on stage in person" (65).

63 *OED*, s.v. "ell," 1a.

64 Vickers, "'The blazon of sweet beauty's best,'" 95. See also Parker, *Literary Fat Ladies*, "Rhetorics of Property: Exploration, Inventory, Blazon" (126–54). For more on the blazon in relation to the "literature of travel and exploration," see Sanford, "A Room Not One's Own," 63, 68–9.

65 Vickers, "'The blazon of sweet beauty's best,'" 96.

66 On Marlowe, see Wilson, "Visible Bullets."

67 Ghani, *Shakespeare, Persia, and the East*, 93–164, and Grogan, *The Persian Empire*, cover additional examples.

68 *The Norton Shakespeare*, 715n9. For the false etymology linking "Tartar" to "Tartarus," see Cogley, "'The Most Vile and Barbarous Nation,'" 798–9. "Tartar" is also used to denote hell in Shakespeare's *Henry V* 2.2.120 and *Twelfth Night* 2.5.179. For Shakespeare's ethnographical references, which tend to be denigrating, see *A Midsummer Night's Dream* 3.2.101 ("Tartar's bow") and 3.2.264 ("tawny Tartar"), *Romeo and Juliet* 1.4.5 ("Tartar's painted bow"), *Merchant of Venice* 4.1.31 ("stubborn Turks and Tartars"), *Merry Wives of Windsor* 4.4.16 ("Bohemian Tartar"), *All's Well That Ends Well* 4.4.7 ("flinty Tartar's bosom"), and *Macbeth* 4.1.29 ("[n]ose of Turk and Tartar's lips").

69 Andrea, "Persia, Tartaria, and Pamphilia," 25.

70 On these treatises, see Rubiés, "Oriental Despotism and European Orientalism."

71 For a case in point, see Dallam, "The Diary," 70–1. Dallam was an organ-maker who played the instrument Queen Elizabeth gifted to the Ottoman Sultan Mehmet III with his back turned towards the sultan, with much anxiety but no repercussions.

72 Rouhi, "A Handsome Boy among Those Barbarous Turks," unpacks this association. For more, see Arvas, "Travelling Sexualities."

73 MacCaffrey, *Elizabeth I*, 4.

74 MacCaffrey, *Elizabeth I*, 75.

75 On the Moroccan embassy, see Harris, "A Portrait of a Moor." The entry for "Embassy History and Previous Ambassadors" on the website for the *Turkish Embassy in London* records that "[t]he Ottoman Empire appointed its first resident envoys to Europe at the end of the 18th century with a view to following the developments in Europe. The first of these ambassadors, Yusuf Agâh Efendi, was posted in London in 1793. There has been a Turkish diplomatic mission in London since then."

76 See the instructions of "The Merchant Adventurers of England, etc., to their Agents in Russia. The 18 Aprill 1567 In London," in Morgan and Coote, *Early Voyages*, 2:217.

77 Romaniello, *The Elusive Empire*, 125.

78 On these lines, see Hall, *Things of Darkness*, 22–34.

79 On England's shift from "postcolonial nation to empire state," see Maley, *Nation, State and Empire*, 31–44. On "imperial envy" and emulation in relation to the Ottomans, see MacLean, *Looking East*, 20–3.

80 On 3 January, the gentlemen of Gray's Inn presented a masque featuring "the Goddess of Amity" to heal the breach with the Inner Temple (*Gesta Grayorum* 25–6).

81 Francis Davison composed this masque, which included music from Thomas Campion (Greg, introduction to *Gesta Grayorum*, vii–viii). On Davison's literary and political career, see McCoy, "Law Sports and the Night of Errors," 294–7. McCoy, in "Lord of Liberty," links this masque to the Earl of Essex's imperial ambitions (218). Albright, "*The Faerie Queene* in Masque at the Gray's Inn Revels," proffers Thomas Campion as co-author of the masque (499–500). On Whitehall Palace as a performance venue, see Astington, *English Court Theatre*, 140–55.

82 Regarding *The Masque of Proteus*, Green remarks in *The Inns of Court*: "It is, thus, at the Inns of Court, that the masque was not only developed but also perfected" (99). For similar assessments, see Welsford, *The Court Masque*, 163–4, and Orgel, *The Jonsonian Masque*, 8–18.

83 Orgel, *The Jonsonian Masque*, is the only literary critic or historian who, to my knowledge, mentions the "Tartar page," albeit in passing (9–10).

84 As Chapman proposes, many of the African performers in English Renaissance plays did not speak ("The Appearance of Blacks" 82). As a result, they, too, have been passed over by most critics.

85 For Queen Henrietta Maria's innovative female-to-male cross-dressing in the dramas she sponsored during the 1630s, see Findlay and Hodgson-Wright, *Women and Dramatic Production*, 48, 142–3, and 170–5. For more, see Britland, *Drama at the Courts of Henrietta Maria*.

86 Cf. Freccero, "Queer Spectrality," in *Queer/Early/Modern*, 69–104.

87 Schwarz, *Tough Love*, 221, in her discussion of Shakespeare's Hippolyta, cites Geoffrey Chaucer's description from "The Knight's Tale" of "Ypolita" (Hippolyta) as "[t]he faire, hardy queene of Scithia." See also DuBois, *Centaurs and Amazons*, who identifies "the Amazons' territory" as "variously placed in the eastern and northern regions of the Black Sea" with specific reference to Hippolyta (33). For more, see Davis-Kimball, *Warrior Women*, 112–31.

5. Signifying Gender and Islam in Late Shakespeare: *Henry VIII* or *All is True* (1613) and British "Masques of Blackness"

1 This play "was initially printed in the First Folio of 1623 ... under the title *The Famous History of the Life of Henry the Eight* and today is generally known as *Henry VIII*"; however, "comments on early performances suggest that it was originally called *All is True*," as per the "Textual Note" to the play in *The Norton Shakespeare*, 3118. Most critics concede that Shakespeare collaborated with John Fletcher on this play; I therefore refer to the play as Shakespeare's for concision rather than to weigh in on the authorship debate, which is not germane to my argument. For those interested in the details, see Richards, "Shakespeare and the Politics of Co-Authorship," 176–94, and Vickers, *Shakespeare, Co-Author*, 333–402. For the occasion of the play, see Rankin, "Henry VIII, Shakespeare, and the Jacobean Royal Court," and Kurland, "*Henry VIII* and James I."

2 Hakluyt, "The Epistle Dedicatorie," in *The Principall Navigations*, sig. *2; Goffman, *The Ottoman Empire and Early Modern Europe*, 8.

3 For historical details, see Russell, *The Field of Cloth of Gold*; for a cultural analysis, see Anglo, *Spectacle, Pageantry, and Early Tudor Policy*, 124–69. More recently, see Richardson, *The Field of Cloth of Gold*.

4 On the early sixteenth-century Franco-Ottoman alliance, see Isom-Verhaaren, *Allies with the Infidel*; for Queen Elizabeth's subsequent alliance with the Ottomans, see Skilliter, *William Harborne and the Trade with Turkey*.

5 Mattingly, *Renaissance Diplomacy*, 148. See also Richardson, *Renaissance Monarchy*.

6 For an earlier articulation of this thesis, see Andrea, "'A noble troop of strangers.'"

7 Smith, *Race and Rhetoric*, 117.

8 Fuchs, "Imperium Studies," 86.

9 Studies that touch on masque elements in Shakespeare's *Henry VIII* include Lindley, "Blackfriars, Music and Masque"; Cho, "Shakespeare's *Henry VIII* and the Politics of the Spectacle"; Hazard, "'Order gave each thing view'"; Berry, *Shakespeare and the Awareness of the Audience*, 128–41; Cox, "*Henry VIII* and the Masque"; and Cutts, "Shakespeare's Song and Masque Hand in *Henry VIII*." See also Chalmers, "'Break Up the Court,'" and Woodcock, "'Their eyes more attentive to the show.'"

10 For a related discussion of "Desdemona's Blackness," see Bovilsky, *Barbarous Play*, 37–65. See also Moore, "'You Turn Me into Nothing'"; Nelson, "Shakespeare's *Henry VIII*: Stigmatizing the 'Disabled' Womb"; Frye, "Queens and the Structure of History in *Henry VIII*"; Carney,

"Queenship in Shakespeare's *Henry VIII*"; Noling, "Grubbing Up the Stock"; and McJannet [Micheli], "'Sit by Us.'"

11 For Elizabeth's assertion of her Englishness, see Loades, *Elizabeth I*, 313. On Anne Boleyn's education in continental European courts, see Ives, *The Life and Death of Anne Boleyn*, 18–36. On Shakespeare's Queen Katherine, see Cerdá, "Patriotism, Presentism, and the Spanish Henry VIII." While Shakespeare renders the queen's name as "Katherine," when referring to the historical queen I follow Mattingly's spelling in *Catherine of Aragon*.

12 For the period of Philip II's reign in England, see Campos, "West of Eden," 250–2; Hadfield, "Peter Martyr, Richard Eden and the New World"; and Gwyn, "Richard Eden."

13 Scarisbrick, *Henry VIII*, 81. Anglo, *Spectacle, Pageantry, and Early Tudor Policy*, concurs: "England was courted by both sides" (137). For an elaboration of this point, see Jardine and Brotton, *Global Interests*, 57–62.

14 See Isom-Verhaaren, *Allies with the Infidel*, "Ottoman Involvement in European Alliances, Diplomacy and the Balance of Power" (23–48). For more on Ottoman relations with France in this era, see Merriman, *Suleiman the Magnificent*, 126–44.

15 On this "quest for peace" in preparation for a new crusade, see Scarisbrick, *Henry VIII*, 67–96. Under Selim I (1512–20), the Ottomans conquered Syria; the Hijaz, including Mecca and Medina; and Egypt from the Mamluks in 1516–17. Under Süleiman I (1520–66), they conquered Belgrade in 1521 and Hungary in 1526. Their first siege of Vienna occurred in 1529; the final siege occurred in 1683.

16 Anglo, *Spectacle, Pageantry, and Early Tudor Policy*, 139, citing *Lordonnance et ordre du tournoy joustes et combat a pied et a cheval*. For "the representation of Egypt" in early modern England, see Archer, *Old Worlds*, 23–62.

17 Anglo, *Spectacle, Pageantry, and Early Tudor Policy*, 137.

18 Russell, *The Field of Cloth of Gold*, 182.

19 On this connection, see Richmond, "Shakespeare's *Henry VIII*: Romance Redeemed by History," 339, and "The Feminism of Shakespeare's *Henry VIII*," 13. As Richardson points out in *The Field of Cloth of Gold*, Norfolk "was not in fact" at Calais for this event (93).

20 Cohen in his introduction to *All is True* (*Henry VIII*) signals, but does not analyse, references to colonialism in the play (3114). Maley, "Postcolonial Shakespeare," touches on *Henry VIII* when addressing internal colonialism in the British Isles (152).

21 In addition to the sources listed above, see Lockey, *Law and Empire*, who traces the anxiety over proto-imperial England's history as a colony – from the Romans to the Normans – expressed by several sixteenth-century

English writers, including William Warner (107–9) and Edmund Spenser (121–4). Critics who register the threat to Jacobean autonomy circa 1613, when "a second Spanish Armada" was looming, include Slights, "The Politics of Conscience in *All is True*," 59; Krantz, "Audience Response to *Henry VIII* ," 142; Baillie, "*Henry VIII*: A Jacobean History," 249–50; and McBride, "*Henry VIII* as Machiavellian Romance," 35–6.

22 Matar, *Turks, Moors and Englishmen*, 10.

23 Andrews, *Trade, Plunder and Settlement*, 13.

24 *The Norton Shakespeare*, 3122n8. For almost verbatim glosses, see *Henry VIII*, ed. Mowat and Werstine, 10, and *The Complete Works of Shakespeare*, ed. Bevington, 898n20 and n21. Foakes's influential edition, *King Henry VIII*, completely elides the colonial resonances in this passage by glossing "heathen gods" as "possibly a biblical allusion" (8) and "India" as "commonly represented a source of fabulous wealth" (9). Editions that follow Foakes include *King Henry VIII* (*All is True*), ed. McMullan, 214; *King Henry VIII, or All is True*, ed. Halio, 76, and *King Henry VIII*, ed. Margeson, 66. Most editors have assigned "the English" as the referent for "they" in line 26; however, "they" could equally refer to "the French" in line 23. Cf. related readings of the ambiguous pronoun in Henry VIII's concluding lines to Act 2, scene 2 – "O, my lord,/Would it not grieve an able man to leave/So sweet a bedfellow? But conscience, conscience–/O, 'tis a tender place, and I must leave her" (2.2.140–3; emphasis added) – with "her" referring either to his repudiated wife or to his conscience.

25 For English anxieties about French cultural imperialism, see Hadfield, *Amazons, Savages, and Machiavels*, 46–52 and 64–80. On the critique of Henrician courtiers who appeared "all French," see Scarisbrick, *Henry VIII*, 117.

26 Warnicke, *The Rise and Fall of Anne Boleyn*, 48.

27 For the Elizabethan Bishop John Aylmer's assertion that "God is English" and "[t]he French Turke," see Andrea, *Women and Islam*, 15. For more, see Devereux, "'The ruin and slaughter of ... fellow Christians.'"

28 Anglo, *Spectacle, Pageantry, and Early Tudor Policy*, 185. On Wolsey's role in crafting the anti-Ottoman "Treaty of London" of 1518, see Mattingly, *Renaissance Diplomacy*, 144–7, and "An Early Nonaggression Pact."

29 Mattingly, *Catherine of Aragon*, 218, citing the queen's communication with Martin de Salinas, envoy of Archduke Ferdinand of Austria, brother of the Holy Roman Emperor Charles V.

30 For the Western Christian association of "Turks" (Ottomans and, more broadly, Muslims) with "pagans," see Meserve, *Empires of Islam*, 22–64, and Tolan, *Saracens*, 105–34.

31 Harris, *Indography*, remarks: "it was only after 1492 ... that 'Indian' became the capacious, portable, and problematic term for diverse peoples around the globe that it continues to be even now" (1).

32 Bray, *Documents of the English Reformation*, 78, citing "Act in Restraint of Appeals, 1533 (24 Henry VIII, c.12)." For more on this epochal declaration, see 134n24 above.

33 As Sen remarks in "Playing an Indian Queen," "Henrietta Maria [the queen consort of Charles I, King James's second son and successor] appeared [in this 1635 masque by William Davenant] before a courtly public as Indamora, sovereign of the Hindu kingdom of Narsinga." Hence, "[h]er predecessor Anne of Denmark was not the only Stuart queen to present herself before a courtly audience as an exotic subject" (209). Sen determines that Henrietta Maria did not play her role in blackface, as did Queen Anna (218–19).

34 Edwards, "The Early African Presence," 9–11, 15–16.

35 Habib, *Black Lives*, 27–8.

36 Fryer, *Staying Power*, 9; Salkeld, *Shakespeare among the Courtesans*, 120, 135, 129–30.

37 Andrea, "Black Skin, The Queen's Masques," 255–67; while I draw on the same primary sources here, the focus of my analysis departs significantly from this earlier piece. For more recent studies that engage similar issues, see Niayesh, "'Cultural Amphibians'" and "The 'Courtly Popular' Orient"; Over, "Alterity and Assimilation" and "Familiarizing the Colonized."

38 Edwards analyses this poem in "The Early African Presence," 21–3. For other renditions, see 143n32 above.

39 Robertson, "Pocahontas at the Masque," 552, and "Writing 'Pocahontas'."

40 Morrison, *Playing in the Dark*, 13; Andrea, "Black Skin, The Queen's Masques," 246, 255. For Jonson as "provisional scriptor" of this masque, see ibid., 254. A year earlier, Queen Anna had sponsored Samuel Daniel's *Vision of Twelve Goddesses* at Hampton Court. For details, see Lewalski, "Enacting Opposition: Queen Anne and the Subversions of Masquing," in *Writing Women*, 15–43.

41 For the epithet "fair ANNA," see Burel, *The Discription*, I.

42 The most detailed account is Stevenson, *Scotland's Last Royal Wedding*.

43 King James's suspicions are recorded in Craig, *Papers Relative to the Marriage*, xiii–xvi. The devil in this account is described as "cled [clad] in a black gown with a blak hat on his head," mimicking a preacher; he ultimately reveals a beastly face (xiii). Blackness is thus ironized rather than racialized here: that is, a pious exterior, signaled by black clothing, is revealed as hypocritical.

44 Williams, *Anne of Denmark*, 18, citing a report to William Cecil, Lord
   Burghley. For an astute analysis, see McManus, "Marriage and the
   Performance of the Romance Quest."

45 Williams, *Anne of Denmark*, 20. For a more recent biography, see Barroll,
   Anna of Denmark, Queen of England.

46 Williams, *Anne of Denmark*, 21. Stevenson, *Scotland's Last Royal Wedding*,
   casts doubt on the extant report (128n12).

47 Hall, *Things of Darkness*, 131, discusses blackness as a foil for white beauty
   in relation to *The Masque of Blackness*.

48 See Kelsey, *Sir John Hawkins*, for details.

49 Smith, in "White Skin, Black Masks," perspicaciously identifies "the
   denigration effect (meaning at once both the 'belittling' and, etymologically,
   the 'blackening' effect) of Hegel's history that installs blackness as the
   undesirable thing that threatens to erupt within whiteness" (41). See also
   Chapman, "The Appearance of Blacks," who asserts that "even though the
   English did find positive connotations in blackness, the positive attitude
   recognizes blacks as objects rather than subjects in English society" (79).

50 Craig, *Papers Relative to the Marriage*, 40. The city records for Edinburgh
   detailing the coronation pageant can be found in Mill, *Mediaeval Plays in
   Scotland*, 202–3. This blackface performance reverses the valence of "repetition
   with a signal difference" as theorized in Gates, *The Signifying Monkey*, xxiv.

51 Burel, *The Discription*, I, IV. In modern English, "hairs like thread of gold
   did glitter [*OED*, 'gleit'],/Their faces fragrant and beautiful or comely
   [*OED*, 'formose']:/White was their hide or skin [*OED*, s.v. 'hýd'] though it
   was hidden/Their coral lips like roses red."

52 Burel, *The Discription*, V. In modern English, "For chains which over their
   shoulders hang:/Gold bracelets on their wrists [*OED*, s.v. 'shackle-bone']
   turn [*OED*, s.v. 'hinge'],/Their fingers full of expensive rings."

53 *A True Report of … the Baptisme*, sig. B.

54 Miller, *Blank Darkness*, 17.

55 Derrida, "That Dangerous Supplement …" in *Of Grammatology*, 141–64. See
   also 133n16 and 134n23 above.

56 *A True Report of … the Baptisme*, sig. C4. "Traces" refers to a "flat plait or
   braid of gold or silver thread, or other material, for trimming a robe"
   (*OED*, s.v. "trace," 2).

57 Hodgen, *Early Anthropology*, 354–430. For an extension of this argument,
   see Pagden, *European Encounters*, 117–40.

58 *A True Report of … the Baptisme*, sig. D. Hall, *Things of Darkness*, relates this
   episode to that of "Snug's lion" in Shakespeare's *A Midsummer Night's
   Dream* (23–4; *MSND* 3.1.25–40).

59 Hall, *The Lives of the Kings*, 15–17. "Pleasauntes" is a "fine gauzelike fabric" (*OED*, s.v. "pleasance"). A "typper" is a "long narrow slip of cloth or hanging part of dress, formerly worn, either attached to and forming part of the hood, head-dress, or sleeve, or loose, as a scarf or the like" (*OED*, s.v. "tippet"). For more, see 144n39 above.

60 See Jones, *Othello's Countrymen*, 145–49, for an indispensable "Chart of Plays, Masques and Pageants Involving African Characters 1510–1638."

61 Andrea, "Black Skin, the Queen's Masques," 267–74.

62 Barthelemy, *Black Face, Maligned Race*, 20.

63 For details, see Smith, "The Textile Black Body"; Stevens, *Inventions of the Skin*, 87–120; Blunt, "The Evolution of Blackface Cosmetics"; Smith, "Othello's Black Handkerchief"; and Vaughan, *Performing Blackness*, 107–29.

64 Orgel, introduction to *Ben Jonson: The Complete Masques*, 1.

65 For more on Prynne, see Barish, *The Antitheatrical Prejudice*, 80–131.

66 Williams, *Anne of Denmark*, 125–6.

67 Winwood, *Memorials* , 2:44.

68 See Andrea, "The Ghost of Leo Africanus," 198–202.

69 Winwood, *Memorials*, 2:44. Cf. Murray, *Like a Film*, 101–13, on the suspect "smudge" of blackness in Laurence Olivier's 1965 film portrayal of Shakespeare's *Othello*.

70 Chapman, "The Appearance of Blacks," convincingly argues that the "blackness" of African women and men created "a confusion prevalent in English culture, the simultaneous visibility and invisibility of blacks" (77).

71 Carleton, *Dudley Carleton*, 68. Carleton further conveys that "[t]he Queen goes to *Greenwich* this Week, to give *Whitehall* some Ayre against that time; and presently after the King goes back *sur ses brisees,* and the Queen returns to *Greenwich* to lay down her great Belly, which is look'd for about three Months hence" (Winwood, *Memorials*, 44). On the pregnant queen's performance as a celebration of African(ist) fertility, see Kelly, "The Challenge of the Impossible."

72 *The Masque of Blackness*, in Jonson, *The Cambridge Edition*, 2:521.

73 As Lindley explains in his introduction, in Jonson, *The Cambridge Edition*, "The *Masque of Beauty* was danced on 10 January 1608 [New Style], in the new Banqueting House at Whitehall. Originally intended for 6 January, the masque was delayed. Chamberlain suggested it was because the hall was not ready ... but the real reason was that Queen Anne had again invited the Spanish ambassador, but not the French, provoking furious complaint" (3:229).

74 *The Masque of Blackness*, in Jonson, *The Cambridge Edition*, 2:521; Andrea, "Black Skin, the Queen's Masques," 274–81.

75 Hall, *The Lives of the Kings*, 15–17. On related productions, see Howard, "'Ascending the Riche Mount'"; Streitberger, *Court Revels*, 65–93; and Axton, "The Tudor Mask."

76 Fradenburg, *City, Marriage, Tournament*, 244–64.

77 Anglo, *Spectacle, Pageantry, and Early Tudor Policy*, 123, citing *Calendar of State Papers* (*Venetian*), 2:918. This is from Francesco Chieregato, the papal nuncio in England, to Isabella d'Este, Marchioness of Mantua.

78 On the English language as "barbarous," see Smith, *Race and Rhetoric*, 16–18; for more on "civilizing Britain," see Floyd-Wilson, *English Ethnicity*, 49–60.

79 Anglo, *Spectacle, Pageantry, and Early Tudor Policy*, 177.

80 Greer, Mignolo, and Quilligan, introduction to *Rereading the Black Legend*, 14. Mignolo adds that during the sixteenth century "[t]heology served as the conceptual framework to argue 'racial differences' in two directions simultaneously: First, Spain, and later England and France, distinguished themselves from the Muslims (in the north of Africa) and the 'Turks' in the East (the Ottoman Empire). Second ... England distinguished itself from the Spaniards, who, the English said, had Moorish blood and acted as barbarians in the New World" ("Afterword," 312–13).

81 Hall, *Things of Darkness*, 2.

82 Loomba and Burton, introduction to *Race in Early Modern England*, 10. For more on the multivalent discourses of blackness during this "era of transition," see Dalton, "Art for the Sake of Dynasty."

83 Krantz's discussion, in "Audience Response to *Henry VIII*," of "'Black' Wolsey" is misleading (137), as the play does not attach these stereotypical terms to the cardinal, even though he is frequently referred to as a devil (cf. 1.1.52–3, 69–72).

84 Sudan, in *Fair Exotics*, remarks that the "*Oxford English Dictionary* identities the first use of the word 'fair' (in England) to refer specifically to lightness of complexion as occurring in 1551" (148). Earlier, "fair" could be applied to the Egyptian queen, Cleopatra, as in Chaucer's *Legend of Good Women*: "Sche [She] was fayr [fair] as is the Rose in may [May]" (*OED*, s.v. "fair," I.1.a); this broader application remained operative, if residual, into the early seventeenth century. Taylor more extensively traces this history in *Buying Whiteness*, specifying 1613 as the year when the "word [white] began to be popularly used in a specific, figurative, physical, ideological, positive, popular, and recognizably modern 'racial' ... sense in London" and thereafter globally (9). Even in an early colonial context blackness could be represented as beauty, which did not mitigate exploitation, on which see Stevenson, "Richard Ligon and the Theater of Empire." For another reading of Ligon, see Feerick, *Strangers in Blood*, 137–72.

85 Wallace, *Premodern Places*, 249; for more on "Blackness, Peasantry, Villainy, Beauty," see ibid., 248–52.

86 In the eighteenth century, Dr Samuel Johnson famously pronounced: "The meek sorrows and virtuous distress of Catherine have furnished some scenes which may be justly numbered among the greatest efforts of tragedy" (Sherbo, *Johnson on Shakespeare*, 657). Bowers, "'The merciful construction of good women,'" traces and challenges this traditional view. This view nevertheless informs Hansen, "'And a Queen of England, Too,'" who argues that "Shakespeare and Fletcher present Catherine as a Griselda-like figure and paragon of English feminine virtue" (91). For more, see Appleford, "Shakespeare's Katherine of Aragon," and Dillon, "Powerful Obedience."

87 Krantz, in "Audience Response to *Henry VIII*," states: "Queen Katherine's championing the cause of the citizenry is a complete invention by Shakespeare" (134). Magnusson, "The Rhetoric of Politeness," describes it as "bold speech action" (401). For more, see Candido, "Katherine of Aragon and Female Greatness."

88 While Griffin does not discuss Shakespeare's play in *English Renaissance Drama and the Specter of Spain*, he offers an important cultural analysis of Catherine of Aragon (30–7). Also consider Queen Hermione's assertion in Shakespeare's late play *The Winter's Tale* , in response to the false charges of adultery from her husband Leontes, the King of Sicilia: "The Emperor of Russia was my father" (3.2.117). On Russians as "proximate Other" for the English, see Palmer, *Writing Russia*, 21, 32.

89 For an influential description of Latin as a "father tongue," see Ong, "Latin Language Study." On the historical Catherine of Aragon's humanist education, see Mattingly, *Catherine of Aragon*, 8–11.

90 On "interpellation" and subject formation, see Althusser, "Ideology and Ideological State Apparatuses," 85–126. On "racial interpellation," see Smith, *Race and Rhetoric*, 152; cf. 138.

91 I agree with Bowers's argument in "'The merciful construction of good women'" that Wolsey taunts Katherine in this scene (38; 47n10). Berry, "*Henry VIII* and the Dynamics of Spectacle," offers a contrary reading.

92 Buckingham is caught in a similar subversion-containment dynamic when he defends himself against "black envy" (*Henry VIII* 2.1.86). For this new historicist paradigm, see Luis-Martínez, "'Maimed Narrations.'"

93 *The Norton Shakespeare*, 3166n5. For a related emphasis on class, see Shakespeare, *Henry VIII*, ed. Mowat and Werstine, 146, 241; *King Henry VIII (All is True)*, ed. McMullan, 350; and *King Henry VIII*, ed. Margeson, 140.

94 Shakespeare, *Henry VIII*, ed. Foakes, 116, citing E. Guilpin's *Skialethia* , sig. B3r; Hall, *Things of Darkness*, 62–122; cf. Shapiro, "Brown – 'Ugly'?"

95 The textual variant for the latter is "earthy cold" (*The Norton Shakespeare*, 3193).

96 *The Norton Shakespeare* glosses "used" in this passage as "signifying chastity" (3177). A comparison with Shakespeare's *Othello*, a play similarly (if more overtly) concerned with the imbrication of blackness and femininity, reveals the double edge of this term (3.3.262–81). For an astute analysis, see Callaghan, *Shakespeare without Women*, 75–96.

97 Fraser, *The Wives of Henry VIII*, 230–1. The autopsy of Catherine "*did reveal a large round black growth on her heart which was itself 'completely black and hideous'*" (229, citing the resident ambassador Eustache Chapuys's report to Charles V). This "blackness" was interpreted as the sign of a broken heart rather than a sign of sin, corruption, or infidelity.

98 On Shakespeare's Anne Bolyen, see Leahy, "'You cannot show me,'" and Hilberdink-Sakamoto, "'O God's Will, Much Better She Ne'er Had Known Pomp.'"

99 Anglo, *Spectacle, Pageantry, and Early Tudor Policy*, 130.

100 Twycross and Carpenter, *Masks and Masking*, 166–7.

101 *The Norton Shakespeare*, 3135.

102 Hall, *Things of Darkness*, 9.

103 Vickers, "'The blazon of sweet beauty's best,'" 96.

104 For the full scope of this injunction, see Hull, *Chaste, Silent, and Obedient*.

105 *The Norton Shakespeare*, 3137. These directions, "Enter King and others as Maskers, habited like Shepheards," are among the few that appear in the First Folio, *Mr. William Shakespeares Comedies, Histories, & Tragedies*, 211.

106 As Mattingly, *Renaissance Diplomacy*, documents, "Nobody in the sixteenth century except an Englishman was expected to speak English, not even the perfect ambassador" (186; cf. 205). For more, see Smith, *Race and Rhetoric*, 92–9.

107 Twycross and Carpenter, *Masks and Masking*, 166; Hall, *The Lives of the Kings*, 15. "Bawdkin" is "[a] rich embroidered stuff, originally made with warp of gold thread and woof of silk" (*OED*, s.v. "baudekin"). "Cimiteries" means "scimitars," or "[a] short, curved, single-edged sword, used among Orientals, esp. Turks and Persians" (*OED*, s.v. "scimitar"). A "bawderike" is "[a] belt or girdle, usually of leather and richly ornamented, worn pendent from one shoulder across the breast and under the opposite arm, and used to support the wearer's sword, bugle, etc." (*OED*, s.v. "baldric").

108 For the proposition that these musicians are African-descent performers and not Englishmen in blackface, see Chapman, "The Appearance of Blacks," 86–92.

109 Hall, *Things of Darkness*, 91, 13.

110 Archer, *Old Worlds*, 122–4, 128–9.

111 *The Norton Shakespeare* glosses "strains" as "embraces" (3171). The *OED*, citing this line, more precisely defines the term as "[t]o clasp tightly in one's arms" (s.v. "strain, v.1"). It also has a bawdy connotation.

112 See Loughnane, "'I Myself Would for Caernarfonshire'" and "*King Henry VIII (All is True)*"; Round, "Rojas' Old Bawd and Shakespeare's Old Lady."

113 For a comparison with *Othello*, see Merriam, "The Old Lady, or All is Not True," 235.

114 On Henry's purported pangs of conscience, see Wegemer, "Henry VIII on Trial."

115 *The Norton Shakespeare*, 3147n3. See also Fizer, "Emballing, Empalling, Embalming, and Embailing."

116 Cohen, introduction to *All is True (Henry VIII)*, 3116.

117 Scarisbrick, *Henry VIII*, points out that Anne's actual title was "marquis of Pembroke (not marchioness, because she held the title in her own right)" (306).

118 Compare the vulgar pun on "common" in Shakespeare's *Hamlet* (1.2.74).

119 For more on *The Masque of Blackness*, see Frye, "Anne of Denmark," and Roper, "Unmasquing the Connections."

120 For an astute analysis, see Richmond, "Elizabeth I in Shakespeare's *Henry VIII*."

121 According to Warnicke, *The Rise and Fall of Anne Boleyn*, 168–9, and Fraser, *The Wives of Henry VIII*, 199, the historical Henry VIII expressed deep disappointment at the news of Elizabeth's birth. Ives, *The Life and Death of Anne Boleyn*, counters: "There is ... no evidence of the crushing psychological blow that some have supposed" (184).

122 *The Norton Shakespeare* glosses "tool" as "genitalia" (3188n5). Critics have described *Henry VIII*'s porter scene in terms of "amoral energy" – as in Cespedes, "'We are one in fortunes,'" 435; Roman saturnalia – Hiscock, "Erotic Sovereignty," 59; and Bakhtinian carnivalesque – McMullan, "'Swimming on Bladders,'" 223–4.

123 On Henry VIII's "incest problems" and their impact on his daughter with Anne Boleyn, the future Queen Elizabeth, see Quilligan, *Incest and Agency*, 33–8.

124 See the essays in Pritchard, *Solomon and Sheba*, esp. Watson, "The Queen of Sheba in Christian Tradition," 115–45. On Sheba as a racialized icon in

early modern England, see Hall, "Object into Object?" 359–66, and *Things of Darkness*, 108–9. Bosman, "Seeing Tears," 474–6, explicates the Sheba reference in Shakespeare's *Henry VIII* alongside Hans Holbein's *Solomon and the Queen of Sheba*. Vanita, "Mariological Memory," 329–30, also addresses the Sheba reference. On Aden as an important port for the East India Company in this period, see Barbour, *The Third Voyage Journals*.

125 In addition, see Felperin, *Shakespearean Romance*, who notes that James as Solomon signified the culmination of the "Tudor myth of British history" (193). For more on James as the New Solomon destined to draw Great Britain under his beneficent imperial rule, see Parry, *The Golden Age Restor'd*, 29–32. For an entertainment featuring the Queen of Sheba that King James arranged for his brother-in-law, Christian IV of Denmark, in 1606, see Butler, *The Stuart Court Masque*, 125–7.

126 Tate, "King James I and the Queen of Sheba," 564; Peck, *The Mental World of the Jacobean Court*, 9.

127 Tate, "King James I and the Queen of Sheba," 565.

128 On this ecumenism and its limits, see Patterson, *King James VI and I and the Reunion of Christendom*, 31–74.

129 *The Norton Shakespeare*, 3191n4. See Bliss, "The Wheel of Fortune," for the double valence of Cranmer's prophecy; however, neither Bliss nor subsequent critics who discuss this prophecy address the imperial theme embedded therein.

130 Andrews, *Trade, Plunder and Settlement*, 13, who continues with the proviso, "James during most of his reign deferred to Spain's pre-emptive claims in the Caribbean, but supported trade and settlement in areas Spain claimed and manifestly did not possess: North America and the East Indies" (13).

6. The Intersecting Paths of Two Women from the Islamic World: Teresa Sampsonia, Mariam Khanim, and the East India Company

1 For the term "presences of women," see Coldiron, "Women in Early English Print Culture," 61.

2 I first made this connection in the course of my collaboration with Bindu Malieckal on the workshop, "Faith Journeys: The Early Seventeenth-Century Travels of Teresa Sampsonia Sherley and Begum Mariam Khan from the Islamic Empires of the East to England," at the 2009 Attending to Early Modern Women symposium, University of Maryland at College Park. I am most grateful to Professor Malieckal for our ongoing collaborations and conversations. I presented a preliminary draft of this chapter at the

2014 conference, Christian-Islamic Interactions: Mobility, Connection, Transformation (1450–1800) (Scuola Normale Superiore, Pisa, Italy). I thank Professor Giuseppe Marcocci profusely for his interest and support.

3 Games, *The Web of Empire*, 103.

4 On native wives of Englishmen in India, see Nocentelli, *Empires of Love*, 115–60.

5 For a fascinating study of Ann Broomfield, General William Keeling's wife, and her attempts to accompany her husband on the 1615 mission to the Mughal court, see Barbour, "Desdemona and Mrs. Keeling."

6 John Dryden's *Amboyna* was initially staged in 1672; the play was published the following year. The subtitle, *"or the Cruelties of the Dutch to the English Merchants"* is listed on page one. Dryden was poet laureate from April 1668 to January 1689 (N.S.).

7 Malieckal, "Mariam Khan," 97. For the honorific "Khanim," see 139n83 above.

8 On Dryden's *Amboyna*, see Nocentelli, *Empires of Love,* 141–50; Ahmed, *The Stillbirth of Capital*, 25–50; Thompson, *Performing Race and Torture*, 99–120; Markley, *The Far East and the English Imagination*, 143–76; and Raman, *Framing "India,"* 189–236.

9 On "the 'exchange of women' model for cultural formation," see Andrea, *Women and Islam*, 13.

10 Fisher, *Counterflows to Colonialism*, 23.

11 Coverte, *A True and Almost Incredible Report*, 42. Hawkins, in "Captaine William Hawkins, his Relations," explains: "because my name was something hard for his [Jahangir's] pronuntiation, hee called me by the name of *English Chan*, that is to say, *English* Lord, but in *Persia*, it is the Title for a Duke, and this went currant throughout the Countrey" (210).

12 Hawkins, "Captaine William Hawkins, his Relations," 211.

13 Coverte, *A True and Almost Incredible Report*, 39.

14 Hawkins, "Captaine William Hawkins, his Relations," 211, 214.

15 Hawkins, "Captaine William Hawkins, his Relations," 215–16. Hawkins uses Old Style dating, with the year starting on March 25; I adjust to New Style in my narration.

16 Robertson, "Mariam Khan, The Resourceful Widow." Robertson is preparing an extended study of "stranger" wives and widows in early modern England, including Mariam Khan, Teresa Sherley, and Pocahontas.

17 Markley, *The Far East and the English Imagination*, 162.

18 Robertson, "Mariam Khan, The Resourceful Widow," details Mariam's struggle to obtain "repayment from the [East India] Company for Hawkins' expenses in India. Administrix of her husband's will, she sought repayment debts of £600." While the EIC rejected this claim for

compensation, it did offer her "200 Jacobus in a purse" as a gift. Robertson concludes that Mariam showed "competence in business affairs in seeking her husband's money and emotional resilience in securing herself a protector and new husband." See also Robertson, "A 'Stranger' Bride."

19 Neill, *Putting History to the Question*, explicates "An Episode of Torture at Bantam in Java, 1604" (285–309). On the "Pamphlet Wars" from the 1620s that influenced Dryden's play fifty years later, see Markley, *The Far East, and the English Imagination* 149–59.

20 Fisher, *Counterflows to Colonialism*, 23n8.

21 Games, *The Web of Empire*, 81–115.

22 Callaghan, "Re-Reading," 163, citing Modeleski, *Feminism Without Women*, 6.

23 As Margaret Cavendish (née Lucas), wife of William Cavendish, Marquis of Newcastle (later Duke), explains in "A True Relation of My Birth, Breeding and Life," "neither did I intend this piece for to delight, but to divulge, not to please the fancy, but to tell the truth, lest after-Ages should mistake, in not knowing I was daughter to one Master *Lucas* of St. *Johns* near *Colchester* in *Essex*, second Wife to the Lord Marquis of *Newcastle*, for, my Lord having had two Wives, I might easily have been mistaken, especially if I should dye, and my Lord Marry again" (391). For a modernized excerpt, see Graham et al., *Her Own Life*, 87–100.

24 Penrose, *The Sherleian Odyssey*, 189; cf. 171. Powell accompanied Anthony and Robert Sherley to the Safavid Empire in 1599; he remained behind with Robert when Anthony absconded in 1600.

25 As Saris records in "The Eighth Voyage," "Captaine *Hawkins* upon distast[e] was come from *Agra*, and with his wife was aboord his ship" (347).

26 Penrose, *The Sherleian Odyssey*, mistakenly states that William Hawkins (and Mariam, whom he does not name) sailed on the *Hector* (190). In fact, they sailed on the *Thomas*, as Hawkins records in "Captaine William Hawkins, his Relations" (215). Hawkins further records that "[s]ome eight days after [his ship's arrival at the Cape] the Expedition came in" (216), bearing letters from the East India Company.

27 Penrose, *The Sherleian Odyssey*, 199.

28 Andrews, *Trade, Plunder and Settlement*, 275. The variant spelling is Steele.

29 For the original, which I have consulted, see the India Office Records and Private Papers in the British Library Archives, "Nicholas Downton at Surat to Sir Robert Sherley" (IOR/E/3/2 ff 124–5: c Nov 1614). For a published version, see Foster, *Letters Received by the East India Company*, 2:209–11.

30 Penrose, *The Sherleian Odyssey*, 199. Gwadar is a port on the Arabian Sea in what is now southwestern Pakistan. The Portuguese sacked and burned it in 1581. Barendse, *The Arabian Seas*, states: "Laribandar, on the mouth of

the Indus ... was the largest center of trade of the Arabian seas" and "[i]t was mainly a port of trade with Persia, both overland and overseas" (54).

31 Chick, *A Chronicle*, 1:145.

32 Lee, in his entry on "Shirley or Sherley, Robert," in *Dictionary of National Biography*, 52: 136–7, comments: "To her [Teresa's] and Sir Robert's only son, Henry, Lady Shirley (his grandmother) left 40*l.* a year in 1623, making at the same time a bequest to a young Persian companion, William Nazerbeg. Henry Shirley was alive in England in 1626, but died there soon afterwards" (137). The minor playwright, Sir Henry Shirley (d. 1627), was the second son of Thomas Sherley, Robert's eldest brother.

33 Penrose, *The Sherleian Odyssey*, 243, 200.

34 Payton, "A Journall," 488. "Tomasin" is of Aramaic origin, which suggests Lady Powell was a Chaldean Christian from the Safavid Empire. For a comparable example of a Western Christian man – in this case, the aristocratic Roman traveller Pietro della Valle (1556–1652) – marrying a Chaldean Christian woman, see Baskins, "Lost in Translation."

35 Fisher, *Counterflows to Colonialism*, 27. Fisher also documents an East India Company proposal to send "an English gentlewoman as a wife" to "the Muslim king of Sumatra." He continues: "One English father volunteered his daughter, who boasted 'most excellent parts for music, her needle and good discourse, and also [was] very beautiful and personable'" (26). He concludes: "While most directors favoured the alliance, the Company's religious advisors opposed it, allegedly fearing the jealousy of the king's other wives towards such an accomplished rival" (26). In other words, the English father was prepared to dispose his daughter into a polygynous non-Christian marriage, a possibility Shakespeare broaches with the marriage of Claribel, daughter of the king of Naples, to the king of Tunis in *The Tempest* (2.1.68–70).

36 Penrose, *The Sherleian Odyssey*, 181n2. Mrs Powell, to recall, was thought to be from Persia; she apparently died in childbirth in India (194).

37 For an important study of this neglected topic, see Sen, "Traveling Companions." For more, see Sen, "Sailing to India."

38 Andrews, *Trade, Plunder and Settlement*, stresses the uncertainty associated with the East India Company from its incorporation in 1600 through the early seventeenth century; as he concludes, "its difficulties persisted until the Restoration [after 1660], when its days of prosperity and grandeur may be said to begin" (279).

Bibliography

Primary Sources

Arber, Edward, ed. *The First Three English Books on America*. Birmingham: Turnbull and Spears, 1885.

Arnold, Janet, ed. *Queen Elizabeth's Wardrobe Unlock'd: The Inventories of the Wardrobe of Robes prepared in July 1600 edited from Stowe MS 557 in the British Library, MS LR 2/121 in the Public Record Office, London, and MS V. b.72 in the Folger Shakespeare Library, Washington DC*. Leeds: Maney, 1988.

Beazley, C. Raymond, ed. *The Texts and Versions of John de Plano Carpini and William de Rubruquis, as Printed for the First Time by Hakluyt in 1598, together with Some Shorter Pieces*. London: Hakluyt Society, 1903.

Berry, Lloyd E., and Robert O. Crummey, eds. *Rude and Barbarous Kingdom: Russia in the Accounts of Sixteenth-Century English Voyagers*. Madison: University of Wisconsin Press, 1968.

Best, George. *A True Discourse of the late voyages of discouerie, for the finding of a passage to Cathaya, by the Northweast, vnder the conduct of Martin Frobisher Generall: Deuided into three Books*. London: Henry Bynnyman, 1578.

Biddulph, William. *The Travels of certaine Englishmen into Africa, Asia, Troy, Bythinia, Thracia, and to the Blacke Sea, and into Syria, Cilicia, Pisidia, Mesopotamia, Damascus, Canaan, Galile, Samaria, Iudea, Palestina, Ierusalem, Iericho, and to the Red Sea: and to sundry other places*. London: Th. Haueland for W. Aspley, 1609.

Bray, Gerald, ed. *Documents of the English Reformation, 1526–1701*. Cambridge: James Clark, 2004.

Burel, John. *The Discription of the Queenis Majesties Maist Honorable Entry into the Tovn of Edinburgh, Upon the 19 Day of Maii 1590*. In Craig, *Papers Relative to the Marriage*, separately paginated.

Carleton, Dudley. *Dudley Carleton to John Chamberlain, 1603–1624: Jacobean Letters*. Ed. Maurice Lee, Jr. New Brunswick, NJ: Rutgers University Press, 1972.

Carpini, Giovanni DiPlano. *The Story of the Mongols Whom We Call the Tartars*. Ed. and trans. Erik Hildinger. Boston: Braden Publishing, 1996.

Cary, Elizabeth. *The Tragedie of Mariam, the Faire Queene of Iewry. Written by that learned, vertuous, and truly noble Ladie, E.C.* London: Thomas Creede for Richard Hawkins, 1613.

– *The Tragedy of Mariam, the Fair Queen of Jewry, with the Lady Falkland Her Life by One of Her Daughters*. Ed. Barry Weller and Margaret W. Ferguson. Berkeley: University of California Press, 1994.

Cavendish, Margaret. "A true Relation of my Birth, Breeding, and Life." In *Natures Pictvres Drawn by Fancies Pencil to the Life. Written by the thrice Noble, Illustrious, and Excellent Princess, the Lady Marchioness of Newcastle*, 368–91. London: J. Martin and J. Allestrye, 1656.

Cerasano, S.P., and Marion Wynne-Davies, eds. *Renaissance Drama by Women: Texts and Documents*. London: Routledge, 1996.

Chick, Herbert, ed. *A Chronicle of the Carmelites in Persia and the Papal Mission of the XVIIth and XVIIIth Centuries*. 2 vols. London: Eyre and Spottiswoode, 1939.

Churchyard, Thomas. *A Discovrse of The Queenes Maiesties entertainment in Suffolk and Norffolk: With a description of many things then presently seene. Deuised by Thomas Churchyarde, Gent. with diuers shewes of his own inuention sette out at Norwich: and some rehearsal of hir Highnesse retourne from Progresse. Wherevnto is adioyned a commendation of Sir Humfrey Gilberts ventrous iourney*. London: Henrie Bynneman, 1578.

– *A Prayse, and Reporte of Maister Martyne Forboishers Voyage to Meta Incognita. (A name giuen by a mightie and most great Personage) in which praise and reporte is written diuers discourses neuer published by any man as yet*. London: Andrew Maunsell, 1578.

Code of Canon Law. Latin-English edition. Vatican: Libreria Editrice Vaticana, 1983. http://www.vatican.va/archive/ENG1104/_INDEX.HTM, last accessed 2 Sept. 2016.

Collinson, Richard, ed. *The Three Voyages of Martin Frobisher*. London: Hakluyt Society, 1867.

Coryat, Thomas. "A Letter of Mr. Thomas Coryat, which trauailed by Land from Ierusalem to the Court of the Great Mogol." In Purchas, *Pvrchas his Pilgrimes*, 592–5.

Coverte, Robert. *A Trve and Almost Incredible report of an Englishman, that (being cast away in the good Ship called the Assention in Cambaya, the farthest part of the East Indies) Trauelled by Land through many vnknowne Kingdomes, and great Cities*. London: William Hall for Thomas Archer and Richard Redmer, 1612.

Craig, J.T. Gibson, ed. *Papers Relative to the Marriage of King James the Sixth of Scotland with the Princess Anna of Denmark*. Edinburgh: The Bannatyne Club, 1828.

Dallam, Thomas. "The Diary of Master Thomas Dallam, 1599–1600." In *Early Voyages and Travels in the Levant*, ed. J. Theodore Bent, 1–98. London: Hakluyt Society, 1893.

Dee, John. *The Limits of the British Empire (Brytanici Imperii Limites, 1578)*. Ed. Ken MacMillan, with Jennifer Abeles. Westport, CT: Praeger, 2004.

The Dictes and Sayings of the Philosophers: A Facsimile Reproduction of the First Book Printed in England by William Caxton, in 1477. Ed. William Blades. London: Elliot Stock, 1877.

Downton, Nicholas. "Nicholas Downton at Surat to Sir Robert Sherley" (IOR/E/3/2 ff 124–5: c Nov 1614). India Office Records and Private Papers in the British Library Archives.

Dryden, John. *Amboyna: A Tragedy. As it is Acted at the Theatre-Royal*. London: T.N. for Henry Herringman, 1673.

Dunbar, William. *The Poems of William Dunbar*. Ed. Priscilla Bawcutt. 2 vols. Glasgow: Association for Scottish Literary Studies, 1998.

– *The Poems of William Dunbar*. Ed. James Kinsley. Oxford: Clarendon Press, 1979.

Elizabeth I. *Elizabeth I: Collected Works*. Ed. Leah S. Marcus, Janel Mueller, and Mary Beth Rose. Chicago: University of Chicago Press, 2000.

– *The Letters of Queen Elizabeth*. Ed. G.B. Harrison. New York: Funk and Wagnalls, 1968.

– *Queen Elizabeth I: Selected Works*. Ed. Steven W. May. New York: Washington Square Press, 2004.

Ellis, Thomas. *A true report of the third and last voyage into Metaincognita: atchieued by the worthie Capteine, M. Martine Frobisher Esquire, Anno. 1578*. London: Thomas Dawson, 1578.

Fletcher, Giles. *Of the Rvsse common wealth. Or, Maner of Gouernement by the Russe Emperour, (commonly called the Emperour of Moskouia) with the manners, and fashions of the people of that Countrey*. London: T.D. for Thomas Charde, 1591.

Foster, William, ed. *Letters Received by the East India Company from its Servants in the East. Transcribed from the "Original Correspondence" Series of the India Office Records*. Vol. 2: 1613–15. London: Sampson Low, Marston and Company, 1897.

Fuller, Thomas. *The History of the Worthies of England, Who for Parts and Learning have been eminent in the several Counties: Together with an Historical*

Narrative of the Native Commodities and Rarities in each County. London: J.G.W.L. and W.G. for Thomas Williams, 1662.

Gesta Grayorum: or, The History of the High and mighty Prince, Henry Prince of Purpoole, Arch-Duke of Stapulia and Bernardia, Duke of High and Nether Holborn, Marquis of St. Giles and Tottenham, Count Palatine of Bloomsbury and Clerkenwell, Great Lord of the Cantons of Islington, Kentish-Town, Paddington and Knights-bridge, Knight of the most Heroical Order of the Helmet, and Sovereign of the Same; Who Reigned and Died, A.D. 1594. Together with a Masque, as it was presented (by His Highness's Command) for the Entertainment of Q. Elizabeth; who, with the Nobles of both Courts, was present thereat. London: W. Canning, 1688.

Gesta Grayorum. Ed. Desmond Bland. Liverpool: Liverpool University Press, 1968.

Gesta Grayorum. Ed. W.W. Greg. Oxford: Oxford University Press, 1914.

Gilbert, Humphrey. *A Discovrse of a Discouerie for a new Passage to Cataia*. London: Henry Middleton for Richarde Ihones, 1576.

Graham, Elspeth, Hilary Hinds, Elaine Hobby, and Helen Wilcox, eds. *Her Own Life: Autobiographical Writings by Seventeenth-Century Englishwomen*. London: Routledge, 1989.

Hadfield, Andrew, ed. *Amazons, Savages, and Machiavels: Travel and Colonial Writing in English, 1550–1630*. Oxford: Oxford University Press, 2001.

Hakluyt, Richard. *Divers voyages touching the discouerie of America, and the Ilands adiacent vnto the same, made first of all by our Englishmen, and afterward by the Frenchmen and Britons*. London: Thomas Woodcocke, 1582.

– *The Principall Navigations, Voiages and Discoueries of the English nation, made by Sea or ouer Land, to the most remote and farthest distant Quarters of the earth at any time within the compasse of these 1500. yeeres*. London: George Bishop and Ralph Newberie, 1589.

– *The Principal Navigations, Voyages, Traffiqves and Discoueries of the English Nation, made by Sea or ouer-land, to the remote and farthest distant quarters of the Earth, at any time within the compasse of these 1600 yeres*. London: George Bishop, Ralph Newberie, and Robert Barker, 1599–1600.

Hall, Christopher. "The first Voyage of M. Martine Frobisher, to the Northwest, for the search of the straight or passage to China, written by Christopher Hall, Master in the Gabriel, and made in the yeere of our Lord 1576." In Stefansson, *Three Voyages*, 1:149–54.

Hall, Edward. *The Lives of the Kings*. Vol. 2: *The Triumphant Reigne of Kyng Henry the VIII*. Ed. Charles Whibley. London: T.C. and E.C. Jack, 1904.

Harriot, Thomas. *A briefe and true report of the new found land of Virginia: of the commodities there found and to be raysed, as well as merchantable, as others for vituall, building and other necessarie vses for those that are and shalbe the planters there; and of the nature and manners of the naturall inhabitants.* London: R. Robinson, 1588.

– *A Briefe and True Report of the New Found Land of Virginia: The Complete 1590 Edition with the 28 Engravings by Theodore de Bry after the Drawings of John White and Other Illustrations.* New York: Dover, 1972.

Hawkins, William. "Captaine William Hawkins, his Relations of the Occurrents which happened in the time of his residence in India, in the County of the Great Mogoll, and of his departure from thence; written to the Company." In Purchas, *Pvrchas his Pilgrimes*, 206–26.

Henderson, Katherine Usher, and Barbara F. McManus, eds. *Half Humankind: Contexts and Texts of the Controversy about Women in England, 1540–1640.* Urbana: University of Illinois Press, 1985.

Herbert, Thomas. *A Relation of Some Yeares Travaile, Begvnne Anno 1626. Into Afrique and the greater Asia, especially the Territories of the Persian Monarchie: and some parts of the Orientall Indies, and Iles adiacent.* London: William Stansby and Jacob Bloome, 1634.

– *Some Years Travels into Divers Parts of Africa, and Asia the Great. Describing more particularly the Empires of Persia and Industan.* London: R. Everingham for R. Scot et al., 1677.

– *Travels in Africa, Persia, and Asia the Great (1677).* Ed. John Anthony Butler. Tempe: Arizona Center for Medieval and Renaissance Studies, 2012.

Jenkinson, Anthony. "The voyage of M. Anthony Jenkinson, made from the citie of Mosco in Russia, to the citie of Boghar in Bactria, in the yere 1558: written by himselfe to the Merchants of London of the Moscovie companie." In Morgan and Coote, *Early Voyages*, 1:41–100.

Jonson, Ben. *Ben Jonson: The Complete Masques.* Ed. Stephen Orgel. New Haven, CT: Yale University Press, 1969.

– *The Cambridge Edition of the Works of Ben Jonson.* 7 vols. Gen. eds. David Bevington, Martin Butler, and Ian Donaldson. Cambridge: Cambridge University Press, 2012.

– *The Characters of Two royall Masques. The one of Blacknesse, The other of Beavtie. Personated by the most magnificent of Queenes, Anne Queene of great Britaine, &c. With her honorable Ladyes, 1605. and 1608. at White hall: and Inuented by Ben: Ionson.* London: Thomas Thorp, 1608.

Knolles, Richard. *The Generall Historie of the Turkes, from The first beginning of that Nation to the rising of the Othoman Familie: with all the notable expeditions of the Christian Princes against them. Together with the Lives and Conquests of the Othoman Kings and Emperours.* London: Adam Islip, 1603.

Lindesay, Robert, of Pitscottie. *The Historie and Cronicles of Scotland: From the Slauchter of King James the First to the Ane thousande fyve hundreith thrie scoir fyftein zeir*. Vol. 1. Ed. Æ.J.G. Mackay. Edinburgh: William Blackwood and Sons, 1899.

Lithgow, William. *A Most Delectable and Trve Discourse, of an admired and painefull peregrination from Scotland, to the most famous Kingdomes in Europe, Asia and Affricke*. London: Nicholas Okes, 1614.

Lok, Michael. "Michael Lok's Account of the First Voyage ... East India by the Northwestw[ard]." In Stefansson, *Three Voyages*, 1:157–66.

Loomba, Ania, and Jonathan Burton, eds. *Race in Early Modern England: A Documentary Companion*. New York: Palgrave Macmillan, 2007.

Middleton, Thomas. "Sir Robert Sherley his Entertainment in Cracovia." Ed. Jerzy Limon and Daniel J. Vitkus. In *Thomas Middleton: The Collected Works*, ed. Gary Taylor and John Lavagnino, 670–8. Oxford: Clarendon Press, 2007.

– *Sir Robert Sherley, Sent ambassadour in the Name of the King of Persia, to Sigismond the third, King of Poland and Swecia, and to other Princes of Evrope. His Royall entertainement into Cracovia, the chiefe Citie of Poland, with his pretended Comming into England. Also, the Honourable praises of the same Sir Robert Sherley, giuen vnto him in that Kingdome, are here likewise inserted.* London: I. Windet for Iohn Budge, 1609.

Montagu, Mary Wortley. *The Turkish Embassy Letters*. Ed. Teresa Heffernan and Daniel O'Quinn. Peterborough, ON: Broadview Press, 2013.

Morgan, E. Delmar, and C.H. Coote, eds. *Early Voyages and Travels to Russia and Persia by Anthony Jenkinson and Other Englishmen. With Some Account of the First Intercourse of the English with Russia and Central Asia by Way of the Caspian Sea*. 2 vols. London: Hakluyt Society, 1886.

Nelson, Alan H., and John R. Elliott, Jr, eds. *Inns of Court*. Records of Early English Drama. 3 vols. Cambridge: D.S. Brewer, 2010.

Nixon, Anthony. *The Three English Brothers: Sir Thomas Sherley his Trauels, with his three yeares imprisonment in Turkie ... Sir Anthony Sherley his Embassage to the Christian Princes. Master Robert Sherley his wars against the Turkes, with his marriage to the Emperour of Persia his Neece*. London: John Hodgets, 1607.

"A note of Sebastian Cabotes voyage of discoverie, taken out of an old Chronicle written by Robert Fabian, som[e]time Alderman of London." In Hakluyt, *Divers voyages*, sig. A3–A3v.

Palmer, Thomas. *An Essay of the Meanes how to make our Trauailes, into forraine Countries, the more profitable and honourable*. London: H.L. for Mathew Lownes, 1606.

Paul, James Balfour, ed. *Accounts of the Lord High Treasurer of Scotland*. Vol. 3: 1506–1507. Edinburgh: H.M. General Register House, 1901.

Payton, Walter. "A Iournall of all principall matters passed in the twelfth Voyage to the East-India, obserued by me Walter Payton, in the good ship

the *Expedition*: the Captaine whereof was M. Christopher Newport, being
set out, *Anno* 1612." In Purchas, *Pvrchas his Pilgrimes*, 488–500.

Prynne, William. *Histrio-Mastix: The Players Scovrge, or, Actors Tragædie*.
London: E.A. and W.I. for Michael Sparks, 1633.

Purchas, Samuel. *Pvrchas his Pilgrimes. In Five Books. The first, Contayning the
Voyages and Peregrinations made by ancient Kings ... The second, a Description
of all the Circum-nauigations of the Globe. The third, Nauigations and Voyages of
English-men, alongst the Coasts of Africa . . . The fourth, English Voyages beyond
the East Indies ... The fifth, Nauigations, Voyages, Traffiques, Discoueries, of the
English Nation in the Easterne parts of the World*. London: William Stansby for
Henrie Fetherstone, 1625.

Ralegh, Walter. *The Discoverie of the Large, Rich and Bewtiful Empyre of Guiana*.
Ed. Neil L. Whitehead. Norman: University of Oklahoma Press, 1997.

– *The Discoverie of the Large, Rich and Bewtiful Empire of Gviana, with a relation
of the great and Golden Citie of Manoa (which the Spanyards call El Dorado) And
the Prouinces of Emeria, Arromaia, Amapaia, and other Countries, with their
riuers, adioyning. Performed in the yeare 1595. By Sir W. Ralegh Knight*. London:
Robert Robinson, 1596.

Rubruck, William. *The Mission of Friar William of Rubruck: His Journey to the
Court of the Great Khan Möngke, 1253–1255*. Ed. and trans. Peter Jackson.
London: Hakluyt Society, 1990.

Saris, John. "The eighth Voyage set forth by the *East-Indian* Societie, wherein
were imployed three Ships, the *Cloue*, the *Hector*, and the *Thomas*, vnder
the Command of Captaine *Iohn Saris*: His Course and Acts to and in the
Red Sea, Iaua, Molucca's, and *Iapan* (by the Inhabitants called *Neffoon*, where
also he first began and setled an *English* Trade and Factorie) with other
remarkable Rarities, collected out of his owne Iournall." In Purchas, *Pvrchas
his Pilgrimes*, 334–84.

Settle, Dionyse. *A true reporte of the laste voyage into the West and Northwest
regions, &c. 1577. worthily atchieued by Capteine Frobisher of the sayde voyage
the first finder and Generall. With a description of the people there inhabiting, and
other circumstances notable. Written by Dionyse Settle, one of the companie in the
sayde voyage.* London: Henry Middleton, 1577.

Shakespeare, William. *The Complete Works of Shakespeare*. Ed. David Bevington.
New York: Longman, 1997.

– *Henry VIII*. Ed. Barbara A. Mowat and Paul Werstine. New York:
Washington Square Press, 2007.

– *King Henry VIII*. Ed. R.A. Foakes. London: Methuen, 1964.

– *King Henry VIII, or All is True*. Ed. Jay L. Halio. Oxford: Oxford University
Press, 1999.

– *King Henry VIII*. Ed. John Margeson. Cambridge: Cambridge University Press, 1990.
– *King Henry VIII (All is True)*. Ed. Gordon McMullan. London: Thompson Learning, 2000.
– *Mr. William Shakespeares Comedies, Histories, & Tragedies. Published according to the True Originall Copies*. London: Isaac Iaggard and Ed. Blount, 1623.
– *The Norton Shakespeare: Based on the Oxford Edition*. Ed. Stephen Greenblatt, Walter Cohen, Jean E. Howard, and Katharine Eisaman Maus. New York: Norton, 1997.
Sidney, Mary. *The Tragedie of Antonie (1595)*. In Cerasano and Wynne-Davies, *Renaissance Drama by Women*, 13–42.
Skinner, John, and Dudley Digges. *A True Relation of the Vniust, Crvell, and Barbarovs Proceedings against the English at Amboyna in the East-Indies, by the Neatherlandish Gouernour and Councel there*. London: H. Lownes for Nathanael Newberry, 1624.
Stefansson, Vilhjalmur, ed. *The Three Voyages of Martin Frobisher. In Search of a Passage to Cathay and India by the North-West A.D. 1576–8*. 2 vols. London: Argonaut Press, 1938.
Stubbes, Philip. *The Anatomie of Abuses. Containing a Description of such notable Vices and enormities, as raigne in many Countries of the World, but especiallie in this Realme of England*. London: Richard Iohnes, 1595.
Timberlake, Henry. *A True and strange discourse of the trauailes of two English Pilgrimes: what admirable accidents befell them in their iourney to Ierusalm, Gaza, Grand Cayro, Alexandria, and other places*. London: Nicholas Oakes for Thomas Archer, 1603.
A Trve Report of the most tryumphant, and Royall accomplishment of the Baptisme of the most Excellent, right High, and mightie Prince, Henry Frederick, By the grace of God, Prince of Scotland, and now Prince of Wales: As it was solemnized the 30. day of August 1594. London: Thomas Creede for Iohn Browne, 1603.
Turler, Jerome. *The Traveiler of Ierome Turler ... A woorke very pleasaunt for all persons to reade, and right profitable and necessarie vnto all such as are minded to traueyll*. London: William How for Abraham Veale, 1575.
Warner, William. *Albions England. A Continued Historie of the same Kingdome, from the Originals of the first Inhabitants thereof: With most the chiefe Alterations and Accidents theare hapning, vnto, and in the happie Raigne of our now most gracious Soueraigne, Queene Elizabeth*. London: Edm. Bollifant for George Potter, 1602.
Willes, Richard. "For. M. Cap. Fvrbyshers Passage by the Northwest." In *The History of Trauayle in the West and East Indies, and other countreys lying eyther way, towardes the fruitfull and ryche Moluccaes. As Moscouia, Persia, Arabia, Syria, AEgypte, Ethiopia, Guinea, China in Cathayo, and Giapan: With a discourse*

of the Northwest passage ...Gathered in parte, and done into Englyshe by Richarde Eden. Newly set in order, augmented, and finished by Richarde Willes, 230-36. London: Richarde Iugge, 1577.

Winwood, Ralph. *Memorials of Affairs of State in the Reigns of Q. Elizabeth and K. James I. Collected (chiefly) from the Original Papers of Sir Ralph Winwood, Kt. Sometime one of the Principal Secretaries of State*. Ed. Edmund Sawyer. 3 vols. London: W.B. for T. Ward, 1725.

Wroth, Mary. *The Countesse of Mountgomeries Urania. Written by the right honorable the Lady Mary Wroath. Daughter to the right Noble Robert Earle of Leicester. And Neece to the ever famous, and renowned Sr. Phillips Sidney knight. And to ye most exele[n]t Lady Mary Countesse of Pembroke late deceased.* London: Ioh[n] Marriott and Iohn Grismand, 1621.

– *The First Part of the Countess of Montgomery's Urania*. Ed. Josephine A. Roberts. Binghamton, NY: Center for Medieval and Early Renaissance Studies, 1995; 2nd printing, Tempe: Arizona Center for Medieval and Renaissance Studies, 2005.

– *Lady Mary Wroth's* Love's Victory: *The Penshurst Manuscript*. Ed. Michael G. Brennan. London: The Roxburghe Club, 1988.

– *Love's Victory (c. 1621)*. In Cerasano and Wynne-Davies, *Renaissance Drama by Women*, 91–126.

– *The Poems of Lady Mary Wroth*. Ed. Josephine Roberts. Baton Rouge: Louisiana State University Press, 1983.

– *The Second Part of the Countess of Montgomery's Urania*. Ed. Josephine A. Roberts; completed by Suzanne Gossett and Janel Mueller. Tempe: Arizona Center for Medieval and Renaissance Studies, 1999.

Secondary Sources

Ahmed, Leila. *Women and Gender in Islam: Historical Roots of a Modern Debate*. New Haven, CT: Yale University Press, 1992.

Ahmed, Shahab. *What Is Islam? The Importance of Being Islamic*. Princeton, NJ: Princeton University Press, 2016.

Ahmed, Siraj. *The Stillbirth of Capital: Enlightenment Writing and Colonial India*. Stanford, CA: Stanford University Press, 2012.

Akbari, Suzanne Conklin. *Idols in the East: European Representations of Islam and the Orient, 1100–1450*. Ithaca, NY: Cornell University Press, 2009.

Akhimie, Patricia. "Bruised with Adversity: Reading Race in *The Comedy of Errors*." In Traub, *Oxford Handbook*, 186–96.

Akhimie, Patricia, and Bernadette Andrea, eds. *Traveling/Travailing Women: Early Modern England and the Wider World*. Lincoln: University of Nebraska Press, forthcoming.

Albright, Evelyn May. "*The Faerie Queene* in Masque at the Gray's Inn Revels." *PMLA* 41 (1926): 497–516.

Alexander, Gavin. *Writing after Sidney: The Literary Response to Sir Philip Sidney 1586–1640.* Oxford: Oxford University Press, 2006.

Allinson, Rayne. *A Monarchy of Letters: Royal Correspondence and English Diplomacy in the Reign of Elizabeth I.* New York: Palgrave Macmillan, 2012.

Alsford, Stephen, ed. *The Meta Incognita Project: Contributions to Field Studies.* Hull, QC: Canadian Museum of Civilization, 1993.

Althusser, Louis. "Ideology and Ideological State Apparatuses." In *Lenin and Philosophy and Other Essays,* trans. Ben Brewster, 127–86. New York: Monthly Review Press, 1971.

Amer, Sahar, and Laura Doyle. "Introduction: Reframing Postcolonial and Global Studies in the Longer *Durée.*" *PMLA* 130.2 (2015): 331–5.

Anderson, Clare. *Subaltern Lives: Biographies of Colonialism in the Indian Ocean World, 1790–1920.* Cambridge: Cambridge University Press, 2012.

Andrea, Bernadette. "Amazons, Turks, and Tartars in the *Gesta Grayorum* and *The Comedy of Errors.*" In Traub, *Oxford Handbook,* 77–92.

– "Assimilation or Dissimulation? Leo Africanus's 'Geographical Historie of Africa' and the Parable of Amphibia." *ARIEL: A Review of International English Literature* 32.3 (2001): 7–29.

– "Black Skin, The Queen's Masques: Africanist Ambivalence and Feminine Author(ity) in the Masques of *Blackness* and *Beauty.*" *English Literary Renaissance* 29.2 (1999): 246–81.

– "The Cultural Biography of a Seventeenth-Century Persianate Woman's Carmelite Relic." In Akhimie and Andrea, *Traveling/Travailing Women,* forthcoming.

– "Elizabeth I and Persian Exchanges." In Beem, *Foreign Relations,* 169–99.

– "English Women's Writing and Islamic Empires, 1610–1690." In *The History of British Women's Writing, 1610–1690,* ed. Mihoko Suzuki, 287–302. New York: Palgrave Macmillan, 2011.

– "The Ghost of Leo Africanus from the English to the Irish Renaissance." In Ingham and Warren, *Postcolonial Moves,* 195–215.

– "Islamic Communities." In *The Handbook of Early Modern English Literature and Religion,* ed. Andrew Hiscock and Helen Wilcox. Oxford University Press, forthcoming.

– "'A noble troop of strangers': Masques of Blackness in Shakespeare's *Henry VIII.*" In *Shakespeare and Immigration,* ed. Ruben Espinosa and David Ruiter, 91–111. Farnham, Eng.: Ashgate, 2014.

– "Persia, Tartaria, and Pamphilia: Ideas of Asia in Mary Wroth's *The Countess of Montgomery's Urania, Part II.*" In *The English Renaissance, Orientalism, and the Idea of Asia*, ed. Debra Johanyak and Walter S.H. Lim, 23–50. New York: Palgrave Macmillan, 2009.

– "The 'Presences of Women' from the Islamic World in Sixteenth- to Early Seventeenth-Century British Literature and Culture." In Wiesner-Hanks, *Mapping Gendered Routes*, 291–306.

– "The Tartar Girl, The Persian Princess, and Early Modern English Women's Authorship from Elizabeth I to Mary Wroth." In *Women Writing Back/ Writing Women Back: Transnational Perspectives from the Late Middle Ages to the Dawn of the Modern Era*, ed. Anke Gilleir, Alicia C. Montoya, and Suzan van Dijk, 257–81. Leiden, The Netherlands: Brill, 2010.

– "The Tartar King's Masque and Performances of Imperial Desire in Mary Wroth's *The Countess of Montgomery's Urania*." In Andrea and McJannet, *Early Modern England and Islamic Worlds*, 73–95.

– "'Travelling Bodyes': Native Women of the Northeast and Northwest Passage Ventures and English Discourses of Empire." In *Rethinking Feminism in Early Modern Studies: Gender, Race, and Sexuality*, ed. Ania Loomba and Melissa E. Sanchez, 135–48. London: Routledge, 2016.

– *Women and Islam in Early Modern English Literature*. Cambridge: Cambridge University Press, 2007.

Andrea, Bernadette, and Linda McJannet, eds. *Early Modern England and Islamic Worlds*. New York: Palgrave Macmillan, 2011.

Andrews, Kenneth R. *Drake's Voyages: A Re-Assessment of their Place in Elizabethan Maritime Expansion*. New York: Charles Scribner's Sons, 1967.

– *Trade, Plunder and Settlement: Maritime Enterprise and the Genesis of the British Empire, 1480–1630*. Cambridge: Cambridge University Press, 1984.

Anglo, Sydney. *Spectacle, Pageantry, and Early Tudor Policy* (1969). Oxford: Clarendon Press, 1997.

Appleford, Amy. "Shakespeare's Katherine of Aragon: Last Medieval Queen, First Recusant Martyr." *Journal of Medieval and Early Modern Studies* 40.1 (2010): 149–72.

Aravamudan, Srinivas. *Tropicopolitans: Colonialism and Agency, 1688–1804*. Durham, NC: Duke University Press, 1999.

Archer, Jayne Elisabeth, Elizabeth Goldring, and Sarah Knight, eds. *The Intellectual and Cultural World of the Early Modern Inns of Court*. Manchester: Manchester University Press, 2011.

Archer, John Michael. "*Love's Labour's Lost*." In *A Companion to Shakespeare's Works: The Comedies*, ed. Richard Dutton and Jean E. Howard, 320–37. Malden, MA.: Blackwell, 2003.

– *Old Worlds: Egypt, Southwest Asia, India, and Russia in Early Modern English Writing*. Stanford, CA: Stanford University Press, 2001.

Arlidge, Anthony. *Shakespeare and the Prince of Love: The Feast of Misrule in the Middle Temple.* London: Giles de la Mare Publishers, 2000.

Armitage, David. *The Ideological Origins of the British Empire.* Cambridge: Cambridge University Press, 2000.

– ed. *Theories of Empire, 1450–1800.* Aldershot, Eng.: Ashgate, 1998.

Arthur, Kate. "'You will say they are Persian but let them be changed': Robert and Teresa Sherley's Embassy to the Court of James." In *Britain and the Muslim World: Historical Perspectives*, ed. Gerald MacLean, 37–51. Newcastle-upon-Tyne, Eng.: Cambridge Scholars Publishing, 2011.

Arvas, Abdulhamit. "Travelling Sexualities, Circulating Bodies, and Early Modern Anglo-Ottoman Encounters." PhD Diss., Michigan State University, 2016.

Ashcroft, Bill, Gareth Griffiths, and Helen Tiffin. *The Empire Writes Back: Theory and Practice in Post-colonial Literatures.* London: Routledge, 1989; 2nd ed. 2002.

Astington, John H. *English Court Theatre, 1558–1642.* Cambridge: Cambridge University Press, 1999.

Axton, Marie. "The Tudor Mask and Elizabethan Court Drama." In *English Drama: Forms and Development*, ed. Marie Axton and Raymond Williams, 24–47. Cambridge: Cambridge University Press, 1977.

Babaie, Sussan, Kathryn Babayn, Ina Baghdiantz-MacCabe, and Massumeh Farhad. *Slaves of the Shah: New Elites of Safavid Iran.* London: I.B. Tauris, 2004.

Baillie, William M. "*Henry VIII*: A Jacobean History." *Shakespeare Studies* 12 (1979): 247–66.

Baker, J.H. "The Third University 1450–1550: Law School or Finishing School?" In Archer et al., *The Intellectual and Cultural World*, 8–24.

Baldwin, Robert C.D. "Colonial Cartography under the Tudor and Early Stuart Monarchies, ca. 1480–ca. 1640." In *The History of Cartography.* Vol. 3, *Cartography in the European Renaissance*, ed. David Woodward, 1754–80. Chicago: University of Chicago Press, 2007.

Barbour, Richmond. *Before Orientalism: London's Theatre of the East, 1576–1626.* Cambridge: Cambridge University Press, 2003.

– "Desdemona and Mrs. Keeling." In Akhimie and Andrea, *Traveling/ Travailing Women*, forthcoming.

– *The Third Voyage Journals: Writing and Performance in the London East India Company, 1607–10.* New York: Palgrave Macmillan, 2009.

Barendse, R.J. *The Arabian Seas: The Indian Ocean World of the Seventeenth Century.* Armonk, NY: M.E. Sharp, 2002.

Barish, Jonas A. *The Antitheatrical Prejudice.* Berkeley: University of California Press, 1981.

Baron, Samuel H. "William Borough and the Jenkinson Map of Russia, 1562." *Cartographica: The International Journal for Geographic Information and Geovisualization* 26 (1989): 72–85.

Barroll, Leeds. *Anna of Denmark, Queen of England: A Cultural Biography.* Philadelphia: University of Pennsylvania Press, 2001.

Barthelemy, Anthony Gerard. *Black Face, Maligned Race: The Representation of Blacks in English Drama from Shakespeare to Southerne.* Baton Rouge: Louisiana State University Press, 1987.

Baskins, Cristelle. "Lost in Translation: Portraits of Sitti Maani Gioerida della Valle in Baroque Rome." *Early Modern Women: An Interdisciplinary Journal* 7 (2012): 241–60.

Bearden, Elizabeth B. *The Emblematics of the Self: Ekphrasis and Identity in Renaissance Imitations of Greek Romance.* Toronto: University of Toronto Press, 2012.

Beattie, Owen, and John Geiger. *Frozen in Time: The Fate of the Franklin Expedition.* New York: MJF Books, 2004.

Beem, Charles, ed. *The Foreign Relations of Elizabeth I.* New York: Palgrave Macmillan, 2011.

Bell, Ilona. *Elizabeth I: The Voice of a Monarch.* New York: Palgrave Macmillan, 2010.

Bennett, Andrew. *The Author.* London: Routledge, 2005.

Bennett, John, and Susan Rowley, eds. *Uqalurait: An Oral History of Nunavut.* Montreal, QC: McGill-Queen's University Press, 2004.

Berry, Edward I. "*Henry VIII* and the Dynamics of Spectacle." *Shakespeare Studies* 12 (1979): 229–46.

Berry, Ralph. *Shakespeare and the Awareness of the Audience.* New York: St Martin's Press, 1985.

Bertolet, Anna Riehl. "The Tsar and the Queen: 'You Speak a Language that I Understand Not.'" In Beem, *Foreign Relations*, 101–23.

Birch, Dinah, and Katy Hooper, eds. *The Concise Oxford Companion to English Literature.* 4th ed. Oxford: Oxford University Press, 2012.

Bliss, Lee. "The Wheel of Fortune and the Maiden Phoenix of Shakespeare's *King Henry the Eighth.*" *ELH: English Literary History* 42.1 (1975): 1–25.

Blow, David. *Shah Abbas: The Ruthless King Who Became an Iranian Legend.* London: I.B. Tauris, 2009.

Blunt, Richard. "The Evolution of Blackface Cosmetics on the Early Modern Stage." In *The Materiality of Color: The Production, Circulation, and Application of Dyes and Pigments, 1400–1800*, ed. Andrea Feeser, Maureen Daly Goggin, and Beth Fowkes Tobin, 217–34. Farnham, Eng.: Ashgate, 2012.

Booth, Marilyn, ed. *Harem Histories: Envisioning Places and Living Spaces.* Durham, NC: Duke University Press, 2010.

Bosbach, Franz. "The European Debate on Universal Monarchy." In Armitage, *Theories of Empire*, 1–98.

Bosman, Anston. "Seeing Tears: Truth and Senses in *All is True*." *Shakespeare Quarterly* 50.4 (1999): 459–76.

Bosworth, Clifford Edmund. *An Intrepid Scot: William Lithgow of Lanark's Travels in the Ottoman Lands, North Africa and Central Europe, 1609–21*. Aldershot, Eng.: Ashgate, 2006.

Bovilsky, Lara. *Barbarous Play: Race on the English Renaissance Stage*. Minneapolis: University of Minnesota Press, 2008.

Bowers, Robin. "'The merciful construction of good women': Katherine of Aragon and Pity in Shakespeare's *King Henry*." *Christianity and Literature* 37 (1988): 29–51.

Brancaforte, Elio. *Visions of Persia: Mapping the Travels of Adam Olearius*. Cambridge, MA: Harvard University Press, 2003.

Brennan, Michael G. "Creating Female Authorship in the Early Seventeenth Century: Ben Jonson and Lady Mary Wroth." In *Women's Writing and the Circulation of Ideas: Manuscript Publication in England, 1550–1800*, ed. George L. Justice and Nathan Tinker, 73–93. Cambridge: Cambridge University Press, 2002.

Brentjes, Sonja. "Immediacy, Mediation, and Media in Early Modern Catholic and Protestant Representations of Safavid Iran." *Journal of Early Modern History* 13 (2009): 173–207.

Bridges, Margaret. "The Reinvention of the Medieval Traveller as Cultural Colonization in Richard Hakluyt's *Principall Navigations, Voiages, Traffiques and Discoveries of the English Nation*." *Zeitsprünge: Forschungen zur Frühen Neuzeit* 7.2–3 (2003): 317–33.

Bridges, Roy. "The Legacy of Richard Hakluyt: Reflections on the History of the Hakluyt Society." In Carey and Jowitt, *Richard Hakluyt*, 309–17.

Brigden, Susan. *New Worlds, Lost Worlds: The Rule of the Tudors, 1485–1603*. New York: Viking, 2000.

Britland, Karen. *Drama at the Courts of Henrietta Maria*. Cambridge: Cambridge University Press, 2006.

Brodeur, Patrice C. "Islam and Other Religions." In Martin, *Encyclopedia*, 1:360–4.

Bromley, James M. *Intimacy and Sexuality in the Age of Shakespeare*. Cambridge: Cambridge University Press, 2012.

Brookes, Kristen G. "A Feminine 'Writing that Conquers': Elizabethan Encounters with the New World." *Criticism* 48.2 (2006): 227–62.

Brotton, Jerry. *The Renaissance Bazaar: From the Silk Road to Michelangelo*. Oxford: Oxford University Press, 2002.

Brown, Kathleen. "Native Americans and Early Modern Concepts of Race." In *Empire and Others: British Encounters with Indigenous Peoples, 1600–1850*, ed. Martin Daunton and Rick Halpern, 79–100. Philadelphia: University of Pennsylvania Press, 1999.

Brown, Pamela Allen. "A New Fable of the Belly: Vulgar Curiosity and the Persian Lady's Loose Bodies." In Callaghan, *The Impact of Feminism*, 171–92.

Brummett, Palmira. "Mapping Trans-Imperial Ottoman Space: Alterity and Attraction." In Fuchs and Weissbourd, *Representing Imperial Rivalry*, 33–57.

Burbank, Jane, and Frederick Cooper. *Empires in World History: Power and the Politics of Difference*. Princeton, NJ: Princeton University Press, 2010.

Burton, Audrey. *The Bukharans: A Dynastic, Diplomatic and Commercial History 1550–1702*. New York: Palgrave Macmillan, 1997.

Burton, Jonathan. "The Shah's Two Ambassadors: *The Travels of the Three Sherley Brothers* and the Global Early Modern." In *Emissaries in Early Modern Literature and Culture: Mediation, Transmission, Traffic, 1550–1700*, ed. Brinda Charry and Gitanjali Shahani, 23–40. Surrey, Eng.: Ashgate, 2009.

– *Traffic and Turning: Islam and English Drama, 1579–1624*. Newark: University of Delaware Press, 2005.

Butler, Judith. *Gender Trouble: Feminism and the Subversion of Identity*. New York: Routledge, 1990.

Butler, Martin. "The Court Masque." In Jonson, *The Cambridge Edition*, 1: cxxxi–cxlii.

– *The Stuart Court Masque and Political Culture*. Cambridge: Cambridge University Press, 2008.

Buzard, James M. "What Isn't Travel?" In *Unravelling Civilisation: European Travel and Travel Writing*, ed. Hagen Schulz-Forberg, 43–61. Brussels: P.I.E-Peter Lang, 2005.

Caison, Gina. "Looking for Loss, Anticipating Absence: Imagining Indians in the Archives and Depictions of Roanoke's Lost Colony." In Harris, *Indography*, 43–56.

Callaghan, Dympna. "Re-Reading Elizabeth Cary's *The Tragedie of Mariam, Faire Queene of Jewry*." In Hendricks and Parker, *Women, "Race," and Writing*, 163–77.

– ed. *The Impact of Feminism in English Renaissance Studies*. New York: Palgrave Macmillan, 2007.

– *Shakespeare without Women: Representing Gender and Race on the Renaissance Stage*. London: Routledge, 2000.

Campbell, Julie D. "Masque Scenery and the Tradition of Immobilization in *The First Part* of *The Countess of Montgomery's Urania*." *Renaissance Studies* 22.2 (2008): 221–39.

Campos, Edmund Valentine. "West of Eden: American Gold, Spanish Greed, and the Discourses of English Imperialism." In Greer et al., *Rereading the Black Legend*, 247–69.

Canby, Sheila R. *Shah 'Abbas: The Remaking of Iran*. London: The British Museum Press, 2009.

Candido, Joseph. "Katherine of Aragon and Female Greatness: Shakespeare's Debt to Dramatic Tradition." *Iowa State Journal of Research* 54.4 (1980): 491–8.

Canny, Nicholas. "The Origins of Empire: An Introduction." In *The Oxford History of the British Empire*. Vol. 1, *The Origins of Empire: British Overseas Enterprise to the Close of the Seventeenth Century*, ed. Canny, 1–33. Oxford: Oxford University Press, 1998.

Carey, Daniel, and Claire Jowitt, eds. *Richard Hakluyt and Travel Writing in Early Modern Europe*. Farnham, Eng.: Ashgate, 2012.

Carney, Jo Eldridge. "Queenship in Shakespeare's *Henry VIII*: The Issue of Issue." In *Political Rhetoric, Power, and Renaissance Women*, ed. Carole Levin and Patricia A. Sullivan, 189–202. Albany: State University of New York Press, 1995.

Cavanagh, Sheila T. *Cherished Torment: The Emotional Geography of Lady Mary Wroth's* Urania. Pittsburgh, PA: Duquesne University Press, 2001.

– "'The Great Cham': East Meets West in Lady Mary Wroth's *Urania*." *Meridian: The La Trobe University English Review* 18.1 (2001): 87–103.

– "Prisoners of Love: Cross-Cultural and Supernatural Desires in Lady Mary Wroth's *Urania*." In *Prose Fiction and Early Modern Sexualities in England, 1570–1640*, ed. Constance C. Relihan and Goran V. Stanivukovic, 93–110. New York: Palgrave Macmillan, 2003.

– "'What ish my nation?' Lady Mary Wroth's Interrogations of Personal and National Identity." In *Early Modern Prose Fiction: The Cultural Politics of Reading*, ed. Naomi Conn Liebler, 98–114. New York: Routledge, 2007.

Cerdá, Juan F. "Patriotism, Presentism, and the Spanish *Henry VIII*: The Tragedy of the Migrant Queen." In *Shakespeare beyond English: A Global Experiment*, ed. Susan Bennett and Christie Carson, 273–81. Cambridge: Cambridge University Press, 2013.

Cespedes, Frank V. "'We are one in fortunes': The Sense of History in *Henry VIII*." *English Literary Renaissance* 10.3 (1980): 413–38.

Chalmers, Hero. "'Break up the court': Power, Female Performance and Courtly Ceremony in *Henry VIII*." *Shakespeare* 7.3 (2011): 257–68.

Chapman, Matthieu A. "The Appearance of Blacks on the Early Modern Stage: *Love's Labour's Lost*'s African Connections to Court." *Early Theatre* 17.2 (2014): 77–94.

Chaudhuri, Nupur, Sherry J. Katz, and Mary Elizabeth Perry, eds. *Contesting Archives: Finding Women in the Sources*. Urbana: University of Illinois Press, 2010.

Cheshire, Neil, Tony Waldron, Alison Quinn, and David Quinn. "Frobisher's Eskimos in England." *Archivaria* 10 (1980): 23–50.

Cho, Kwang Soon. "Shakespeare's *Henry VIII* and the Politics of the Spectacle." *The Shakespeare Review* 30 (1997): 197–216.

Cixous, Hélène. "Sorties." Trans. Ann Liddle. In *New French Feminisms: An Anthology*, ed. Elaine Marks and Isabelle de Courtivron, 90–8. New York: Schocken Books, 1981.

Cixous, Hélène, and Catherine Clement. *The Newly Born Woman.* Trans. Betsy Wing. Minneapolis: University of Minnesota Press, 1986.

Cogley, Richard W. "'The Most Vile and Barbarous Nation of all the World': Giles Fletcher the Elder's *The Tartars Or, Ten Tribes* (ca. 1610)." *Renaissance Quarterly* 58 (2005): 781–814.

Cohen, Walter. "The Discourse of Empire in the Renaissance." In *Cultural Authority in Golden Age Spain*, ed. Marina S. Brownlee and Hans Ulrich Gumbrecht, 260–83. Baltimore, MD: Johns Hopkins University Press, 1995.

– Introduction to *All is True (Henry VIII)*. In Shakespeare, *The Norton Shakespeare*, 3111–18.

– Introduction to *Antony and Cleopatra*. In Shakespeare, *The Norton Shakespeare*, 2619–26.

– "The Literature of Empire in the Renaissance." *Modern Philology* 102.1 (2004): 1–34.

Coldiron, A.E B. *Printers without Borders: Translation and Textuality in the Renaissance*. Cambridge: Cambridge University Press, 2015.

– "Women in Early English Print Culture." In *The History of British Women's Writing, 1500–1610*, ed. Caroline Bicks and Jennifer Summit, 60–83. New York: Palgrave Macmillan, 2010.

Cole, Mary Hill. *The Portable Queen: Elizabeth I and the Politics of Ceremony*. Amherst: University of Massachusetts Press, 1999.

Colley, Linda. *Captives: Britain, Empire, and the World, 1600–1850*. New York: Random House, 2002.

Collinson, Patrick. "Elizabethan and Jacobean Puritanism as Forms of Popular Culture." In *The Culture of English Puritanism, 1560–1700*, ed. Christopher Durston and Jacqueline Eales, 32–57. New York: St Martin's Press, 1996.

Connell, C.W. "Western Views of the Origin of the 'Tartars': An Example of the Influence of Myth in the Second Half of the Thirteenth Century." *Journal of Medieval and Renaissance Studies* 3.1 (1973): 115–37.

– "Western Views of the Tartars, 1240–1340." PhD diss., Rutgers University, 1969.

Cormack, Bradin. "Locating *The Comedy of Errors*: Revels Jurisdiction at the Inns of Court." In Archer et al., *The Intellectual and Cultural World*, 264–85.

Cormack, Lesley B. "Britannia Rules the Waves? Images of Empire in Elizabethan England." *Early Modern Literary Studies* 4.2 (1998): 10.1–20. http://purl.oclc.org/emls/04-2/cormbrit.htm, last accessed 4 Sept. 2016.

– *Charting an Empire: Geography at the English Universities, 1580–1620*. Chicago: University of Chicago Press, 1997.

Cox, John D. "*Henry VIII* and the Masque." *ELH: English Literary History* 45 (1978): 390–409.

Craton, Michael. "Slavery and Slave Society in the British Caribbean." In *The Slavery Reader*, ed. Gad Heuman and James Walvin, 103–11. London: Routledge, 2003.

Cutts, John P. "Shakespeare's Song and Masque Hand in *Henry VIII*." *Shakespeare-Jahrbuch* 99 (1963): 184–95.

Dale, Stephen F. *The Muslim Empires of the Ottomans, Safavids, and Mughals*. Cambridge: Cambridge University Press, 2010.

Dallal, Ahmad S. "Hijri Calendar." In Martin, *Encyclopedia*, 1:299–300.

Dalton, Karen C.C. "Art for the Sake of Dynasty: The Black Emperor in the Drake Jewel and Elizabethan Imperial Imagery." In Erickson and Hulse, *Early Modern Visual Culture*, 178–214.

Dandelet, Thomas James. *The Renaissance of Empire in Early Modern Europe*. Cambridge: Cambridge University Press, 2014.

Das, Nandini. "'Apes of Imitation': Imitation and Identity in Sir Thomas Roe's Embassy to India." In Singh, *Companion*, 114–28.

Davies, D.W. *Elizabethans Errant: The Strange Fortunes of Sir Thomas Sherley and His Three Sons*. Ithaca, NY: Cornell University Press, 1967.

Davis, Natalie Zemon. *Trickster Travels: A Sixteenth-Century Muslim between Worlds*. New York: Hill and Wang, 2006.

– *Women on the Margins: Three Seventeenth-Century Lives*. Cambridge, MA: Harvard University Press, 1995.

Davis, Natalie Zemon, and Arlette Farge, eds. *A History of Women in the West*. Vol. 3, *Renaissance and Enlightenment Paradoxes*. Cambridge, MA: Harvard University Press, 1993.

Davis-Kimball, Jeannine, with Mona Behan. *Warrior Women: An Archaeologist's Search for History's Hidden Heroines*. New York: Warner Books, 2002.

Degenhardt, Jane Hwang. *Islamic Conversion and Christian Resistance on the Early Modern Stage*. Edinburgh: Edinburgh University Press, 2010.

Derrida, Jacques. *Of Grammatology*. Trans. Gayatri Chakravorty Spivak. Baltimore, MD.: Johns Hopkins University Press, 1974.

Devereux, Andrew W. "'The ruin and slaughter of ... fellow Christians': The French as a Threat to Christendom in Spanish Assertions of Sovereignty in Italy, 1479–1516." In Fuchs and Weissbourd, *Representing Imperial Rivalry*, 101–25.

Dillon, Janette. "Powerful Obedience: *Godly Queen Hester* and Katherine of Aragon." In *Interludes and Early Modern Society: Studies in Gender, Power and Theatricality*, ed. Peter Happé and Wim Hüsken, 117–39. Amsterdam: Rodopi, 2007.

Dimmock, Matthew. "Converting and Not Converting 'Strangers' in Early Modern London." *Journal of Early Modern History* 17 (2013): 457–78.

– "Guns and Gawds: Elizabethan England's Infidel Trade." In Singh, *Companion*, 207–22.

– *New Turkes: Dramatizing Islam and the Ottomans in Early Modern England*. Aldershot, Eng.: Ashgate, 2005.

Distiller, Natasha. *Desire and Gender in the Sonnet Tradition*. New York: Palgrave Macmillan, 2008.

– Review of *A Companion to the Global Renaissance: English Literature and Culture in the Era of Expansion*, ed. Jyotsna G. Singh. *Shakespeare Quarterly* 61.4 (2010): 600–4.

Dolan, Frances E. *True Relations: Reading, Literature, and Evidence in Seventeenth-Century England*. Philadelphia: University of Pennsylvania Press, 2013.

DuBois, Page. *Centaurs and Amazons: Women and the Pre-History of the Great Chain of Being*. Ann Arbor: University of Michigan Press, 1982.

Dubrow, Heather. *Echoes of Desire: English Petrarchism and Its Counterdiscourses*. Ithaca, NY: Cornell University Press, 1995.

Duncan, Sarah. *Mary I: Gender, Power, and Ceremony in the Reign of England's First Queen*. New York: Palgrave Macmillan, 2012.

– "The Two Virgin Queens." *Explorations in Renaissance Culture* 30.1 (2004): 77–88.

Duncan-Jones, Katherine. *Sir Philip Sidney: Courtier Poet*. New Haven, CT: Yale University Press, 1991.

Edwards, Paul. "The Early African Presence in the British Isles." In *Essays on the History of Blacks in Britain: From Roman Times to the Mid-Twentieth Century*, ed. Jagdish S. Gundara and Ian Duffield, 9–29. Aldershot, Eng.: Avebury, 1992.

Edwards, Paul, and James Walvin. "Africans in Britain, 1500–1800." In *The African Diaspora: Interpretive Essays*, ed. Martin L. Kilson and Robert I. Rotberg, 172–204. Cambridge, MA: Harvard University Press, 1976.

Elliott, G.R. "Weirdness in *The Comedy of Errors*" (1939). In Miola, *The Comedy of Errors*, 57–70.

Elsner, Jaś, and Joan-Pau Rubiés, eds. *Voyages and Visions: Towards a Cultural History of Travel*. London: Reaktion Books, 1999.

Elton, G.R. *England under the Tudors*. 3rd ed. London: Routledge, 1991.

– "The Reformation in England." In *The New Cambridge Modern History*. Vol. 2, *The Reformation, 1520–1559*, ed. Elton, 226–50. Cambridge: Cambridge University Press, 1958.

"Embassy History and Previous Ambassadors," from the *Turkish Embassy in London* website. http://london.emb.mfa.gov.tr/MissionChiefHistory.aspx, last accessed 4 Sept. 2016.

Epstein, Mortimer. *The Early History of the Levant Company* (1908). New York: Augustus M. Kelley, 1968.

Epstein, Stephen A. *Speaking of Slavery: Color, Ethnicity, and Human Bondage in Italy*. Ithaca, NY: Cornell University Press, 2001.

Erickson, Peter, and Clark Hulse, eds. *Early Modern Visual Culture: Representation, Race, and Empire in Renaissance England*. Philadelphia: University of Pennsylvania Press, 2000.

Eskandari-Qajar, Manoutchehr. "Persian Ambassadors, Their Circassians, and the Politics of Elizabethan and Regency England." *Iranian Studies: Journal of the International Society for Iranian Studies* 44.2 (2011): 251–71.

Euben, Roxanne L. *Journeys to the Other Shore: Muslim and Western Travelers in Search of Knowledge*. Princeton, NJ: Princeton University Press, 2006.

Fabian, Johannes. *Time and the Other: How Anthropology Makes Its Object* (1983). New York: Columbia University Press, 2002.

Faizer, Rizwi. "Hijra." In Martin, *Encyclopedia*, 1:299.

Feerick, Jean E. *Strangers in Blood: Relocating Race in the Renaissance*. Toronto: University of Toronto Press, 2010.

Felperin, Howard. *Shakespearean Romance*. Princeton, NJ: Princeton University Press, 1972.

Ferguson, Margaret W. *Dido's Daughters: Literacy, Gender, and Empire in Early Modern England and France*. Chicago: University of Chicago Press, 2003.

Findlay, Alison. *Playing Spaces in Early Women's Drama*. Cambridge: Cambridge University Press, 2006.

Findlay, Alison, and Stephanie Hodgson-Wright, with Gweno Williams. *Women and Dramatic Production, 1550–1700*. Harlow, Eng.: Longman, 2000.

Finkel, Caroline. *Osman's Dream: The Story of the Ottoman Empire, 1300–1923*. New York: Basic Books, 2005.

– "'The Treacherous Cleverness of Hindsight': Myths of Ottoman Decay." In *Re-Orienting the Renaissance: Cultural Exchanges with the East*, ed. Gerald MacLean, 148–74. New York: Palgrave Macmillan, 2005.

Finkelpearl, Philip J. *John Marston of the Middle Temple: An Elizabethan Dramatist in His Social Setting*. Cambridge, MA: Harvard University Press, 1969.

Fisher, Michael H. *Counterflows to Colonialism: Indian Travellers and Settlers in Britain, 1600–1857*. Delhi, India: Permanent Black, 2004.

Fizer, Irene. "Emballing, Empalling, Embalming, and Embailing Anne Bullen: The Annotation of Shakespeare's Bawdy Tongue after Samuel Johnson." In *Reading Readings: Essays on Shakespeare Editing in the Eighteenth Century*, ed.

Joanna Gondris, 281–95. Madison, NJ: Fairleigh Dickinson University Press, 1998.

Flannery, John M. *The Mission of the Portuguese Augustinians to Persia and Beyond (1602–1747)*. Leiden, The Netherlands: Brill, 2013.

Fleissner, Robert F. "William Dunbar's Sultry Pre-Shakespearean Dark Lady." *The Upstart Crow* 3 (1980): 88–96.

Floyd-Wilson, Mary. *English Ethnicity and Race in Early Modern Drama*. Cambridge: Cambridge University Press, 2003.

Forbes, Jack D. *The American Discovery of Europe*. Urbana: University of Illinois Press, 2007.

Forte, Maximilian C. "Introduction: 'Who Is an Indian?' The Cultural Politics of a Bad Question." In Forte, *Who Is an Indian?* 3–51.

– ed. *Who Is an Indian? Race, Place, and the Politics of Indigeneity in the Americas*. Toronto: University of Toronto Press, 2013.

Foster, William. *England's Quest of Eastern Trade* (1933). New York: Barnes and Noble, 1967.

Fradenburg, Louise Olga. *City, Marriage, Tournament: Arts of Rule in Late Medieval Scotland*. Madison: University of Wisconsin Press, 1991.

Fraser, Antonia. *The Wives of Henry VIII*. New York: Vintage Books, 1994.

Freccero, Carla. *Queer/Early/Modern*. Durham, NC: Duke University Press, 2006.

Freud, Sigmund. *The Interpretation of Dreams* (1900). Trans. and ed. James Strachey. New York: Avon Books, 1965.

Froude, James Anthony. "England's Forgotten Worthies." In *Short Studies on Great Subjects*, 1:358–405. New York: Charles Scribner, 1868.

Frye, Susan. "Anne of Denmark and the Historical Contextualisation of Shakespeare and Fletcher's *Henry VIII*." In *Women and Politics in Early Modern England, 1450–1700*, ed. James Daybell, 181–93. Aldershot, Eng.: Ashgate, 2004.

– *Elizabeth I: The Competition for Representation*. New York: Oxford University Press, 1993.

– *Pens and Needles: Women's Textualities in Early Modern England*. Philadelphia: University of Pennsylvania Press, 2010.

– "Queens and the Structure of History in *Henry VIII*." In *A Companion to Shakespeare's Works: The Poems, Problem Comedies, Late Plays*, ed. Richard Dutton and Jean E. Howard, 427–44. Malden, MA: Blackwell, 2003.

Fryer, Peter. *Staying Power: Black People in Britain since 1504*. Atlantic Highlands, NJ: Humanities Press, 1984.

Fuchs, Barbara. "Imperium Studies: Theorizing Early Modern Expansion." In Ingham and Warren, *Postcolonial Moves*, 71–90.

– *Romance*. New York: Routledge, 2004.

Fuchs, Barbara, and Emily Weissbourd, eds. *Representing Imperial Rivalry in the Early Modern Mediterranean*. Toronto: University of Toronto Press, 2015.

Fuller, Mary C. "Arctics of Empire: The North in *Principal Navigations* (1598–1600)." In Regard, *The Quest for the Northwest Passage*, 15–29.

– *Voyages in Print: English Travel to America, 1576–1624*. Cambridge: Cambridge University Press, 1995.

– "Where was Iceland in 1600?" In Singh, *Companion*, 149–62.

Fumerton, Patricia. *Unsettled: The Culture of Mobility and the Working Poor in Early Modern England*. Chicago: University of Chicago Press, 2006.

Games, Alison. *The Web of Empire: English Cosmopolitans in an Age of Expansion, 1560–1660*. Oxford: Oxford University Press, 2008.

Garber, Marjorie. *Vested Interests: Cross-Dressing and Cultural Anxiety*. New York: Routledge, 1992.

Gates, Henry Louis. *The Signifying Monkey: A Theory of African American Literary Criticism* (25th Anniversary Edition). Oxford: Oxford University Press, 2014.

Ghani, Cyrus. *Shakespeare, Persia, and the East*. Washington, DC: Mage Publishers, 2008.

Gillies, John, and Virginia Mason Vaughan, eds. *Playing the Globe: Genre and Geography in English Renaissance Drama*. Madison, WI: Fairleigh Dickinson University Press, 1998.

Ginzburg, Carlo. *The Cheese and the Worms: The Cosmos of a Sixteenth-Century Miller* (1976). Trans. John and Anne Tedeschi. Baltimore, MD.: Johns Hopkins University Press, 1980.

– *Threads and Traces: True, False, Fictive*. Trans. Anne C. Tedeschi and John Tedeschi. Berkeley: University of California Press, 2012.

A Global Report on Trafficking in Persons. United Nations Office on Drugs and Crime, February 2009. https://www.unodc.org/unodc/en/human-trafficking/global-report-on-trafficking-in-persons.html, last accessed 3 Sept. 2016.

Godman, Maureen. "'Plucking a Crow' in *The Comedy of Errors*." *Early Theatre* 8.1 (2005): 53–68.

Godzich, Wlad. "Forward: The Further Possibility of Knowledge." In *Heterologies: Discourse on the Other*. By Michel de Certeau. Trans. Brian Massumi, vii–xxi. Minneapolis: University of Minnesota Press, 1986.

Goffman, Daniel. *Britons in the Ottoman Empire, 1642–1660*. Seattle: University of Washington Press, 1998.

– *The Ottoman Empire and Early Modern Europe*. Cambridge: Cambridge University Press 2002.

Gómez, Nicolás Wey. *The Tropics of Empire: Why Columbus Sailed South to the Indies*. Cambridge, MA: MIT Press, 2008.

Gossett, Suzanne, and Janel Mueller. "Textual Introduction." In Wroth, *The Second Part*, xvii–xliv.

Green, A. Wigfall. *The Inns of Court and Early English Drama*. New York: Benjamin Blom, 1931.

Greenblatt, Stephen. *Marvelous Possessions: The Wonder of the New World*. Chicago: University of Chicago Press, 1991.

Greene, Roland. *Unrequited Conquests: Love and Empire in the Colonial Americas*. Chicago: University of Chicago Press, 1999.

Greer, Margaret R., Walter D. Mignolo, and Maureen Quilligan, eds. *Rereading the Black Legend: Discourses of Religious and Racial Difference in the Renaissance Empires*. Chicago: University of Chicago Press, 2007.

Griffin, Eric J. *English Renaissance Drama and the Specter of Spain: Ethnopoetics and Empire*. Philadelphia: University of Pennsylvania Press, 2009.

Grogan, Jane. *The Persian Empire in English Renaissance Writing, 1549–1622*. New York: Palgrave Macmillan, 2014.

Grosrichard, Alain. *The Sultan's Court: European Fantasies of the East*. Trans. Liz Heron. London: Verso, 1998.

Gwyn, David. "Richard Eden: Cosmographer and Alchemist." *The Sixteenth Century Journal* 15.1 (1984): 13–34.

Habib, Imtiaz. *Black Lives in the English Archives, 1500–1677: Imprints of the Invisible*. Aldershot, Eng.: Ashgate, 2008.

– "'Hel's Perfect Character' or the Blackamoor Maid in Early Modern English Drama: The Postcolonial History of a Dramatic Type." *LIT: Literature Interpretation Theory* 11 (2000): 277–304.

– "Reading Black Women Characters of the English Renaissance: Colonial Inscription and Postcolonial Recovery." In *Renaissance Papers 1996*, ed. George Walton Williams and Philip Rollinson, 67–80. Rochester, NY: Camden House, 1997.

Hadfield, Andrew. "Peter Martyr, Richard Eden and the New World: Reading, Experience and Translation." *Connotations* 5.1 (1995/96): 1–22.

Hagerman, Anita M. "'But Wroth pretends': Discovering Jonsonian Masque in Lady Mary Wroth's *Pamphilia to Amphilanthus*." *Early Modern Literary Studies* 6.3 (January, 2001): 4.1–17. http://purl.oclc.org/emls/06-3/hagewrot.htm, last accessed 4 Sept. 2016.

Hall, Kim F. "Object into Object? Some Thoughts on the Presence of Black Women in Early Modern Culture." In Erickson and Hulse, *Early Modern Visual Culture*, 346–79.

– "Reading What Isn't There: 'Black' Studies in Early Modern England." *Stanford Humanities Review* 3.1 (1993): 23–33.

– *Things of Darkness: Economies of Race and Gender in Early Modern England.* Ithaca, NY: Cornell University Press, 1995.

Hannay, Margaret P. *Mary Sidney, Lady Wroth.* Farnham, Eng.: Ashgate, 2010.

– *Philip's Phoenix: Mary Sidney, Countess of Pembroke.* New York: Oxford University Press, 1990.

Hansen, Matthew C. "'And a Queen of England, Too': The 'Englishing' of Catherine of Aragon in Sixteenth-Century English Literary and Chronicle History." In Levin et al., *"High and Mighty Queens,"* 79–99.

Harris, Bernard. "A Portrait of a Moor." In *Shakespeare and Race,* ed. Catherine M.S. Alexander and Stanley Wells, 23–36. Cambridge: Cambridge University Press, 2000.

Harris, Jonathan Gil. *The First Firangis: Remarkable Stories of Heroes, Healers, Charlatans, Courtesans and other Foreigners Who Became Indian.* New Delhi: Aleph Book Co., 2015.

– ed. *Indography: Writing the "Indian" in Early Modern England.* New York: Palgrave Macmillan, 2012.

– *Sick Economies: Drama, Mercantilism, and Disease in Shakespeare's England.* Philadelphia: University of Pennsylvania Press, 2004.

Hazard, Mary E. "'Order gave each thing view': 'shows, pageants, and sights of honour' in *King Henry VIII.*" *Word and Image* 3.1 (1987): 95–103.

Headley, John M. "The Habsburg World Empire and the Revival of Ghibellinism." In Armitage, *Theories of Empire,* 5–79.

Hearn, Karen. *Dynasties: Painting in Tudor and Jacobean England, 1530–1630.* London: Tate Publishing, 1995.

Hellie, Richard. *Slavery in Russia, 1450–1725.* Chicago: University of Chicago Press, 1982.

Hellinga, Lotte. *Caxton in Focus: The Beginning of Printing in England.* London: The British Library, 1982.

Hendricks, Margo. "Feminist Historiography." In *A Companion to Early Modern Women's Writing,* ed. Anita Pacheco, 361–76. Oxford: Blackwell, 2002.

Hendricks, Margo, and Patricia Parker, eds. *Women, "Race," and Writing in the Early Modern Period.* London: Routledge, 1994.

Hertel, Ralf. "Ousting the Ottomans: The Double Vision of the East in *The Travels of the Three English Brothers* (1607)." In *Early Modern Encounters with the Islamic East: Performing Cultures,* ed. Sabine Schülting, Sabine Lucia Müller, and Ralf Hertel, 135–51. Farnham, Eng.: Ashgate, 2012.

Hilberdink-Sakamoto, K. "'O God's Will, Much Better She Ne'er Had Known Pomp': The Making of Queen Anne in Shakespeare's *Henry VIII.*" *Shakespeare Studies* (Shakespeare Society of Japan) 37 (1999): 21–44.

Hildinger, Erik. Preface. In Carpini, *The Story of the Mongols,* 6–29.

Hiscock, Andrew. "Erotic Sovereignty: Crises of Desire and Faith in *The Winter's Tale* and *Henry VIII*." *Cahiers Elisabéthains* 52 (1997): 53–62.

Hodgen, Margaret T. *Early Anthropology in the Sixteenth and Seventeenth Centuries*. Philadelphia: University of Pennsylvania Press, 1964.

Hodgson, Marshall G.S. *Rethinking World History: Essays on Europe, Islam, and World History*. Ed. Edmund Burke III. Cambridge: Cambridge University Press, 1993.

– *The Venture of Islam: Conscience and History in a World Civilization*. 3 vols. Chicago: University of Chicago Press, 1974.

Holmberg, Eva Johanna. "In the Company of Franks: British Identifications in the Early Modern Levant *c*. 1600." *Studies in Travel Writing* 16.4 (2012): 363–74.

Hopkins, Lisa. *Writing Renaissance Queens: Texts by and about Elizabeth I and Mary, Queen of Scots*. Newark: University of Delaware Press, 2002.

Householder, Michael. *Inventing Americans in the Age of Discovery: Narratives of Encounter*. Farnham, Eng.: Ashgate, 2011.

Howard, Jean E. *The Stage and Social Struggle in Early Modern England*. London: Routledge, 1994.

Howard, Skiles. "'Ascending the Riche Mount': Performing Hierarchy and Gender in the Henrician Masque." In *Rethinking the Henrician Era: Essays on Early Tudor Texts and Contexts*, ed. Peter C. Herman, 16–39. Urbana: University of Illinois Press, 1994.

Hull, Suzanne W. *Chaste, Silent and Obedient: English Books for Women, 1475–1640*. San Marino, CA: Huntington Library, 1982.

Hulme, Peter. *Colonial Encounters: Europe and the Native Caribbean, 1492–1797*. London: Methuen, 1986.

Ingham, Patricia Clare, and Michelle R. Warren, eds. *Postcolonial Moves: Medieval through Modern*. New York: Palgrave Macmillan, 2003.

Isom-Verhaaren, Christine. *Allies with the Infidel: The Ottoman and French Alliance in the Sixteenth Century*. London: I.B. Tauris, 2013.

Ives, Eric. *The Life and Death of Anne Boleyn*. Malden, MA: Blackwell, 2004.

Iyengar, Sujata. *Shades of Difference: Mythologies of Skin Color in Early Modern England*. Philadelphia: University of Pennsylvania Press, 2005.

Jackson, Peter. Introduction. In Rubruck, *The Mission*, 1–55.

Jaimoukha, Amjad. *The Circassians: A Handbook*. New York: Palgrave, 2001.

Jardine, Lisa, and Jerry Brotton. *Global Interests: Renaissance Art between East and West*. Ithaca, NY: Cornell University Press, 2000.

Jones, Ann Rosalind, and Peter Stallybrass. *Renaissance Clothing and the Materials of Memory*. Cambridge: Cambridge University Press, 2000.

Jones, Eldred. *Othello's Countrymen: The African in English Renaissance Drama*. London: Oxford University Press 1965.

Jones, Pamela M. "Envisioning a Global Environment for Blessed Teresa of Avila in 1614: The Beatification Decorations for S. Maria della Scala in Rome." In Wiesner-Hanks, *Mapping Gendered Routes*, 131–56.

Jowitt, Claire. "'Et in Arcadia Ego': The Politics of Pirates in the *Old Arcadia, New Arcadia* and *Urania*." *Early Modern Literary Studies* 13.2 (2007): 5.1–36. URL: http://purl.oclc.org/emls/si-16/jowiarca.htm, last accessed 4 Sept. 2016.

– *Voyage Drama and Gender Politics, 1589–1642*. Manchester: Manchester University Press, 2003.

Kelly, Ann Cline. "The Challenge of the Impossible: Ben Jonson's *The Masque of Blackness*." *College Language Association Journal* 20 (1977): 341–55.

Kelsay, John. "Dar al-Islam." In Martin, *Encyclopedia*, 1:169–70.

Kelsey, Harry. *Sir John Hawkins: Queen Elizabeth's Slave Trader*. New Haven, CT: Yale University Press, 2003.

Kennedy, William J. *The Site of Petrarchism: Early Modern National Sentiment in Italy, France, and England*. Baltimore, MD: Johns Hopkins University Press, 2003.

Khodarkovsky, Michael. *Russia's Steppe Frontier: The Making of a Colonial Empire, 1500–1800*. Bloomington: Indiana University Press, 2002.

Kinney, Arthur F. "Shakespeare's *Comedy of Errors* and the Nature of Kinds" (1988). In Miola, *The Comedy of Errors*, 155–81.

Knapp, Margaret, and Michal Kobialka. "Shakespeare and the Prince of Purpoole: The 1594 Production of *The Comedy of Errors* at Gray's Inn Hall." In Miola, *The Comedy of Errors*, 431–45.

Knobler, Adam. "Missions, Mythologies and the Search for Non-European Allies in Anti-Islamic Holy War, 1291–c.1540." PhD diss., University of Cambridge, 1989.

– *The Power of Distance: Mythology and Diplomacy in the Age of Exploration*. Notre Dame, IN: University of Notre Dame Press, forthcoming.

– "Pseudo-Conversions and Patchwork Pedigrees: The Christianization of Muslim Princes and the Diplomacy of Holy War." *Journal of World History* 7.2 (1996): 181–97.

Krantz, Susan E. "Audience Response to *Henry VIII* and Cultural Destabilization." *University of Dayton Review* 22.1 (1993): 133–46.

Kuin, Roger. "Querre-Muhau: Sir Philip Sidney and the New World." *Renaissance Quarterly* 51.2 (1998): 549–85.

Kupperman, Karen Ordahl. *Indians and English: Facing Off in Early America*. Ithaca, NY: Cornell University Press, 2000.

– *The Jamestown Project*. Cambridge, MA: Harvard University Press, 2007.

Kurland, Stuart M. "*Henry VIII* and James I: Shakespeare and Jacobean Politics." *Shakespeare Studies* 19 (1987): 203–17.

Kusunoki, Akiko. *Gender and Representations of the Female Subject in Early Modern England*. New York: Palgrave Macmillan, 2015.
– "Gender and Representations of Mixed-Race Relationships in English Renaissance Literature." *Essays and Studies in British and American Literature* 52 (2006): 21–35.
Lal, Ruby. *Domesticity and Power in the Early Mughal World*. Cambridge: Cambridge University Press, 2005.
Lamb, Mary Ellen. *Gender and Authorship in the Sidney Circle*. Madison: University of Wisconsin Press, 1990.
Lanier, Douglas. "'Stigmatical in Making': The Material Character of *The Comedy of Errors*" (1993). In Miola, *The Comedy of Errors*, 299–334.
Laoutaris, Chris, and Yasmin Arshad. "'Still renewing wronges': The Persian Lady Revealed." *British Art Journal* (2017), forthcoming.
Larson, Katherine R., and Naomi J. Miller, with Andrew Strycharski, eds. *Re-Reading Mary Wroth*. New York: Palgrave Macmillan, 2015.
Leahy, William. "'You cannot show me': Two Tudor Coronation Processions, Shakespeare's *King Henry VIII*, and the Staging of Anne Boleyn." *EnterText* 3.1 (2003): 132–44.
Lee, Sidney, ed. *Dictionary of National Biography*. New York: Macmillan, 1897.
Lemercier-Goddard, Sophie. "George Best's Arctic Mirrors: *A True Discourse of the Late Voyages of Discoverie of … Martin Frobisher* (1578)." In Regard, *The Quest for the Northwest Passage*, 55–70.
Leonidas, Eric. "Theatrical Experiment and the Production of Knowledge in the Gray's Inn Revels." In *Early Modern Academic Drama*, ed. Jonathan Walker and Paul D. Streufert, 115–28. Farnham, Eng.: Ashgate, 2008.
Lestringant, Frank. *Cannibals: The Discovery and Representation of the Cannibal from Columbus to Jules Verne*. Trans. Rosemary Morris. Berkeley: University of California Press, 1997.
Levin, Carole. "Women in the Renaissance." In *Becoming Visible: Women in European History*. 3rd ed. Ed. Renate Bridenthal, Susan Mosher Stuard, and Merry E. Wiesner, 153–72. Boston: Houghton Mifflin, 1998.
Levin, Carole, Debra Barrett-Graves, and Jo Eldridge Carney, eds. *"High and Mighty Queens" of Early Modern England: Realities and Representations*. New York: Palgrave Macmillan, 2003.
Levine, Laura. *Men in Women's Clothing: Anti-theatricality and Effeminization, 1579–1642*. Cambridge: Cambridge University Press, 1994.
Levy, Philip. "Man-Eating and Menace on Richard Hore's Expedition to America." *Atlantic Studies* 2.2 (2005): 129–51.
Lewalski, Barbara Kiefer. "Authorship and Author-Characters in Sidney and Wroth." In Larson and Miller, *Re-Reading Mary Wroth*, 35–51.

– *Writing Women in Jacobean England*. Cambridge, MA: Harvard University Press, 1993.

Lindley, David. "Blackfriars, Music and Masque: Theatrical Contexts of the Last Plays." In *The Cambridge Companion to Shakespeare's Last Plays*, ed. Catherine M. S. Alexander, 29–45. Cambridge: Cambridge University Press, 2009.

– Introduction to *The Masque of Beauty*. In Jonson, *The Cambridge Edition*, 3:229–31.

Loades, David. *Elizabeth I*. London: Hambledon Continuum, 2003.

– *England's Maritime Empire: Seapower, Commerce and Policy, 1490–1690*. Harlow, Eng.: Longman, 2000.

– *Henry VIII: Court, Church and Conflict*. Kew, Eng.: The National Archives, 2007.

– *Mary Tudor: A Life*. Cambridge, MA: Blackwell, 1989.

Lockey, Brian C. *Law and Empire in English Renaissance Literature*. Cambridge: Cambridge University Press, 2006.

Lockhart, Laurence. "European Contacts with Persia, 1350–1736." In *The Cambridge History of Iran*. Vol. 6: *The Timurid and Safavid Periods*, ed. Peter Jackson and Laurence Lockhart, 373–411. Cambridge: Cambridge University Press, 1986.

Loewenstein, Joseph. *Ben Jonson and Possessive Authorship*. Cambridge: Cambridge University Press, 2002.

Loomba, Ania. "Early Modern or Early Colonial?" *The Journal for Early Modern Cultural Studies* 14.1 (2014): 143–8.

Loomba, Ania, and Jonathan Burton, Introduction to *Race in Early Modern England: A Documentary Companion*, ed. Loomba and Burton, 1–36. New York: Palgrave Macmillan, 2007.

Loughnane, Rory. "'I myself would for Caernarfonshire': The Old Lady in *King Henry VIII*." In *Celtic Shakespeare: The Bard and the Borderers*, ed. Willy Maley and Rory Loughnane, 185–202. Farnham, Eng.: Ashgate, 2013.

– "*King Henry VIII (All is True)*: Semi-Choric Devices and the Framework for Playgoer Response in *King Henry VIII*." In *Late Shakespeare, 1608–1613*, ed. Andrew J. Power and Rory Loughnane, 108–23. Cambridge: Cambridge University Press, 2013.

Luis-Martínez, Zenón. "'Maimed Narrations': Shakespeare's *Henry VIII* and the Task of the Historian." *Explorations in Renaissance Culture* 27.2 (2001): 205–43.

Lynch, Kathleen. "Whatever Happened to Dinah the Black? And Other Questions about Gender, Race, and the Visibility of Protestant Saints." In *Conversions: Gender and Religious Change in Early Modern Europe*, ed. Simon Ditchfield and Helen White, 258–80. Manchester: Manchester University Press, 2017.

Lyne, Raphael. "Churchyard, Thomas." In *Oxford Dictionary of National Biography*, vol. 6, ed. H.C.G. Matthew and Brian Harrison, 687–90. Oxford: Oxford University Press, 2004.

MacCaffrey, Wallace T. *Elizabeth I: War and Politics, 1588–1603*. Princeton, NJ: Princeton University Press, 1992.

– *Queen Elizabeth and the Making of Policy, 1572–1588*. Princeton, NJ: Princeton University Press, 1981.

Macdougall, Norman. *James IV*. East Lothian, Scotland: Tuckwell Press, 1997.

MacLean, Gerald. "East by North-east: The English among the Russians, 1553–1603." In Singh, *Companion*, 163–77.

– *Looking East: English Writing and the Ottoman Empire before 1800*. New York: Palgrave Macmillan, 2007.

– *The Rise of Oriental Travel: English Visitors to the Ottoman Empire, 1580–1720*. New York: Palgrave Macmillan, 2004.

MacLean, Gerald, and Nabil Matar. *Britain and the Islamic World, 1558–1713*. Oxford: Oxford University Press, 2011.

MacMillan, Ken. "Introduction: Discourse on History, Geography, and Law." In Dee, *The Limits of the British Empire*, 1–29.

– *Sovereignty and Possession in the English New World: The Legal Foundations of Empire, 1576–1640*. Cambridge: Cambridge University Press, 2006.

Madariaga, Isabel de. *Ivan the Terrible: First Tsar of Russia*. New Haven, CT: Yale University Press, 2005.

Maggio, J. "'Can the Subaltern Be Heard?' Political Theory, Translation, Representation, and Gayatri Chakravorty Spivak." *Alternatives: Global, Local, Political* 32.4 (2007): 419–43.

Magnusson, Lynne A. "The Rhetoric of Politeness and *Henry VIII*." *Shakespeare Quarterly* 43.4 (1992): 391–409.

Maguire, Laurie. "The Girls from Ephesus" (1997). In Miola, *The Comedy of Errors*, 355–91.

Makdisi, Saree. *Making England Western: Occidentalism, Race and Imperial Culture*. Chicago: University of Chicago Press, 2014.

Maley, Willy. *Nation, State and Empire in English Renaissance Literature: Shakespeare to Milton*. New York: Palgrave Macmillan, 2003.

– "Postcolonial Shakespeare: British Identity Formation and *Cymbeline*." In *Shakespeare's Late Plays: New Readings*, ed. Jennifer Richards and James Knowles, 145–57. Edinburgh: Edinburgh University Press, 1999.

Malieckal, Bindu. "Mariam Khan and the Legacy of Mughal Women in Early Modern Literature of India." In Andrea and McJannet, *Early Modern England and Islamic Worlds*, 97–121.

– "Slavery, Sex, and the Seraglio: 'Turkish' Women and Early Modern Texts." In *The Mysterious and the Foreign in Early Modern England*, ed. Helen Ostovich, Mary V. Silcox, and Graham Roebuck, 58–73 . Newark: University of Delaware Press, 2008.

Mancall, Peter C. *Hakluyt's Promise: An Elizabethan's Obsession for an English America*. New Haven, CT: Yale University Press, 2007.

Manz, Beatrice Forbes. *The Rise and Rule of Tamerlane*. Cambridge: Cambridge University Press, 1989.

Manz, Beatrice Forbes, and Masashi Handeda. "Čarkas [Circassians]." *Encyclopaedia Iranica* Online, 1990. http://www.iranicaonline.org/articles/carkas, last accessed 4 Sept. 2016.

Markley, Robert. *The Far East and the English Imagination, 1600–1730*. Cambridge: Cambridge University Press, 2006.

Martin, Richard C., ed. *Encyclopedia of Islam and the Muslim World*. 2 vols. New York: Macmillan, 2004.

Maslen, R.W. "Sidneian Geographies." *Sidney Journal* 20.2 (2002): 45–56.

Masood, Hafiz Abid. "From Cyrus to Abbas: Staging Persia in Early Modern England." PhD diss., University of Sussex, 2011.

Matar, Nabil. *Britain and Barbary, 1589–1689*. Gainesville: University Press of Florida, 2005.

– *In the Land of the Christians: Arabic Travel Writing in the Seventeenth Century*. New York: Routledge, 2003.

– *Turks, Moors, and Englishmen in the Age of Discovery*. New York: Columbia University Press, 1999.

Matei-Chesnoiu, Monica. *Geoparsing Early Modern English Drama*. New York: Palgrave Macmillan, 2015.

Matthee, Rudolph P. [Rudi] "Christians in Safavid Iran: Hospitality and Harassment." *Studies in Persianate Societies* 3 (2005): 3–43.

– *The Politics of Trade in Safavid Iran: Silk for Silver, 1600–1730*. Cambridge: Cambridge University Press, 1999.

– "Was Safavid Iran an Empire?" *Journal of the Social and Economic History of the Orient* 53 (2010): 233–65.

Mattingly, Garrett. *Catherine of Aragon* (1941). New York: Quality Paperback Books, 1990.

– "An Early Nonaggression Pact." *The Journal of Modern History* 10.1 (1938): 1–30.

– *Renaissance Diplomacy* (1955). New York: Dover Publications, 1988.

Mayers, Kit. *North-East Passage to Muscovy: Stephen Borough and the First Tudor Explorations*. Phoenix Mill, Eng.: Sutton Publishing, 2005.

McBride, Tom. "*Henry VIII* as Machiavellian Romance." *Journal of English and Germanic Philology* 76.1 (1977): 26–39.

McCoy, Richard C. "Law Sports and the Night of Errors: Shakespeare and the Inns of Court." In Archer et al., *The Intellectual and Cultural World*, 286–301.
– "Lord of Liberty: Francis Davison and the Cult of Elizabeth." In *The Reign of Elizabeth I: Court and Culture in the Last Decade*, ed. John Guy, 212–28. Cambridge: Cambridge University Press, 1995.
McDermott, James. "The Company of Cathay: The Financing and Organization of the Frobisher Voyages." In Symons, *Meta Incognita*, 1:147–78.
– *Martin Frobisher: Elizabethan Privateer*. New Haven, CT: Yale University Press, 2001.
McGough, Laura J. *Gender, Sexuality, and Syphilis in Early Modern Venice*. New York: Palgrave Macmillan, 2011.
McJannet, Linda. "Genre and Geography: The Eastern Mediterranean in *Pericles* and *The Comedy of Errors*." In Gillies and Vaughan, *Playing the Globe*, 86–106.
– "Pirates, Merchants, and Kings: Oriental Motifs in English Court and Civic Entertainments, 1510–1659." In *The Mysterious and the Foreign in Early Modern England*, ed. Helen Ostovich, Mary V. Silcox, and Graham Roebuck, 249–65. Newark: University of Delaware Press, 2008
– [McJ. Micheli]. "'Sit by Us': Visual Imagery and the Two Queens in *Henry VIII*." *Shakespeare Quarterly* 38.4 (1987): 452–66.
McManus, Clare. "'Defacing the Carcass': Anne of Denmark and Jonson's *Masque of Blackness*." In *Refashioning Ben Jonson: Gender, Politics, and the Jonsonian Canon*, ed. Julie Sanders, with Kate Chedgzoy and Susan Wiseman, 93–113. New York: St Martin's Press, 1998.
– "Marriage and the Performance of the Romance Quest: Anne of Denmark and the Stirling Baptismal Celebrations for Prince Henry." In *A Palace in the Wild: Essays on Vernacular Culture and Humanism in Late-Medieval and Renaissance Scotland*, ed. L.A.J.R. Houwen, A.A. MacDonald, and S.L. Mapstone, 175–98. Leuven, Belguim: Peeters, 2000.
– *Women on the Renaissance Stage: Anna of Denmark and Female Masquing in the Stuart Court (1590–1619)*. Manchester: Manchester University Press, 2002.
McMullan, Gordon. "'Swimming on bladders': The Dialogics of Reformation in Shakespeare and Fletcher's *Henry VIII*." In *Shakespeare and Carnival: After Bakhtin*, ed. Ronald Knowles, 211–27. New York: St Martin's Press, 1998.
McRae, Andrew. *Literature and Domestic Travel in Early Modern England*. Cambridge: Cambridge University Press, 2009.
Mehdizadeh, Nedda. "Translating Persia: Safavid Iran and Early Modern English Writing." PhD diss., George Washington University, 2013.
Merriam, Thomas. "The Old Lady, or All is Not True." *Shakespeare Survey* 54 (2001): 234–45.

Merriman, Roger Bigelow. *Suleiman the Magnificent, 1520–1566*. Cambridge, MA: Harvard University Press, 1944.

Meserve, Margaret. *Empires of Islam in Renaissance Historical Thought*. Cambridge, MA: Harvard University Press, 2008.

Meshkat, Kurosh. "The Journey of Master Anthony Jenkinson to Persia, 1562–1563," *Journal of Early Modern History* 13 (2009): 209–28.

Mignolo, Walter D. "Afterword: What Does the Black Legend Have to Do with Race?" In Greer et al., *Rereading the Black Legend*, 312–24.

– *The Darker Side of the Renaissance: Literacy, Territoriality, and Colonization*. 2nd ed. Ann Arbor: University of Michigan Press, 2003.

– *The Darker Side of Western Modernity: Global Futures, Decolonial Options*. Durham, NC: Duke University Press, 2011.

– *Local Histories/Global Designs: Coloniality, Subaltern Knowledges, and Border Thinking*. Princeton, NJ: Princeton University Press, 2000.

Mill, Anna Jean. *Mediaeval Plays in Scotland*. Edinburgh: William Blackwood and Sons, 1927.

Miller, Christopher L. *Blank Darkness: Africanist Discourse in French*. Chicago: University of Chicago Press, 1985.

Miller, Naomi J. *Changing the Subject: Mary Wroth and Figurations of Gender in Early Modern England*. Lexington: University Press of Kentucky, 1996.

Miola, Robert S., ed. *The Comedy of Errors: Critical Essays*. New York: Garland, 1997.

– "The Play and the Critics." In Miola, *The Comedy of Errors*, 3–51.

Mitchell, Colin Paul. *Sir Thomas Roe and the Mughal Empire*. Karachi, Pakistan: Area Study Centre for Europe, 2000.

Modeleski, Tania. *Feminism without Women: Culture and Criticism in a "Postfeminist" Age*. New York: Routledge, 1991.

Montgomery, Marianne. "'All that glisters': The Moral Meanings of Gold in the Frobisher Narratives and *The Merchant of Venice*." *Studies in Travel Writing* 17.3 (2013): 250–63.

Montrose, Louis. *The Subject of Elizabeth: Authority, Gender, and Representation*. Chicago: University of Chicago Press, 2006.

– "The Work of Gender in the Discourse of Discovery." *Representations* 33 (1991): 1–41.

Moore, Gaywyn. "'You Turn Me into Nothing': Reformation of Queenship on the Jacobean Stage." *Mediterranean Studies* 21.1 (2013): 27–56.

Moore, Mary B. *Desiring Voices: Women Sonneteers and Petrarchism*. Carbondale: Southern Illinois University Press, 2000.

Morris, Rosalind C., ed. *Can the Subaltern Speak? Reflections on the History of an Idea*. New York: Columbia University Press, 2010.

Morrison, Toni. *Playing in the Dark: Whiteness and the Literary Imagination*. New York: Vintage, 1993.

Morton, Margaret B. Graham. *The Jenkinson Story*. Glasgow: William Maclellan, 1962.

Morton, Stephen. *Gayatri Spivak: Ethics, Subalternity and the Critique of Postcolonial Reason*. Cambridge: Polity Press, 2007.

Moss, Grant. "'Are you now or have you ever been Queen of England?' Elizabeth, the 'Persian Lady' and the Vagaries of (Mis)Identification." Paper presented at the South Central Renaissance Conference/Queen Elizabeth I Society Annual Meeting, 10 March 2006.

Mottram, Stewart. *Empire and Nation in Early English Renaissance Literature*. Cambridge: D.S. Brewer, 2008.

Muir, Edward. "Introduction: Observing Trifles." In *Microhistory and the Lost Peoples of Europe*, ed. Edward Muir and Guido Ruggiero, vii–xxviii. Baltimore, MD.: Johns Hopkins University Press, 1991.

Mullaney, Steven. *The Place of the Stage: License, Play, and Power in Renaissance England*. Chicago: University of Chicago Press, 1988.

Murray, Timothy. *Like a Film: Ideological Fantasy on Screen, Camera and Canvas*. London: Routledge, 1993.

Murrin, Michael. *Trade and Romance*. Chicago: University of Chicago Press, 2014.

Nadwi, Mohammad Akram. *Al-Muhaddithat: The Women Scholars in Islam*. Oxford: Interface Publications, 2007.

Nashat, Guity, and Lois Beck, eds. *Women in Iran from the Rise of Islam to 1800*. Urbana: University of Illinois Press, 2003.

Natho, Kadir I. *Circassian History*. Lexington, KY: Xlibris, 2009.

Neill, Michael. *Putting History to the Question: Power, Politics, and Society in English Renaissance Drama*. New York: Columbia University Press, 2000.

Nelson, Mary K. "Shakespeare's *Henry VIII*: Stigmatizing the 'Disabled' Womb." *Disability Studies Quarterly* 29.4 (2009). http://dsq-sds.org/article/view/995/1179, last accessed 4 Sept. 2016.

Newman, Andrew J. *Safavid Iran: Rebirth of a Persian Empire*. London: I.B. Tauris, 2009.

Newman, Karen. *Cultural Capitals: Early Modern London and Paris*. Princeton, NJ: Princeton University Press, 2007.

Nezam-Mafi, Mohammad Taghi. "Persian Recreations: Theatricality in Anglo-Persian Diplomatic History, 1599–1828." PhD diss., Boston University, 1999.

Niayesh, Ladan. "From Myth to Appropriation: English Discourses on the Strait of Anian (1566–1628)." In Regard, *The Quest for the Northwest Passage*, 31–9.

– "The 'Courtly Popular' Orient of Ben Jonson's Court Masques." *Cahiers Elisabéthains* 73 (2008): 31–6.

– "'Cultural Amphibians': Impersonating the Alien in Jacobean Court Masques." In *Selfhood on the Early Modern Stage*, ed. Pauline Blanc, 86–99. Newcastle: Cambridge Scholars Publishing, 2008.

– "Muscovites and 'Black-amours': Alien Love Traders in *Love's Labour's Lost*." *Actes des congrès de la Société française Shakespeare* 32 (2015). http:// shakespeare.revues.org/3158, last accessed 4 Sept. 2016.

Niebrzydowski, Sue. "The Sultana and Her Sisters: Black Women in the British Isles before 1530." *Women's History Review* 10.2 (2001): 187–210.

Nocentelli, Carmen. *Empires of Love: Europe, Asia, and the Making of Early Modern Identity*. Philadelphia: University of Pennsylvania Press, 2013.

– "Teresa Sampsonia Sherley: Amazon, Wife, and Traveler." In Akhimie and Andrea, *Traveling/Travailing Women*, forthcoming.

Noling, Kim H. "Grubbing Up the Stock: Dramatizing Queens in *Henry VIII*." *Shakespeare Quarterly* 39.3 (1988): 291–306.

Oakley-Brown, Liz. "Churchyard, Thomas." In *The Encyclopedia of English Renaissance Literature*, vol. 1, ed. Garrett A. Sullivan Jr. and Alan Stewart, 189–90. Malden, MA: Blackwell, 2012.

– "Taxonomies of Travel and Martial Identity in Thomas Churchyard's *A generall rehearsall of warres* and 'A Pirates Tragedie' (1579)." *Studies in Travel Writing* 12.1 (2008): 67–83.

Oberg, Michael Leroy. *The Head in Edward Nugent's Hand*: *Roanoke's Forgotten Indians*. Philadelphia: University of Pennsylvania Press, 2008.

Ogborn, Miles. *Global Lives: Britain and the World, 1550–1800*. Cambridge: Cambridge University Press, 2008.

O'Hara, Susan Lauffer. "Sonnets as Theater: The Performance of Ideal Love and the Negation of Marriage in Mary Wroth's Masque." *Explorations in Renaissance Culture* 29.1 (2003): 59–99.

– *The Theatricality of Mary Wroth's* Pamphilia to Amphilanthus: *Unmasking Conventions in Context*. Selinsgrove, PA: Susquehanna University Press, 2011.

Ong, Walter J. "Latin Language Study as a Renaissance Puberty Rite." *Studies in Philology* 56.2 (1959): 103–24.

Orgel, Stephen. *Impersonations: The Performance of Gender in Shakespeare's England*. Cambridge: Cambridge University Press, 1996.

– *The Jonsonian Masque*. Cambridge, MA: Harvard University Press, 1965.

Over, William. "Alterity and Assimilation in Jonson's Masques of *Blackness* and *Beauty*." *Cultura, Lenguaje y Representatión/Culture, Language and Representation* 1 (2004): 43–54.

– "Familiarizing the Colonized in Ben Jonson's Masques." *Partial Answers: Journal of Literature and the History of Ideas* 2.2 (2004): 27–50.

Pagden, Anthony. *European Encounters with the New World: From Renaissance to Romanticism*. New Haven, CT: Yale University Press, 1993.

– *Lords of All the World: Ideologies of Empire in Spain, Britain and France, c. 1500–c. 1800*. New Haven, CT: Yale University Press, 1995.

Palmer, Daryl W. *Writing Russia in the Age of Shakespeare*. Aldershot, Eng.: Ashgate, 2004.

Parker, Charles H. *Global Interactions in the Early Modern Age, 1400–1800*. Cambridge: Cambridge University Press, 2010.

Parker, Patricia. *Literary Fat Ladies: Rhetoric, Gender, Property*. London: Methuen, 1987.

– *Shakespeare from the Margins: Language, Culture, Context*. Chicago: University of Chicago Press, 1996.

Parry, Graham. *The Golden Age Restor'd: The Culture of the Stuart Court, 1603–42*. Manchester: Manchester University Press, 1981.

Patrick, Donna. "Inuitness and Territoriality in Canada." In Forte, *Who Is an Indian?* 52–70.

Patterson, W.B. *King James VI and I and the Reunion of Christendom*. Cambridge: Cambridge University Press, 1997.

Payne, Anthony. "Richard Hakluyt's *Divers Voyages* (1582) & *Principal Navigations* (1589; 1598/9 to 1600): A Census of Surviving Copies." *The Hakluyt Society* website. http://www.hakluyt.com/hakluyt_census.htm, last accessed 3 Sept. 2016.

Peck, Linda Levy, ed. *The Mental World of the Jacobean Court*. Cambridge: Cambridge University Press, 1991.

Peirce, Leslie P. "An Imperial Caste: Inverted Racialization in the Architecture of Ottoman Sovereignty." In Greer et al., *Rereading the Black Legend*, 27–47.

– *The Imperial Harem: Women and Sovereignty in the Ottoman Empire*. New York: Oxford University Press, 1993.

Penrose, Boies. *The Sherleian Odyssey: Being a Record of the Travels and Adventures of Three Famous Brothers during the Reigns of Elizabeth, James I, and Charles I*. London: Simpkin Marshall, 1938.

Peyré, Yves. "Marlowe's Argonauts." In *Travel and Drama in Shakespeare's Time*, ed. Jean-Pierre Maquerlot and Michèle Willems, 106–23. Cambridge: Cambridge University Press, 1996.

Phillips, Kim M. *Before Orientalism: Asian Peoples and Cultures in European Travel Writing, 1245–1510*. Philadelphia: University of Pennsylvania Press, 2014.

Prest, Wilfrid R. *The Inns of Court under Elizabeth I and the Early Stuarts, 1590–1640*. London: Longman, 1972.

Pritchard, James B., ed. *Solomon and Sheba*. London: Phaidon, 1974.

Probasco, Nate. "Cartography as a Tool of Colonization: Sir Humphrey Gilbert's 1583 Voyage to North America." *Renaissance Quarterly* 67.2 (2014): 425–72.

– "Sir Humphrey Gilbert, Elizabeth I, and the Anglo-Spanish Conflict." *Explorations in Renaissance Culture* 37 (2011): 119–35.

Publicover, Laurence. "Strangers at Home: The Sherley Brothers and Dramatic Romance." *Renaissance Studies* 24.5 (2010): 694–709.

Quilligan, Maureen. *Incest and Agency in Elizabeth's England*. Philadelphia: University of Pennsylvania Press, 2005.

Quinn, David Beers. *England and the Discovery of America, 1481–1620*. New York: Alfred A. Knopf, 1973.

– "Frobisher in the Context of Early English Northwest Exploration." In Symons, *Meta Incognita*, 1: 7–18.

– *North America from Earliest Discovery to First Settlements: The Norse Voyages to 1612*. New York: Harper and Row, 1975.

Raman, Shankar. *Framing "India": The Colonial Imaginary in Early Modern Culture*. Stanford, CA: Stanford University Press, 2001.

Rankin, Mark. "Henry VIII, Shakespeare, and the Jacobean Royal Court." *SEL: Studies in English Literature, 1500–1900* 51 (2011): 349–66.

Ravelhofer, Barbara. *The Early Stuart Masque: Dance, Costume, and Music*. Oxford: Oxford University Press, 2006.

Regard, Frédéric, ed. *The Quest for the Northwest Passage: Knowledge, Nation and Empire, 1576–1806*. London: Pickering and Chatto, 2013.

Rhatigan, Emma K. "Audience, Actors, and 'Taking Part' in the Revels." In *Imagining the Audience in Early Modern Drama, 1558–1642*, ed. Jennifer A. Low and Nova Myhill, 151–69. New York: Palgrave Macmillan, 2011.

Richards, Jennifer. "Shakespeare and the Politics of Co-Authorship: *Henry VIII*." In *Shakespeare and Early Modern Political Thought*, ed. David Armitage, Conal Condren, and Andrew Fitzmaurice, 176–94. Cambridge: Cambridge University Press, 2009.

Richardson, Glenn. *The Field of Cloth of Gold*. New Haven, CT: Yale University Press, 2013.

– *Renaissance Monarchy: The Reigns of Henry VIII, Francis I and Charles V*. London: Arnold, 2002.

Richmond, Hugh Macrae. "Elizabeth I in Shakespeare's *Henry VIII*." In *Queen Elizabeth I: Past and Present*, ed. Christa Jansohn, 45–58. Münster: LIT Verlag, 2004.

– "The Feminism of Shakespeare's *Henry VIII*." *Essays in Literature* 6 (1979): 11–20.

– "Shakespeare's *Henry VIII*: Romance Redeemed by History." *Shakespeare Studies* 4 (1968): 334–49.

Rivlin, Elizabeth. "Theatrical Literacy in *The Comedy of Errors* and the *Gesta Grayorum*." *Critical Survey* 14.1 (2002): 64–78.

Roberts, Josephine A. "Critical Introduction." In Wroth, *The First Part*, xv–xcviii.

– "'The Knott Never to Bee Untied': The Controversy Regarding Marriage in Mary Wroth's *Urania*." In *Reading Mary Wroth: Representing Alternatives in Early Modern England*, Naomi J. Miller and Gary Waller, 109–31. Knoxville: University of Tennessee Press, 1991.

Robertson, Karen. "A 'Stranger' Bride: Mariam Khan and the East India Company." In Akhimie and Andrea, *Traveling/Travailing Women*, forthcoming.

– "Mariam Khan, the Resourceful Widow: Generic Shadows in the Archive." Paper presented at Shakespeare Association of America conference, New Orleans, March 2016.

– "Pocahontas at the Masque." *Signs: Journal of Women in Culture and Society* 21.3 (1996): 551–83.

– "Writing 'Pocahontas at the Masque'." *Medieval Feminist Newsletter* 16.1 (1993): 17–20.

Robinson, Benedict. *Islam and Early Modern English Literature: The Politics of Romance from Spenser to Milton*. New York: Palgrave Macmillan, 2007.

Romaniello, Matthew P. *The Elusive Empire: Kazan and the Creation of Russia, 1552–1671*. Madison: University of Wisconsin Press, 2012.

Roper, Louis H. "Unmasquing the Connections between Jacobean Politics and Policy: The Circle of Anna of Denmark and the Beginning of the English Empire, 1614–18." In Levin et al., *"High and Mighty Queens,"* 45–59.

Rosenthal, Franz. "Al-Mubashshir ibn Fâtik: Prolegomena to an Abortive Edition." *Oriens* 13/14 (1960/1): 132–58.

– *The Classical Heritage in Islam*. Trans. Emile and Jenny Marmorstein. London: Routledge, 1975.

Ross, E. Denison. *Sir Anthony Sherley and His Persian Adventure*. London: Routledge, 1933.

Rouhi, Leyla. "A Handsome Boy among Those Barbarous Turks: Cervantes's Muslims and the Art and Science of Desire." In *Islamicate Sexualities: Translations across Temporal Geographies of Desire*, ed. Kathryn Babayan and Afsaneh Najmabadi, 41–71. Cambridge, MA: Harvard University Press, 2008.

Round, Nicholas G. "Rojas' Old Bawd and Shakespeare's Old Lady: Celestina and the Anglican Reformation." *Celestinesca* 21 (1997): 93–109.

Rowley, Susan. "Frobisher Miksanut: Inuit Accounts of the Frobisher Voyages." In *Archeology of the Frobisher Voyages*, ed. William W. Fitzhugh and Jacqueline S. Olin, 27–40. Washington, DC: Smithsonian Institution Press, 1993.
– "Inuit Oral History: The Voyages of Martin Frobisher, 1576–78." In Alsford, *The Meta Incognita Project*, 211–19.
Rubiés, Joan-Pau. "Late Medieval Ambassadors and the Practice of Cross-Cultural Encounters, 1250–1450." In *The "Book" of Travels: Genre, Ethnology, and Pilgrimage, 1250–1700*, ed. Palmira Brummett, 37–112. Leiden, The Netherlands: Brill, 2009.
– "Oriental Despotism and European Orientalism: Botero to Montesquieu." *Journal of Early Modern History* 9 (2005): 109–80.
Russell, Joycelyne G. *The Field of Cloth of Gold: Men and Manners in 1520*. New York: Barnes and Noble, 1969.
Said, Edward W. *Culture and Imperialism*. New York: Vintage Books, 1993.
– *Orientalism* (25th Anniversary Edition). New York: Vintage Books, 1994.
Salih, Sara. *Judith Butler*. London: Routledge, 2002.
– "On Judith Butler and Performativity." In *Sexualities and Communication in Everyday Life*, ed. Karen E. Lovaas and Mercilee M. Jenkins, 55–67. Thousand Oaks, CA: Sage, 2007.
Salkeld, Duncan. *Shakespeare among the Courtesans: Prostitution, Literature, and Drama, 1500–1650*. Farnham, Eng.: Ashgate, 2012.
Salzman, Paul. *Reading Early Modern Women's Writing*. Oxford: Oxford University Press, 2006.
Salzman, Paul, and Marion Wynne-Davies, eds. *Mary Wroth and Shakespeare*. New York: Routledge, 2015.
Sanchez, Melissa E. *Erotic Subjects: The Sexuality of Politics in Early Modern English Literature*. Oxford: Oxford University Press, 2011.
Sanford, Rhonda Lemke. "A Room Not One's Own: Feminine Geography in *Cymbeline*." In Gillies and Vaughan, *Playing the Globe*, 63–85.
Saunders, A.C. de C.M. *A Social History of Black Slaves and Freedmen in Portugal, 1441–1555*. Cambridge: Cambridge University Press, 1982.
Savory, Roger. *Iran under the Safavids*. Cambridge: Cambridge University Press, 1980.
Scarisbrick, J.J. *Henry VIII*. London: Methuen, 1968.
Schelling, Felix E. *Elizabethan Drama, 1558–1642*. New York: Houghton Mifflin, 1908.
Schwarz, Kathryn. *Tough Love: Amazon Encounters in the English Renaissance*. Durham, NC: Duke University Press, 2000.
Scott, Tom. *Dunbar: A Critical Exposition of the Poems*. New York: Barnes and Noble, 1966.

Seaver, Kirsten A. "How Strange is a Stranger? A Survey of Opportunities for Inuit-European Contact in the Davis Strait before 1576." In Symons, *Meta Incognita*, 2:523–52.

Sedgwick, Eve Kosofsky. *Between Men: English Literature and Male Homosocial Desire*. New York: Columbia University Press, 1985.

Sen, Amrita. "Playing an Indian Queen: Neoplatonism, Ethnography, and *The Temple of Love*." In Harris, *Indography*, 209–22.

– "Sailing to India: Women, Travel, and Censorship in the Seventeenth Century." In Akhimie and Andrea, *Traveling/Travailing Women*, forthcoming.

– "Traveling Companions: Women, Trade, and the Early East India Company." *Genre: Forms of Discourse and Culture* 48.2 (2015): 193–214.

Shami, Seteney. "Circassians." In *Encyclopedia of the Modern Middle East and North Africa*, ed. Philip Mattar, 1:599–600. 2nd ed. New York: Macmillan, 2004.

Shapiro, I.A. "Brown– 'Ugly'?" *Notes and Queries* 39 (1992): 445–6.

Sherbo, Arthur, ed. *Johnson on Shakespeare*. New Haven, CT: Yale University Press, 1968.

Sherman, William H. "John Dee's Role in Martin Frobisher's Northwest Enterprise." In Symons, *Meta Incognita*, 1:283–98.

– *John Dee: The Politics of Reading and Writing in the English Renaissance*. Amherst: University of Massachusetts Press, 1995.

– "Strirrings and Searchings (1500–1720)." In *The Cambridge Companion to Travel Writing*, ed. Peter Hulme and Tim Youngs, 7–36. Cambridge: Cambridge University Press, 2002.

Shohet, Lauren. *Reading Masques: The English Masque and Public Culture in the Seventeenth Century*. Oxford: Oxford University Press, 2010.

Shvarts, Elena. "Putting Russia on the Globe: The Matter of Muscovy in Early Modern English Travel Writing and Literature." PhD diss., Stanford University, 2004.

Singh, Jyotsna G. "Introduction: The Global Renaissance." In Singh, *Companion*, 1–27.

– ed. *A Companion to the Global Renaissance: English Literature and Culture in the Era of Expansion*. Malden, MA: Wiley-Blackwell, 2009.

Skilliter, Susan A. "Catherine de' Medici's Turkish Ladies-in-Waiting: A Dilemma in Franco-Ottoman Diplomatic Relations." *Turcica* 7 (1975): 188–204.

– *William Harborne and the Trade with Turkey, 1578–1582: A Documentary Study of the First Anglo-Ottoman Relations*. Oxford: Oxford University Press, 1977.

Skretkowicz, Victor. *European Erotic Romance: Philhellene Protestantism, Renaissance Translation, and English Literary Politics*. Manchester: Manchester University Press, 2010.

Slights, Camille Wells. "The Politics of Conscience in *All is True* (or *Henry VIII*)." *Shakespeare Survey* 43 (1991): 59–68.

Smith, Cassander L. "'For They are Naturally Born': Quandaries of Racial Representation in George Best's *A True Discourse*." *Studies in Travel Writing* 17.3 (2013): 233–49.

Smith, Ian. "Othello's Black Handkerchief." *Shakespeare Quarterly* 64.1 (2013): 1–25.

– *Race and Rhetoric in the Renaissance: Barbarian Errors*. New York: Palgrave Macmillan, 2009.

– "The Textile Black Body: Race and 'shadowed livery' in *The Merchant of Venice*." In Traub, *Oxford Handbook*, 170–85.

– "White Skin, Black Masks: Racial Cross-Dressing on the Early Modern Stage." *Renaissance Drama* 32 (2003): 33–67.

Sousa, Geraldo U. ed. *Shakespeare's Cross-Cultural Encounters*. New York: St Martin's Press, 1999.

Snook, Edith. *Women, Beauty and Power in Early Modern England: A Feminist Literary History*. New York: Palgrave Macmillan, 2011.

Spiller, Elizabeth. *Reading and the History of Race in the Renaissance*. Cambridge: Cambridge University Press, 2011.

Spivak, Gayatri Chakravorty. "Can the Subaltern Speak?" (1988). In Morris, *Can the Subaltern Speak?* 237–91.

– "Can the Subaltern Speak?" rev. ed. (1999). In Morris, *Can the Subaltern Speak?* 21–78.

– *A Critique of Postcolonial Reason: Toward a History of the Vanishing Present*. Cambridge, MA: Harvard University Press, 1999.

– "Subaltern Talk: Interview with the Editors (29 October 1993)." In *The Spivak Reader*, ed. Donna Landry and Gerald MacLean, 287–308. New York: Routledge, 1996.

– "Translator's Preface." In Derrida, *Of Grammatology*, ix–lxxxvii.

Stallybrass, Peter. "Marginal England: The View from Aleppo." In *Center or Margin: Revisions of the English Renaissance in Honor of Leeds Barroll*, ed. Lena Cowen Orlin, 27–39. Selinsgrove, PA: Susquehanna University Press, 2006.

Stanivukovic, Goran. *Knights in Arms: Prose Romance, Masculinity, and Eastern Mediterranean Trade in Early Modern England, 1565–1655*. Toronto: University of Toronto Press, 2016.

Stapleton, Kristiane. "Measuring Authorship: Framing Forms, Genres, and Authors in *Urania*." In Larson and Miller, *Re-Reading Mary Wroth*, 103–17.

Steckley, John L. *White Lies about the Inuit*. Peterborough, ON: Broadview Press, 2008.

Stevens, Andrea Ria. *Inventions of the Skin: The Painted Body in Early English Drama, 1400–1642*. Edinburgh: Edinburgh University Press 2013.

Stevenson, David. *Scotland's Last Royal Wedding: The Marriage of James VI and Anne of Denmark*. Edinburgh: John Donald Publishers, 1997.

Stevenson, Jane. "Richard Ligon and the Theater of Empire." In *Shaping the Stuart World, 1603–1714: The Atlantic Connection*, ed. Allan I. MacInnes and Arthur H. Williamson, 285–309. Leiden: Brill, 2006.

Streitberger, W.R. *Court Revels, 1485–1559*. Toronto: University of Toronto Press, 1994.

Strong, Roy. *Gloriana: The Portraits of Queen Elizabeth I*. London: Thames and Hudson, 1987.

– "'My Weepinge Stagg I Crowne': The Persian Lady Reconsidered." In *The Art of the Emblem*, ed. Michael Bath, John Manning, and Alan R. Young, 103–37. New York: AMS Press, 1993.

Sturtevant, William C., and David Beers Quinn. "This New Prey: Eskimos in Europe in 1567, 1576, and 1577." In *Indians and Europe: An Interdisciplinary Collection of Essays*, ed. Christian F. Feest, 61–140. Lincoln: University of Nebraska Press, 1989.

Subrahmanyam, Sanjay. "Connected Histories: Notes towards a Reconfiguration of Early Modern Eurasia." *Modern Asian Studies* 31.3 (1997): 735–62.

– *Explorations in Connected History: From the Tagus to the Ganges*. Delhi: Oxford University Press, 2004.

– *Explorations in Connected History: Mughal and Franks*. Delhi: Oxford University Press, 2004.

– *Three Ways to Be Alien: Travails and Encounters in the Early Modern World*. Waltham, MA: Brandeis University Press, 2011.

Sudan, Rajani. *Fair Exotics: Xenophobic Subjects in English Literature, 1720–1850*. Philadelphia: University of Pennsylvania Press, 2002.

Suranyi, Anna. *The Genius of the English Nation: Travel Writing and National Identity in Early Modern England*. Newark: University of Delaware Press, 2008.

Symons, Thomas H.B., ed. *Meta Incognita: A Discourse of Discovery, Martin Frobisher's Arctic Expeditions, 1576–1578*. 2 vols. Hull, QC: Canadian Museum of Civilization, 1999.

– "The Significance of the Frobisher Expeditions of 1576–1578." In Symons, *Meta Incognita*, 1:xix–xxxiv.

Szuppe, Maria. "Status, Knowledge, and Politics: Women in Sixteenth-Century Safavid Iran." In Nashat and Beck, *Women in Iran*, 140–69.

Tate, William. "King James I and the Queen of Sheba." *English Literary Renaissance* 26.3 (1996): 561–85.

Taylor, E.G.R. "Master Hore's Voyage of 1536." *The Geographical Journal* 77.5 (1931): 469–70.

Taylor, Gary. *Buying Whiteness: Race, Culture, and Identity from Columbus to Hip Hop.* New York: Palgrave Macmillan, 2005.

Tharps, Lori L. "The Case for Black with a Capital B." *The New York Times*, 18 November 2014. http://www.nytimes.com/2014/11/19/opinion/the-case-for-black-with-a-capital-b.html, last accessed 4 Sept. 2016.

Thompson, Ayanna. *Performing Race and Torture on the Early Modern Stage.* New York: Routledge, 2008.

Thrush, Coll. *Indigenous London: Native Travelers at the Heart of Empire.* New Haven, CT: Yale University Press, 2016.

Tlostanova, Madina V., and Walter D. Mignolo. *Learning to Unlearn: Decolonial Reflections from Eurasia and the Americas.* Columbus: Ohio State University Press, 2012.

Tolan, John V. *Saracens: Islam in the Medieval European Imagination.* New York: Columbia University Press, 2002.

Toledano, Ehud R. *Slavery and Abolition in the Ottoman Middle East.* Seattle: University of Washington Press, 1997.

Tomlinson, Sophie. *Women on Stage in Stuart Drama.* Cambridge: Cambridge University Press, 2005.

Tommaso, Laura. "'Th' receiving earth': Shakespeare and the Land/Woman Trope." *Textus* 18 (2005): 267–82.

Traub, Valerie, ed. *The Oxford Handbook of Shakespeare and Embodiment: Gender, Sexuality, and Race.* Oxford: Oxford University Press, 2016.

Trimingham, J. Spencer. *A History of Islam in West Africa.* Oxford: Oxford University Press, 1962.

Tuan, Yi-Fu. *Dominance and Affection: The Making of Pets.* New Haven, CT: Yale University Press, 1984.

Twycross, Meg, and Sarah Carpenter. *Masks and Masking in Medieval and Early Tudor England.* Aldershot, Eng.: Ashgate, 2002.

Van Den Berg, Sara. "Dwarf Aesthetics in Spenser's *Faerie Queene* and the Early Modern Court." In *Recovering Disability in Early Modern England*, ed. Allison P. Hobgood and David Houston Wood, 23–42. Columbus: Ohio State University Press, 2013.

Van Elk, Martine. "'This sympathizèd one day's error': Genre, Representation, and Subjectivity in *The Comedy of Errors*." *Shakespeare Quarterly* 60.1 (2009): 47–72.

Vanita, Ruth. "Mariological Memory in *The Winter's Tale* and *Henry VIII*." *SEL: Studies in English Literature, 1500–1900* 40.2 (2000): 311–37.

Van Note, Beverley M. "Performing 'fitter means': Marriage and Authorship in *Love's Victory*." In Larson and Miller, *Re-Reading Mary Wroth*, 69–81.

Vásáry, István. *Turks, Tatars and Russians in the 13th–16th Centuries*. Aldershot, Eng.: Ashgate, 2007.

Vaughan, Alden T. *Transatlantic Encounters: American Indians in Britain, 1500–1766*. Cambridge: Cambridge University Press, 2006.

Vaughan, Virginia Mason. *Performing Blackness on English Stages, 1500–1800*. Cambridge: Cambridge University Press, 2005.

Vickers, Brian. *Shakespeare, Co-Author: A Historical Study of Five Collaborative Plays*. Oxford: Oxford University Press, 2002.

Vickers, Nancy. "'The blazon of sweet beauty's best': Shakespeare's *Lucrece*." In *Shakespeare and the Question of Theory*, ed. Geoffrey H. Hartman and Patricia Parker, 95–115. New York: Methuen, 1985.

Vitkus, Daniel. "'The Common Market of All the World': English Theater, the Global System, and the Ottoman Empire in the Early Modern Period." In *Global Traffic: Discourses and Practices of Trade in English Literature and Culture from 1550 to 1700*, ed. Barbara Sebek and Stephen Deng, 19–37. New York: Palgrave Macmillan, 2008.

– "The New Globalism: Transcultural Commerce, Global Systems Theory, and Spenser's Mammon." In Singh, *Companion*, 31–49.

Vizenor, Gerald. *Manifest Manners: Narratives on Postindian Survivance*. Lincoln: University of Nebraska Press, 1999.

– *Native Liberty: Natural Reason and Cultural Survivance*. Lincoln: University of Nebraska Press, 2009.

Wade, Mara R. "The Queen's Courts: Anna of Denmark and her Royal Sisters – Cultural Agency at Four Northern European Courts in the Sixteenth and Seventeenth Centuries." In *Women and Culture at the Courts of the Stuart Queens*, ed. Clare McManus, 49–80. New York: Palgrave Macmillan, 2003.

Wall, Wendy. *The Imprint of Gender: Authorship and Publication in the English Renaissance*. Ithaca, NY: Cornell University Press, 1993.

Wallace, David. *Premodern Places: Calais to Surinam, Chaucer to Aphra Behn*. Malden, MA: Blackwell, 2004.

Waller, Gary. *The Sidney Family Romance: Mary Wroth, William Herbert and the Early Modern Construction of Gender*. Detroit, MI: Wayne State University Press, 1993.

Warnicke, Retha M. *The Rise and Fall of Anne Boleyn*. Cambridge: Cambridge University Press, 1989.

Waterfield, Robin E. *Christians in Persia: Assyrians, Armenians, Roman Catholics and Protestants*. New York: Harper and Row, 1973.

Watson, Paul F. "The Queen of Sheba in Christian Tradition." In Pritchard, *Solomon and Sheba*, 115–45.

Watt, James, and Ann Savours. "The Captured 'Countrey People': Their Depiction and Medical History." In Symons, *Meta Incognita*, 2:553–62.

Weatherford, Jack. *Genghis Khan and the Making of the Modern World*. New York: Broadway Books, 2004.

Wegemer, Gerard B. "Henry VIII on Trial: Confronting Malice and Conscience in Shakespeare's *All is True*." In *Shakespeare's Last Plays: Essay in Literature and Politics*, ed. Stephen W. Smith and Travis Curtright, 73–90. London: Lexington Books, 2002.

Welsford, Enid. *The Court Masque: A Study in the Relationship between Poetry and the Revels* (1927). New York: Russell and Russell, 1964.

Wheatcroft, Andrew. *The Habsburgs: Embodying Empire*. New York: Penguin, 1995.

White, Hayden. *Figural Realism: Studies in the Mimesis Effect*. Baltimore, MD: Johns Hopkins University Press, 1999.

– *Tropics of Discourse: Essays in Cultural Criticism*. Baltimore, MD: Johns Hopkins University Press, 1978.

Whitehead, Neil L. "Introduction." In Ralegh, *The Discoverie*, 3–116.

Whitworth, Charles. "Rectifying Shakespeare's *Errors*: Romance and Farce in Bardeditry" (1991). In Miola, *The Comedy of Errors*, 227–60.

Wiesner-Hanks, Merry. "Early Modern Gender and the Global Turn." In Wiesner-Hanks, *Mapping Gendered Routes*, 55–74.

– *Women and Gender in Early Modern Europe*. 3rd ed. Cambridge: Cambridge University Press, 2008.

– ed. *Mapping Gendered Routes and Spaces in the Early Modern World*. Farnham, Eng.: Ashgate, 2015.

Willan, T.S. *The Early History of the Russia Company, 1553–1603*. Manchester: Manchester University Press, 1956.

– *The Muscovy Merchants of 1555* (1953). Clifton, NJ: Augustus M. Kelley, 1973.

Williams, Ethel Carleton. *Anne of Denmark: Wife of James VI of Scotland: James I of England*. London: Longman, 1970.

Williams, Raymond. Keywords: *A Vocabulary of Culture and Society*. Rev. ed. New York: Oxford University Press, 1983.

– *Marxism and Literature*. Oxford: Oxford University Press, 1977.

Wilson, Richard. "Visible Bullets: Tamburlaine the Great and Ivan the Terrible." *ELH: English Literary History* 62.1 (1995): 47–68.

Wood, Alfred C. *A History of the Levant Company* (1935). London: Frank Cass, 1964.

Woodbridge, Linda. *Vagrancy, Homelessness, and English Renaissance Literature.* Urbana: University of Illinois Press, 2001.

Woodcock, Matthew. "'Their eyes more attentive to the show': Spectacle, Tragedy and the Structure of *All Is True (Henry VIII)*." *Shakespeare* 7.1 (2011): 1–15.

– *Thomas Churchyard: Pen, Sword, and Ego.* Oxford: Oxford University Press, 2016.

Woolley, Benjamin. *The Queen's Conjurer: The Science and Magic of Dr. John Dee, Adviser to Queen Elizabeth I.* New York: Henry Holt, 2001.

Yarnall, Judith. *Transformations of Circe: The History of an Enchantress.* Champaign: University of Illinois Press, 1994.

Yates, Frances A. *Astraea: The Imperial Theme in the Sixteenth Century.* London: Routledge, 1975.

Zilfi, Madeline C. *Women and Slavery in the Late Ottoman Empire.* Cambridge: Cambridge University Press, 2010.

Zurcher, Amelia. "Civility and Extravagance in *Timon of Athens* and *Urania*." In Salzman and Wynne-Davies, *Mary Wroth and Shakespeare*, 95–109.

Index